Wellington's Campaigns
Volume 2
The Waterloo Campaign, 1815

WELLINGTON IN THE FIELD.

After a Portrait by Sir Thomas Lawrence.

This was Wellington's favourite campaigning costume. The frock-coat was dark blue, the cloak grey lined with white. The telescope he carried all through Spain and Belgium and afterwards gave to Lord Stanhope.

Wellington's Campaigns
Volume 2
The Waterloo Campaign, 1815

The Tactics, Terrain, Commanders and
Armies Assessed

Illustrated with Maps

C. W. Robinson

LEONAUR

Wellington's Campaigns
Volume 2
The Waterloo Campaign, 1815
The Tactics, Terrain, Commanders and Armies Assessed
Illustrated with Maps
by C. W. Robinson

First published under the Title
Wellington's Campaigns 1808-15

Leonaur is an imprint of Oakpast Ltd
Copyright in this form © 2017 Oakpast Ltd

ISBN: 978-1-78282-598-2 (hardcover)
ISBN: 978-1-78282-599-9 (softcover)

http://www.leonaur.com

Publisher's Notes

The views expressed in this book are not necessarily
those of the publisher.

Contents

Introduction

Campaign in Belgium, or Waterloo Campaign, 1815

Many volumes have been written upon the campaign of Waterloo. They have appeared in many countries, in various languages, and have been contributed by able pens both of soldiers and civilians; and yet there is no campaign, although its broad facts are so well known, as to some of the incidents in which, with their causes, more contradictory assertions are still made, and conflicting opinions expressed.

The interest in the operations of the campaign appears to grow with years; every decade throws more light upon them, or introduces, in connection with them, new matter for discussion. It may be of use, therefore, to the military student that we should commence this brief account of the chief movements which took place by saying something as to how it is that certain incidents, and certain orders issued, should, after the lapse of nearly a century, be still subjects of controversy; and also as to what are the chief topics of debate and criticism at the present day.

The uncertainty which surrounds some of the details of the campaign, and the very different opinions held and expressed as to why movements were made, or were not made, are attributable partly perhaps to the accidents of war of which there were many; partly to the fact that historians of different nations have written, as is natural, from points of view, with feelings, and from sources of information, which are dissimilar; and partly to the circumstance, as far as Wellington's operations are concerned, that no really full and standard British military history of the campaign appeared in England until many years after Waterloo had been fought.

As to the "accidents of war," the decisive struggle of the campaign was crowded into three days of great strain—from the evening of the 15th to the evening of the 18th of June, 1815. Some orders to corps and divisions of each army were given verbally, and some written ones lost, of which the time of despatch and receipt, as well as the exact nature, are open to dispute. The original instructions of the Duke of Wellington for the movements of his army, issued on June 15th, 16th, and 17th, were lost, they being in possession of Sir William De Lancey, his quartermaster-general, who was mortally wounded on the 18th. (*Wellington Despatches*, vol. viii.). Sir William De Lancey's papers were also lost. Thus, although some of his orders of movements based on the Duke's instructions, and also copies of the latter have been preserved by those who received them, some details which would not otherwise have been matters of doubt now remain so.

With respect to the uncertainty which surrounds the motives of some of the French movements, this has been increased by Ney, who was opposed to Wellington at Quatre Bras, having been put to death shortly afterwards by D'Erlon, Grouchy, and other leaders having been obliged to leave France; by Napoleon having been sent to St. Helena; and by what is narrated in the *Mémoires* compiled there as to instructions given to Ney, Grouchy, D'Erlon, etc., being, on several points, in conflict with the statements of others.

As to the standpoint from which the historians of various nations have viewed the contest not being exactly similar, it must be remembered that for France the operations had terminated in a crushing defeat; Napoleonic and anti-Napoleonic feeling has been strong; there were blunders to be accounted for, and great military reputations to be defended.

Prussia, although she had contributed largely to the crowning victory of Waterloo, had to account for a reverse at Ligny.

Great Britain, though she had been hard pressed, had repulsed the French throughout, and had thus comparatively little to explain to the nation.

Histories of the war by English writers came out, under the circumstances, but slowly.

Alison writes, (*Some Account of my Life and Writings*, autobiography of Sir Archibald Alison, vol. ii.), referring to the year 1842, that up to that time "no correct or detailed account of Waterloo had yet appeared on the English side."

The chief military and critical works upon the campaign read in England for many years were by Continental authors, such as Jomini, (*Precis politique et militaire de la campagne de 1815, par le general Jomini*); Clausewitz, (*Der Feldzug von* 1815, by General Carl von Clausewitz);

and Von Damitz. (*Geschichte des Feldzuges von* 1815, by Major von Damitz, from the papers of General von Grolman, Q.M.G. to the Prussian Army in 1815). Siborne's *History of the War in France and Belgium in* 1815 did not come out until 1844.

This brings us to the manner in which the literature of the campaign has grown up. In a sense we may regard it as divided into two periods—*i.e.* previous to, and subsequent to, the death of the Duke of Wellington in 1852. Between this last date and the present time, 1906, especially within the past thirty years, many additions have been made to it, fresh sources of information have become available, and some journals of private conversations, etc., with Wellington have been published which would not in his lifetime have seen the light.

The following remarks, bearing upon this literature, may assist students in turning to various accounts of the campaign, as well as direct their attention to present topics of discussion and criticism.

Wellington, up to the day of his death, considered (and his attitude can be very well understood) that, with due regard to national and individual interests and susceptibilities, the time had not come when a true history could be written, although he sanctioned the publication of his despatches by Colonel Gurwood, the first edition of which was completed by 1839.

He would never encourage historians to bring out works upon the campaign; nor accept the dedication of any to him, lest he should be imagined to endorse their contents; nor consent to become the arbiter upon any disputed point, no matter how trivial.

Any unfavourable comments on individuals, stamped, however indirectly, with his approval, would have been most keenly felt by those concerned; he had said all which he deemed essential; he and Blücher, in command of the Prussian Army, had worked together, from first to last, in cordial concert; there was between them a warm feeling of regard and confidence; and in his Waterloo despatch he had acknowledged fully how essentially the Prussians had contributed to the victory. He considered, no doubt, that such despatches and letters as he had permitted to be published afforded all the information which it was proper that he should give.

The most complete memorandum left behind him in his own hand, which bears upon criticisms of his own operations, was put together when he was seventy-three years of age—*i.e.* twenty-seven years after the Battle of Waterloo, and was not then written as an official paper, or addressed to anyone.

★★★★★★

It has appeared since, also, in the *Wellington Supplementary Des-patches* (1863), and is of course of much value; but should not justly be regarded as a State Paper, in which exact accuracy as to details of distances, hours, etc., is expected.

★★★★★★

After 1852 the second period of the Waterloo literature opens.

A new edition of the *Wellington Despatches* was completed by about this year, some corrections in previous ones being made; and a paper was added which has been the subject of much criticism. This was apparently contributed by Sir De Lacy Evans to the compiler (Colonel Gurwood), and is said to have been drawn up by Sir William De Lancey, the Quartermaster-General of the army, killed at Waterloo. It relates to the disposition of Wellington's troops at 7 a.m. on June 16th, 1815, the day on which the Battles of Ligny and Quatre Bras were fought.

In 1853 there appeared in England the translation by Colonel Philip Yorke of *Aus meinem Leben* (Passages from my Life), by General the Baron von Müffling, who had died in 1851; he having directed that it should be published, as:

He felt bound to leave behind him explanations or corrections relating to the particular events of which he had been an eye-witness, and to which an European interest attached.

This work will always be of value in connection with Wellington's movements in the campaign, from the official knowledge and status of its author.

Müffling, while Quartermaster-General upon Blücher's staff, and after much experience of war, was sent as commissioner to the head-quarters of Wellington in 1815, and held this appointment, being in the full confidence of both Wellington and Blücher, throughout the operations. His work is not a history, but it enters into some important incidents in the campaign, and throws several sidelights upon them.

He states that he took up his duties very reluctantly, having found a predecessor at the British headquarters displeased with the brusque manners of some staff-officers, and having been also warned by General Gneisenau, chief of the staff to Marshal Blücher, to be much on his guard against the Duke of Wellington:

For that from his relations with India, and transactions with the deceitful *nabobs*, this distinguished general had so accustomed

10

himself to duplicity, that he had at last become such a master of the art, as even to outwit the *nabobs* themselves.

He adds, however, that before he left his appointment he had learnt Wellington's real character; and valued the proofs he had received of his personal confidence more highly than the honours, (the Order of the Bath—*Passages from my Life*), conferred upon him by the British Crown.

Between 1853 and 1875 several contributions, foreign and English, were added to the history of the campaign. Among these were the valuable "*Supplementary*" *Wellington Despatches*, completed in twelve volumes by 1865, and edited by the then Duke of Wellington; a new series appearing in 1867-72.

The following works, among others, also came out: *Histoire du Duc de Wellington*, by Colonel Brialmont; *Histoire de Campaigne de* 1815, by Colonel Charras; *Waterloo*, by the Rev. G. R. Gleig; *Notes on the Battle of Waterloo*, by General Sir James Shaw-Kennedy; *Waterloo, or the Downfall of the First Empire*, by George Hooper. A discussion of the campaign in the *Operations of War*, by Sir Edward Hamley; *Waterloo Lectures*, by Colonel C. C. Chesney, in which the share taken by the Prussians is specially emphasised.

In 1876 was published in Berlin *Geschichte des Feldzuges von* 1815, by General von Ollech, in which, for the first time, appeared a letter, with a photograph of it, written in French by Wellington to Blücher, from near Quatre Bras, at 10.30 a.m. on June 16th, 1815—*i.e.* just after he had ridden up from Brussels, and observed the country to the south from this point. This letter had been preserved in the Archives of the Prussian General Staff at Berlin.

It relates to the positions and movements of Wellington's troops, and the opinion is expressed by General von Ollech that the effect of the letter had been to make the Prussians count upon assistance from Wellington at Ligny, which was not given to them.

No mention of this letter appears to have been made by Wellington, Blücher, or Müffling, but the reason possibly is, that it was followed up immediately by a personal interview between Wellington and Blücher, close to Ligny.

In 1880, Dr. Hans Delbrück, in his *Life of Marshal Gneisenau*, published in Berlin, suggests that this letter was sent by Wellington, with the knowledge that its statements were incorrect, in order to induce Blücher, in the interests of Wellington's unconcentrated army, to stand

and fight, as he did, at Ligny; and (to conclude the subject) we may say here that in a very recent work (1904) *Napoleon's Untergang*, 1815, by General von Lettow-Vorbeck, (forming part of *Geschichte der Befreiungskriege*, 1813-15), this view again appears.

Opinion in England, where the absolutely straightforward, truthful character of Wellington is well established, will not be affected by this; but in Germany, where there is less knowledge of him as a man, it may be so, which is much to be regretted.

Several more works than the above two have come out since 1876, and some have gone critically into an examination of all the evidence available upon various questions—such, for instance, as *The Campaign of Waterloo*, by Ropes, an American author (1893).

We may mention, among many others, "Waterloo," in *Great Campaigns*, edited by Captain C. Cooper-King, from the writings of Major Adams; *Great Commanders of Modern Times*, by W. O'Connor Morris; *Wellington and Waterloo*, with an introduction by Lord Wolseley, and excellent illustrations, by Major Arthur Griffiths; *The Decline and Fall of Napoleon*, by Lord Wolseley; *The Rise of Wellington*, by Lord Roberts; *Cavalry in the Waterloo Campaign*, by Sir Evelyn Wood; articles in *The United Service Magazine* (in 1890 and 1891), by Sir Frederick Maurice; *The Story of Waterloo*, by Major-General H. D. Hutchinson; *Waterloo*, a narrative and criticism, by E. L. Horsburgh; and *Waterloo*, 1815, by Henry Houssaye, a work thought much of in France.

In 1891, *Waterloo Letters* came out, edited by Major-General H. T. Siborne. These letters, the originals of which are now in the British Museum, were, with the sanction of the commander-in-chief, written by various officers, from Lord Fitzroy Somerset and Lord Anglesey, (Lord Uxbridge at the time of Waterloo), downwards, to Captain Siborne, the editor's father, when he was compiling his *History* (brought out in 1844), and constructing his model of Waterloo, now in the Royal United Service Institution, (this model, it is interesting to mention, was inspected by the Duke of Wellington himself, who considered it an accurate representation of the ground). Much of what is in them was embodied in Captain Siborne's *History*, but not all their details.

Napoleon's Untergang, 1815, by General von Lettow-Vorbeck (1904), we have already referred to.

Another work is *La critique de la Campagne de* 1815, by A. Grouard (1904), and it is said that one is now near its completion by Colonel Stoffel, which should be, when it appears, of interest. (Article by General Zurlinden, "Ligny and Waterloo," in *Revue des deux Mondes*, January, 1906. Colonel Stoffel is well known from his able reports upon the Prussian Army when French military *attaché* at Berlin, before the outbreak of the Franco-German War of 1870).

It can be seen, therefore, that the military student of today who wishes to examine into the campaign of Waterloo, and understand how certain questions with respect to it are now regarded, must consult recent works, as well as the older ones; and, it may be added, should not accept hastily the views expressed by any one author.

Among the topics which are still those of debate and criticism is the question whether the wide dispersion of the armies of both Wellington and Blücher in their cantonments, when the French invaded Belgium, on June 15th, 1815, was necessarily or wisely continued up to the time it was—*i.e.* until the moment when the real point of attack became certain. It is indisputable that Napoleon fell upon both armies before they had completely concentrated, and defeated Blücher at Ligny before Wellington, hard pressed at Quatre Bras, had united with him.

On the other hand, the Allies had a long frontier line to defend; Wellington had important interests to safeguard, as well as to effect this union; and he, and Blücher also, met Napoleon on the 16th with such a resistance as he had not contemplated having so soon to encounter.

Wellington, it is true, did not fight at Ligny, nor Blücher at Quatre Bras; but their two armies were, during these battles, little over three miles apart. They did act in concert, though not in actual touch; they did indirectly aid one another; and the result of Napoleon's attack was that he was beaten upon his left at Quatre Bras, and though successful on his right at Ligny after a desperate battle, he was so severely handled there, that his victory, weakly followed up, was inconclusive.

There is, therefore, much connected with Wellington's dispositions on June 15th, and with what the two Allied armies did not, and did, accomplish on the 16th, which lends itself to discussion.

More is known now than was the case sixty years ago as to whether Napoleon's assumption of the offensive, and invasion of Belgium, came as "a surprise" to the Allies. The evidence appears against this; but the main cause why the two Allied armies had not effected a union before his attack was delivered is still a debated point,—*i.e.* whether it was due entirely to the position of Wellington's troops and of his own headquarters on June 15th; to the treachery of spies; to the tardy and inadequate information received at Brussels from his own and the Prussian outposts; to an inexperienced staff; to the accidents of war; or to other causes, avoidable and unavoidable.

The fact that the fields of Ligny and Quatre Bras were so close together as they were has not apparently been generally realised, though it is important. They formed, in a great measure, but one battlefield, and the troops at Ligny could until nightfall be seen with a glass from Quatre Bras. We have endeavoured to show their proximity on the one plan of both the battles.

Almost every work upon the campaign necessarily enters into the relative share which is due to the armies of Wellington and Blücher for the great triumph of the Battle of Waterloo itself on June 18th—a matter upon which there has existed, in the past at all events, among some of the people both of England and Germany, opinions based upon incomplete knowledge and prejudice.

But among educated men in this country the important part which the Prussians took in the whole campaign is well understood. It was always recognised by Wellington himself, and there is no necessity on either side for the exaggeration and jealousy which has at times found expression.

Recently the memorandum of Sir William De Lancey as to the disposition of Wellington's army at 7 a.m. on June 16th, and in association with it the duke's letter to Blücher at 10.30 a.m. on that day from near Quatre Bras, have been much referred to. Therefore, they are entered upon further than would otherwise have been the case in the following pages.

Before concluding this introduction to the campaign, we may add that what may seem perplexing occasionally to some in connection with certain events and movements between June 15th and 18th will often appear less so, if they remember—a difficult thing, in reality, to do—that the actors on the field at the time had not the knowledge of the situation on both sides that we now possess; also that the Waterloo campaign was in its essence, though not technically, a continuation of those of the Peninsula—the concluding act, in fact, after a brief interval and change of scene to Belgium, of the great seven years' drama of that war. Many of the chief actors in the armies of Wellington and Napoleon were the same, and had, on their respective sides, met in battle repeatedly in Spain and Portugal.

The British regiments, though the old Peninsular Army was but weakly represented, were all imbued with Peninsular traditions; they had confidence in their generals, and implicit trust in Wellington, based on Peninsular contests. In truth, this trust was of that kind which, from all accounts which have come down to us, was absolute, and knew no doubt. This was an immeasurable advantage.

Napoleon himself had also been in Spain, but there was this special difference between his experience there and that of his lieutenants, that he had never met Wellington nor the British troops in battle; and that his operations against the latter had been confined to the Corunna campaign, when Sir John Moore necessarily retired before his overwhelming numbers. From circumstances and temperament, he underrated his enemy; but his generals were naturally more or less influenced by their own experience, which they could not forget because he did not share in it.

The campaign of Waterloo is full of practical military lessons, which it is one object of this short account to bring out. Colonel Chesney, writing in 1874, (*Waterloo Lectures*), says:

> Time was when it was treasonable to doubt whether what Wellington arranged was the best thing possible on his part.

Apparently this has not been the case now for many years. Criticism as to movements on Wellington's part in the Waterloo campaign has been keen enough. The desire to do full justice to Napoleon and the defeated side has contributed to this; and Wellington's good fortune and the valour of his troops have been perhaps more dwelt upon than his military genius and skill.

All successful generals owe something to fortune and much to the valour of their troops. Wellington was no exception to this rule, and never pretended to be so. "When I made mistakes," he said, "my men pulled me through."

We see him in this campaign, a skilful organiser applying ably his means, which were far from ample, to the facts of the position; cool and cautious at the outset (some have thought too much so); afterwards, when he had decided to act, bold and self-reliant; quick in handling his troops; vigilant and undaunted on the battlefield; and completely triumphant at the close.

He was as great a servant of the State on land as Nelson was at sea, and it seems even doubtful whether, in spite of the high place given to him among the military leaders of the world, Lord Roberts is not right in considering that he has, nevertheless, as a commander, been "greatly underrated." (*The Rise of Wellington*, by Lord Roberts).

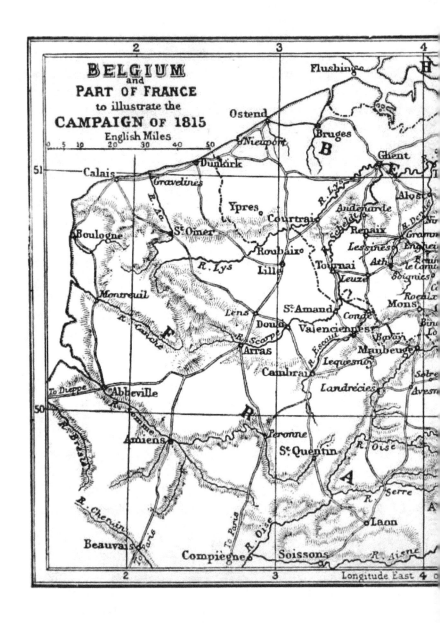

BELGIUM
and
PART OF FRANCE
to illustrate the
CAMPAIGN OF 1815
English Miles

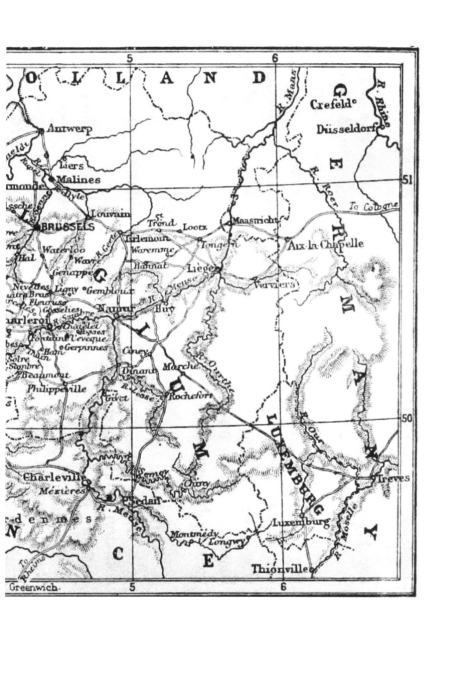

CHAPTER 1

The Armies & the Topography

By the treaty of peace, signed at Paris on April 11th, 1814, and notified to Wellington shortly after the Battle of Toulouse, Napoleon renounced for himself, and his descendants, the throne of France, and was permitted, with a small retinue, and about a thousand of his Old Guard, to reside in the island of Elba, the nominal sovereignty of which was conceded to him.

The armies of the Allied Powers were then withdrawn beyond the boundaries of France; a British, Hanoverian, and Dutch force, under Lord Lynedoch, remained in occupation of the Netherlands; the Prussians and Germans held the territory bordering the Rhine; and a European Congress met at Vienna (September 25th, 1814) to settle many important questions connected with the re-constitution of Europe, and the future limits of the European states, which Napoleon's conquests had reduced to confusion. At this Congress Talleyrand represented France, and Lord Castlereagh England. The progress made by the Congress was slow, it being difficult to reconcile the divergent interests of the powers, and so by the close of the year 1814 little had been definitely settled. Balls, dinners, and conferences went on continuously; but, as Talleyrand said:

The Congress danced, but did not move forward.

Wellington, in the meantime, after a short stay in England, had, in July 1814, been appointed Ambassador Extraordinary to the Court of France; and it is interesting to note that in August, at the desire of the British Government, he visited the entire line of the Franco-Belgian frontier, accompanied by Colonels Carmichael Smyth, Chapman, and Pasley of the Royal Engineers, and afterwards drew up a memorandum upon its defence, (enclosed with a letter to Lord Bathurst, dated

Paris, September 22nd, 1814. *Wellington Despatches*, vol. vii.), in which the following passage occurs touching upon the position upon which the Battle of Waterloo was subsequently fought:

> About Nivelle, and between that and Binche, there are many advantageous positions; and the entrance of the *Forêt de Soignies*, on the high road which leads to Brussels from Binche, Charleroi, and Namur, (it was here that the Battle of Waterloo took place), would, if worked upon, afford others.

In January, 1815, he proceeded from Paris to succeed Lord Castlereagh at the Congress of Vienna, where a deadlock had ensued.

> The combatants, still breathless and bleeding from the struggle, (*i.e.* of the war which had been terminated by the Treaty of Paris), snarled over the prey which they had just compelled the common enemy (France) to abandon. . . . Prussia extended her clutch towards Saxony, while Russia growled over the well-mumbled bone of Poland. The western Powers—England, France, and Austria—were on the point of forming in self-defence a league against the two northern monopolists, when a common peril once more united them—Buonaparte had escaped from Elba.—*Wellington's Career*, by Sir Edward Hamley.

The watch kept by the powers over his movements in that island had been culpably negligent; and upon the ground that the powers themselves were not intending to keep to the Treaty of Paris, he threw his own obligations under it to the winds. Confident that the army in France, if not the entire nation, would rally round his standard, he set sail from Elba with his Guard in a few small vessels, landed at Cannes on March 1st, 1815, and from thence proceeded to Grenoble and Lyons.

The troops sent by King Louis XVIII. to oppose him, with few exceptions welcomed him, as did also several of his former marshals, Ney among them; on March 20th he entered Paris, and King Louis fled to Ghent.

But his appearance in France had an effect which he had not looked for. He had counted upon the dissensions among the Powers at the Congress as an element in his favour, and did not anticipate that all peaceful overtures on his part would be rejected.

For the moment he desired peace, in order, if not from any higher motives, to consolidate his position and increase his army; but his escape from Elba was felt to have been such a flagrant breach of treaty engagements, and confidence had been so entirely destroyed in his good faith, that the powers declined to negotiate, and in a proclamation, on March 13th, 1815, declared him to be the "enemy and disturber of the world," and abandoned him to "public justice."

All Europe sprang again to arms, and on every road leading towards France troops were set in motion. The Prussians marched to co-operate with Great Britain and the King of the Netherlands in Belgium; the Austrians and Bavarians gathered on the Rhine; the Sardinians in the Appennines; the Swiss in the Alps; Spain and Portugal threatened to cross the Pyrenees; the Russians advanced from Poland; and Denmark and Sweden joined the Coalition. It was to be a struggle to the death between the Allied Powers of Europe and Napoleon, whom they had outlawed.

Wellington was at once appointed to command the "Anglo-Belgian" (or "Anglo-Allied") Army in the Netherlands, and arrived at Brussels on April 5th, 1815.

★★★★★★

Wellington's army is sometimes spoken of as the "Army of Flanders," the "Anglo-Dutch," the "Anglo-Belgian," and the "Anglo-Allied" Army. It is important to remember that it was far from a purely British one, being composed of about one-third British and two-thirds foreigners. In these pages it will be termed the "Anglo-Allied Army," or "Army of Wellington."

★★★★★★

Great Britain, in addition to her naval and military assistance in the war, agreed to pay large money subsidies to the Continental Powers. (In 1815 the expenditure of Great Britain upon the war on Navy, Army, and in subsidies, is stated to have been one hundred and ten millions sterling—Alison's *History of Europe*, vol. xix.).

MILITARY STRENGTH OF THE COALITION

It was the design of the powers forming the Coalition against Napoleon to invade France in concert as soon as possible; and it was agreed that the following armies were to be brought into the positions and to the strength mentioned:—

The 1st Army (Army of the Upper Rhine),—see Part of Europe Map further on—under Schweidnitz, composed chiefly of Austrians and Bavarians, was to assemble about Coblentz and along the southern limits of Germany.

Strength about   255,000

The 2nd Army (Army of the Lower Rhine), under Blücher, composed of Prussians and Saxons, was to connect the Army of the Upper Rhine with an army under Wellington in the Netherlands. It was to extend, by Cologne, along the Lower Rhine and the Meuse.

Strength about   155,000

The 3rd Army ("Anglo-Allied Army," or "Army of Flanders"), under Wellington, composed of British and other Allied troops, was to assemble in the Netherlands (Holland and Belgium).

Strength about   155,000

The 4th Army, under Barclay de Tolly, composed of Russians, at some distance in Saxon Poland, was to move forward in reserve.

Strength about   170,000
                              ————
        Total   735,000

Of the above forces it was calculated that 600,000 men could be brought to bear upon the frontier of France, but it soon became clear that some time must elapse before they could cross it.

Before entering further into the campaign of 1815, it may be well to explain that it is occasionally spoken of as the "campaign in Flanders," the campaign in "Belgium," in "Holland," in the "Low Countries," in the "Netherlands," in "Holland and Belgium," and in "France and Belgium."

The reason of this is that Flanders was, and still is, a portion of Belgium, comprising much of the ground occupied by Wellington in 1815; that "Holland" (the Hollow-land), the "Netherlands," and the "Low Countries," are all terms for that low-lying territory to the north of Belgium bordering the North Sea; that Belgium in 1815 was united to, and therefore formed part of, "The Netherlands," or "Holland," but in 1830 it became separated from it. Thus writers after 1830 speak of the campaign as being in "Holland *and* Belgium." Finally, after the Battle of Waterloo, the Allies advanced through France and occupied Paris.

Thus all the above designations of the campaign may be said to be in a sense correct, although sometimes, without an explanation, they are confusing.

MILITARY STRENGTH OF THE FRENCH

When Napoleon reached Paris he found, although the conscription of previous years had largely exhausted the youth of the country, an armed force ready to join him of about 224,000 men, which would give him an effective in the field of some 155,000. This he immediately bent all his great energy to organise and augment.

He completed the fortifications and armament of Paris; supplied the frontier fortresses with provisions for six months; fortified Lyons and other provincial towns, and also the passes of the Jura and the Vosges Mountains; re-organised the Imperial Guard; raised 200 new battalions of National Guards; and by unceasing labour soon largely increased his army, a valuable portion of which consisted of old soldiers of the Empire, who, after holding out in various garrisons, or having been prisoners of war on the Continent, had returned to France at the conclusion of the peace of 1814.

Both sides now hurried on their preparations to take the field.

When the clouds of war are rolling up in dense masses, the natural and all-absorbing question is, "Where will the storm burst?" and the campaign of Waterloo forms an excellent illustration of what has been said in connection with the Peninsular War,—*viz.* of how nothing but a knowledge of the circumstances of the hostile powers, and of the topography of the territory where they may come into contact, will enable us to answer it; and how, with the possession of such knowledge, we may usually do so fairly correctly.

It was tolerably certain,—

First, that France, or her *borders on the north and east*, would at the outset become the theatre of war;

Next, that the storm would probably burst near her north-eastern frontier; and,

Finally, that it would do so towards the portion of that frontier west of the River Meuse.

The explanation of this is that France had few colonies or out-lying possessions, and that her navy had been destroyed at Trafalgar. Therefore, the campaign would be mainly a military one. If Napoleon assumed the offensive, the powers would protect their own borders; while if he acted on the defensive, they would endeavour to reach Paris, the French capital, and the centre of the power and national life of France.

Why the north-east border of France, adjoining Belgium, especially that portion between the Meuse and the sea, would probably become, early, a main theatre of the war, arose from the topography of the French borders, and other considerations which we now must touch upon.

Turning to the map, we see that France was in 1815 thus bounded, beginning at the south-west extremity, at the Pyrenees. On the west and north-west by the Bay of Biscay and the English Channel; on the north-east, from Dunkirk to the Rhine, by Belgium (Flanders), Prussia, or German Territory; on the east by Germany, Switzerland, and Italy; on the south by the Mediterranean and Spain.

The main watershed of France runs chiefly along the high ground close to the eastern and southern frontiers. From this the great rivers flow on the west towards the English Channel and the Bay of Biscay—for instance, the Seine (on which lies Paris, the capital), the Loire, and the Garonne; and on the east to the Rhine and the Mediterranean—for instance, the Meuse, the Moselle, and the Rhone.

Thus to the west or north-west lay the sea; to the east and south, the difficult, and comparatively defensible, country of the Vosges Mountains towards Germany, the Jura towards Switzerland, the Alps towards Italy, and the Pyrenees towards Spain; while on the east flowed also the broad River Rhine and the Rhone.

On the north-eastern frontier, therefore, France was most open to attack. This was particularly the case to the west of the River Meuse, because to the east of that river lay the broken hilly district of the Ardennes. Between Namur on the Meuse and the sea to the west the country was by nature open, though protected by certain fortresses and walled towns. Paris was close to this frontier; while for England— a naval power, and already in occupation of Belgium—Ostend and Antwerp afforded convenient ports from which British troops could co-operate with the Army of the Lower Rhine.

Moreover, the armies of Wellington and Blücher were the nearest to Paris, and thus threatened it the most directly. It would be much to the advantage of Napoleon if he could defeat them before the armies of the Upper Rhine, and of Russia, or of other powers, could arrive; while on the other hand, he could scarcely march against these latter and more distant armies, leaving his capital exposed to Wellington and Blücher.

Holland, too, had been but a short time before under the rule of France. Many of its people, French in language, custom, and habits, were Dutch only by compulsion. Some sympathised with Napoleon, while all had a dread of his military genius. It was extremely probable that any decided success gained in the Netherlands would turn many of his enemies there into allies.

Let us now, therefore, consider more particularly that part of the

Belgian frontier which was expected to be, and did become, the theatre of war, describing the communications which traverse or give access to it, and the defences which guarded it.

Topography of the Franco-Belgian Frontier, from the Sea to the Meuse

RIVERS

The boundary which here separated France and Belgium in 1815 is indicated on the map, at the front of the appendices, of part of Belgium and the French frontier. Of the chief rivers which flow across it, beginning from the sea on the west, we may mention the following rising in France:—

The Lys.—Flows by Courtray, and enters the Scheldt at Ghent; navigable with the aid of numerous canals communicating with it.

The Scheldt.—Flows by Cambray, Valenciennes, and Tournay, to Ghent and Antwerp, beyond which it enters the North Sea; navigable for large ships as far as Antwerp, and for small vessels for the whole distance to the French frontier.

The Sambre.—Flows by Maubeuge in a north-easterly direction, joining the Meuse (or Maas) at Namur; navigable for barges throughout the greater part of its course; communicates by canal with the Scheldt.

The Meuse (or Maas).—Rises in the department of the Vosges; passes by Givet, Namur, Liege, and Moestricht; navigable to far south of the French frontier.

The rivers named below have both their rise and source in Belgium :—

The Dender.—An affluent of the Scheldt; passes Ath, Grammont, Ninove, and Alost, joining the Scheldt at Termonde; navigable by the help of numerous sluices up to Ath.

The Haine.—Rises near Binche and flows westward by Mons to join the Scheldt.

The Serine.—Rises near Soignies and passes by Hal and Brussels to the Dyle.

The Dyle.—Rises east of the Charleroi-Brussels road, and flows by Wavre, Louvain, and Malines. Numerous small affluents join the Dyle, and the whole district bordering it becomes in wet weather swampy and deep in mud.

ROADS AND COMMUNICATIONS

The wide *chaussées* of France and Belgium, as the high roads

24

are termed, are excellent; the cross roads numerous and fairly good, though often roughly paved. Canals link together the sea, the Meuse, the Scheldt, and most of the chief towns.

Close to the frontier line, on the French side, good roads connect the strong places of Lille, Valenciennes, Maubeuge, Beaumont, Philippeville, and Givet; and from these, roads lead northward towards Ghent, Brussels, Namur, Liege, etc.

Among the most important of these are:—

West of where the Sambre crosses the frontier,—

1. From Lille, up the valley of the Lys, by Courtray, to Ghent.

2. From Valenciennes: (1) by Tournay, up the Scheldt past Audenarde to Ghent; (2) by Condé to Ghent, and through Ath to Brussels; (3) by Mons to Brussels.

3. From Maubeuge by Mons to Brussels.

East of where the Sambre crosses the frontier,—

4. From Beaumont by Mons, or Binche.

5. From Philippeville by Charleroi, or Châtelet to Brussels; or up the Meuse to Namur; and by Dinant and Ciney to Liege.

Several bridges spanned the River Sambre between Maubeuge and Namur—for instance, at Merbes-le-Château, Solre-sur-Sambre, Thuin, Marchienne-au-Pont, Charleroi, and Châtelet.

In Belgium excellent roads ran from Brussels north to Antwerp; west to Ghent, Bruges, and Ostend; and east by Louvain to Moestricht, These, with good bridges over the rivers, linked together the various high roads leading northwards. The latter are sufficiently indicated on the map, but we may allude more particularly to the road leading from Audenarde by Grammont, Enghien, Nivelles, Quatre Bras, and Sombref to Namur; and also the Roman road running by Binche, across the Charleroi-Brussels road, towards Moestricht. Thus the communications throughout Belgium were generally very good, but there were districts of wooded, or broken and enclosed, as well as wet and swampy country, over which roads or tracks were either few or bad.

On the whole, the surface of Belgium is flat or undulating; near the coast large tracks have been recovered from the sea, and are fenced off by dykes. To the east of the Meuse are the forest-covered hills of the Ardennes; and south of Brussels lies the forest of Soignies, a wooded tract of some extent.

An example of the broken, enclosed country is found in the space between the Charleroi-Quatre Bras and the Charleroi-Fleurus roads, the latter of which continues on to the east of Ligny and Sombref. These two roads branch off further from each other as they lead northward from Charleroi, and between them no good road runs to the north.

An example of the wet, swampy country is found a little further to the north, along the banks of the River Dyle, which runs through Wavre, to the east of the Charleroi–Brussels road.

The topography of this portion of Belgium exercised a great influence upon the campaign.

FORTRESSES, FORTIFIED TOWNS, AND POSTS OF IMPORTANCE

The open country bordering the north-eastern frontier of France, to the west of the Meuse, had been strengthened long before 1815 by several fortresses and fortified towns, a good many of which were designed by the well-known engineer Vauban.

The general principle governing their situation appears to have been this (Lavallee's *Military Geography*, 1868):—

The country was considered as divided into sections by the rivers which traverse the boundary, such as the Lys, Scheldt, Sambre, and Meuse.

As a rule, the chief roads and arteries of communication run along the river valleys; and fortresses, walled towns, or defensive works of some description were placed at convenient spots commanding these roads, either at or adjacent to cross roads, the passages of rivers, or the junction of their affluents.

If we look at the boundary, beginning from the west, we see, on the French side, Dunkirk, Lille, Valenciennes with Condé, Maubeuge, Beaumont, Philippeville, and Givet (on the Meuse); on the Belgian side, Nieuport, Ypres, Courtray (on the Lys), Tournay, Audenarde and Ghent (on the Scheldt), Ath (on the Dender), Mons (north of Maubeuge), Charleroi (north of Philippeville), and Namur (on the Meuse)—all of which places form the junction of roads, and lie on, or near, rivers.

★★★★★★

The same principle was carried out between the Meuse and the Rhine, where we find Sedan, Thionville, Metz, and Strasbourg (the two last now in the possession of Germany); with, on the Rhine, the, fortifications at Cologne (Ehrenbreitsten),

Coblentz, and Mayence.

★★★★★★

In France, between her frontiers and the capital, there were various fortified towns, while Paris itself formed a great central citadel to the whole.

Many of the strong places and walled towns towards the frontier had been permitted to fall out of repair—Charleroi, for instance, among them; but several had citadels, ramparts, and ditches, and possessed the means of inundating, if necessary, the surrounding country. They were of value also, especially when strengthened by earthworks, as rallying points for the field army watching the borders, forming posts which could not be readily taken by a *coup-de-main*.

Ghent, Bruges, and Nieuport, in Belgium, were important places; Ostend, on the sea, was a large port with a considerable trade, and Antwerp was a harbour of great value and strongly fortified.

CLIMATE, RESOURCES, ETC.

Little need be said about the climate of France or Belgium. It was good and temperate, though hot occasionally in summer, the period of the year when the more active part of this campaign went on. Marching in the sultry and dry weather, upon the roads choked with dust, or after heavy thunderstorms, over the low-lying deep country, became exceedingly toilsome for heavily laden troops.

The western portion of Belgium was the most fertile part. Wheat, oats, rye, potatoes, and various root crops were freely cultivated. Cattle were numerous, and the transport throughout the country, by means of horses, carts, and canal-boats, sufficiently good.

EVENTS OF THE CAMPAIGN

Wellington took command of the Anglo-Allied Army early in April, 1815, and was at once overwhelmed with work in organising his composite force, and arranging for the defence of Belgium, in co-operation with the armies of his allies. Garrisons, some under British officers, were assigned to Antwerp, Ghent, Ostend, Nieuport, Ypres Tournay, Ath, Mons, etc., and measures were taken to strengthen these fortresses or fortified towns. Namur fell to the Prussian Army to occupy.

At first he was anxious to assume the offensive as quickly as possible in France, and in urging this upon the authorities at home he writes, on April 10th, 1815:

This point is so clear that it would be a useless waste of your time and mine to discuss it.

And again on April 12th:

Every day's experience convinces me that we ought not to lose a moment which could be spared.

But he soon saw that he must abandon the prompt realisation of this idea. Unexpected delays occurred in the preparations to take the field; and it was held desirable that the powers should wait to enter France till they could all move in concert, while the strength of Napoleon's army daily increased.

Upon first reaching Brussels he found that General von Kleist, who before Blücher's arrival was in command of the Prussian troops (then cantoned to the east of the Meuse), desired that, in the event of Napoleon's invading Belgium, he (Wellington) should fall back behind Brussels; the Prussians co-operating with him by advancing across the Meuse: the two armies to join about Tirlemont or St. Trond (east of Louvain).

This scheme, of course, would have yielded up a large portion of Belgium to the army of Napoleon; and Wellington, looking upon the matter from more than the military aspect alone, deprecated it. He proposed instead that he himself should take up a more forward position, and that the Prussians, in order to co-operate with him and better cover Brussels, should approach closer, and occupy Huy, Namur, and Charleroi.

Writing to General ———— (name not given, but, from the context, clearly the officer in command of the Prussian troops at Namur, *Wellington Despatches*, vol. viii.), he says:

It is not possible to entirely separate political considerations from purely military ones, especially under the circumstances in which we now find ourselves, and in an affair such as that on which we are about to engage. But it is also true that we must not sacrifice military considerations and conveniences to those purely political.

About this time—that is, long before the opening of the campaign—he anticipates the possibility of what he was always afterwards on his guard against—*viz.* that Bonaparte might make an attempt to reach Ghent or Brussels with his light troops, because it would be of the greatest importance to him to drive away the King of France (then at Ghent) with the Royal family, and cause the King of the Nether-lands to retire from Brussels, he writes:

That would have a terrible effect on public opinion in France and here.

Wellington's plan naturally commended itself to the King of the Netherlands; but General von Kleist, as Müffling tells us, (*Passages from my Life*), replied respecting it, that with the best will he could not con-cur, as the subsistence of the Prussian troops was not ensured beyond the limits of the Government of the Lower Rhine, also that he had no money at his disposal to live on the Meuse by purchases; neither could he draw supplies from magazines.

Now this question of supplies became, from the very first, a trou-blesome one in Belgium, and we allude to it here for a reason which will appear later on. Wellington tells us in his correspondence that the Prussians were often in difficulties as to supplies, and he viewed it as a matter of paramount military consequence that the Prussian Army should be in close touch with him. The armies of the Allies were, it is true, on Belgian territory, in the interests of the King of the Nether-lands as well as in their own; but naturally they were, in certain senses at all events, a burden upon the people whose villages and lands were about to be made the battlefield of Europe; and therefore, for reasons of state, as well as mere convenience of supply, it was desirable not to make that burden greater than military exigencies clearly demanded.

Wellington arranged that the King of the Netherlands should furnish and pay for the supplies of the Prussian Army, the Prussian Government settling the financial debt later on, instead of paying for supplies upon the spot. The Prussians then crossed the Meuse, and concentrated about Liege, Namur, and Charleroi.

But such friction subsequently arose upon the matter of supplies and the payment for them, that the question of Blücher's withdrawal from his cantonments was at one time raised. This Wellington was very much averse to, and for military reasons, no doubt, again became mediator, and the matter was settled.

How strong the Prussian feeling was upon this subject, how Wel-lington was more or less viewed as responsible for the arrangements made, and what worry the supply question caused generally, comes out in the following allusions by Müffling and Sir Henry Hardinge to it. Müffling writes, as to the supply difficulties:

Field-Marshal Blücher inherited from his predecessor in com-

MAP OF
part of
EUROPE
showing boundaries of France
and adjoining Countries in
1815.

mand, General von Kleist, troublesome difficulties with the authorities of the Netherlands.

And Colonel Sir H. Hardinge, British Commissioner at Blücher's headquarters, writes thus to Wellington on May 25th, 1815 (*Supplementary Despatches*, vol. x.):—

> I spoke with General Gneisenau on the subject of the subsistence of the Prussian troops by the King of the Netherlands. His reasoning on the question was, that when circumstances rendered it expedient that the Prussian troops should enter Belgium, it was stipulated that their subsistence should be provided at the expense of the King of the Netherlands, and that your lordship was the party, or the guarantee, to this stipulation, and the principal cause of the readiness with which the movement was made, without magazines or means to supply their troops... During this conversation strong expressions were used towards the Belgian Government, showing the acrimony and bad understanding which exist between the two courts.

On May 1st, 1815, Wellington concentrated his own troops somewhat more together in their cantonments; and they then occupied much the same positions which they did when the campaign actually opened in the following June.

As the weeks went by, it was at times expected that the opponents of the Imperial regime in Paris would be strong enough to overthrow Napoleon, and that it might never come to a contest in the field.

On May 25th it seemed as if the powers would soon be able to assume the offensive. Prince Wrede, writing from Manheim on that date, says:

> I think that about the 10th June at the latest we will be able to commence operations. We are losing much time, and wearing out the country on which we are cantoned.

On June 7th instructions were sent to all the governors of the Belgian fortresses, that the moment the enemy entered Belgium a state of siege was to be proclaimed.

On June 14th, in answer to a letter from the Czar of Russia (requiring a reply), Wellington entered fully into his views as to invading France, should the powers take the offensive. Thus, preparations either to defend Belgium or to invade France alike went on; but it is sufficiently evident, as will be shown in the next chapter, that Wellington was well aware of the possibility that Napoleon would attack; and also that the Allies had a very approximate idea indeed of the strength and position of his forces.

The initiative, however, and choice of the point of attack rested at this date with Napoleon; the powers not being yet ready to enter France.

Before describing the dispositions of the armies of Wellington, Blücher, and Napoleon, or entering into the plans of their leaders, we must give a few more particulars respecting the composition of the three armies about to come into collision.

The Army of Wellington

The army of Wellington, by June 1815, numbered about 106,000, of whom 14,000 were cavalry, with 196 guns. This, however, includes over 12,000 troops garrisoning various places.

About 34,000 (not including garrison troops) were British, the remainder consisting of mixed nationalities. These included some excellent German troops (the King's German Legion); Hanoverians and Brunswickers (good troops, but having among them many young soldiers); and a large body (25,000) of Nassauers, Dutch, and Belgians. Upon these latter, on account of the doubtful attachment of some of them towards the Allied cause, too much reliance could not be placed.

Of Wellington's old Peninsular army, the regiments despatched from the south of France to America had not yet returned, and many of the private soldiers had been discharged; so that the British force was largely made up of second battalions, and of militiamen incorporated into the line.

Still, all the regiments were imbued with the Peninsular traditions of the army, and had full confidence in Wellington.

Several of the Peninsular leaders also held commands, such as Hill, Picton, Uxbridge, Alten, Kempt, Pack, etc., not to mention other juniors, such as Colborne.

Upon the headquarter staff Lord FitzRoy Somerset, the military secretary, Sir William De Lancey, the deputy quartermaster-general, and a few more had Peninsular experience; but as a whole the staff was untrained and inexperienced.

Wellington more than once remonstrated upon the manner in which his requests for certain staff-officers had not been complied with. He did not want more staff officers, but to obtain those whom he desired; and his annoyance at not having been given more choice in their selection comes out strongly in the following letter, (to Sir H.

I think it much better that this correspondence upon the staff should cease. The commander-in-chief has the right to appoint whom he chooses, and those whom he appoints shall be employed. It cannot be expected that I should declare myself satisfied with these appointments, till I shall find the persons as fit for their situations as those whom I should have recommended to His Royal Highness.

Often in Wellington's correspondence we find strong expressions as to the bad army and the inexperienced staff which he had at Waterloo. Once he writes, (to Lord Stewart, May 8th, 1815):

I have got an infamous army, very weak and ill-equipped, and a very inexperienced staff.

It should always be remembered that, when he does this, he speaks of the composition, strength, and equipment of his heterogeneous force of all nations, not of their courage; and of the experience, not the zeal, of his staff. Also that these expressions (used before the battle of Waterloo had taken place) were probably made all the stronger by his recollection of his old Peninsular Army, not now available.

Some of the British battalions were very weak, except those of the Guards and 52nd, who had each about 1,000 men in their ranks. There were only four over 700 strong, many under 600, and a few under 400.

The organisation of his mixed force gave Wellington much trouble, and what was accomplished in the way of welding it into that army which won the day at Waterloo speaks volumes for the exertions of all concerned, and the administrative power of the directing mind.

To combine the regiments into a workable effective machine, without interfering too much with national feeling, was most difficult, and required both ability, tact, and judgment.

Wellington writes as to it:

No troops can be employed in an allied army excepting each corps and detachment be under the immediate command of its own national officers. It was necessary to organise these troops in brigades, divisions, and *corps d'armée*, with those better disciplined and more accustomed to war, in order to derive from their numbers as much advantage as possible. The organisation and formation of corps to serve together, and under the command and direction of *what officer*, becomes therefore, and became in this case, a matter which required great attention and labour, and was of great difficulty.—"Memorandum upon the Battle of Waterloo," in *Personal Reminiscences of the Duke of Wellington*, by the Earl of Ellesmere.

In connection with this organisation we can only allude to a very few among the points which will strike those who examine and reflect upon the details given in the tables in Appendix A.

Battalions of different nationalities were not mixed together in brigade. Brigades were of one nation, and, with one or two exceptions, under an officer of that nation.

On the other hand, each division, with the exception of the 1st (composed entirely of British Guards) and the Dutch-Belgians, was made up partly of British, and partly of German and Hanoverian brigades. Thus the latter fought in division side by side with the British.

The Dutch-Belgian Infantry, though formed into divisions under their own officers, were distributed between the 1st and 2nd corps.

The whole force was divided into two corps (*i.e. corps d'armée*), under the Prince of Orange and Lord Hill; the cavalry, organised by brigades under Lord Uxbridge, being, with a strong reserve, under Wellington's more direct command.

The reserve, with the cavalry—a great part of which was kept together—practically constituted a body of the three arms at Wellington's disposal, which was evidently provided as the result of his Peninsular experience; for he writes to the military secretary from Brussels, April 21st, 1815:

> In the Peninsula, I always kept three or four divisions under my own immediate command, which, in fact, was the working part of the army, thrown as necessary upon one flank or the other. It might be convenient to have something of the same kind now.

There was no reserve of cavalry or artillery with either *corps d'armée*, but two batteries of field artillery were as a rule attached to each division of infantry, and one horse artillery to each brigade of cavalry.

THE ARMY OF BLÜCHER

The army of Blücher numbered about 117,000, with 312 guns. It consisted largely of *Landwehr*, and in the regular battalions there were many young soldiers. Very recently a portion of the troops from the Saxon and Rhenish provinces, which had lately come under Prussian rule, had broken out into grave breaches of discipline; but this had no influence on others, and the army as a whole was animated with an enthusiastic patriotism, as well as a bitter hatred of Napoleon.

Gneisenau, the Chief of the Staff, was a man of marked ability, but of a difficult temper. Apparently he was not on cordial terms with all of the Prussian leaders, and had conceived an extreme distrust of Wellington.

Fortunately, this was balanced by the frankness and loyal character of Blücher, which bore with great importance upon the conduct of the campaign.

The general staff had possibly more experience and knowledge than the British, although it was not in those days what it has since become.

Müffling, writing of the year 1814, says, (*Passages from my Life*):

The ordinary daily duties of the general staff had grown somewhat lax during the last three campaigns. This I endeavoured to remedy.

He adds the result being that when Napoleon reappeared in France in 1815, many of the officers were then "fit to be employed—*i.e.* after a year's training—on staff duty."

The army was organised into four *corps d'armée*, with a reserve of cavalry and artillery attached to each. These corps consisted of large brigades, which were in reality of the strength, or more than the strength, of French or British divisions. Several battalions were between 800 and 900 strong.

There was no special reserve retained under Blücher's direct command, although, of course, he could, as commander-in-chief, employ any portion of the army as he desired upon any day.

THE ARMY OF NAPOLEON

The field army of Napoleon numbered about 123,000, with 344 guns.

Having determined to assume the offensive against Wellington and Blücher, and left a large body of men to occupy various posts in France and watch the frontiers to the south and east, he pushed forward his columns behind the screen of his fortresses close to the Belgian frontier. By June 14th they had assembled between Maubeuge and Philippeville; he left Paris himself early on June 12th, arrived at Beaumont on the 14th, and issued orders to cross the Sambre upon the following day.

His army contained a greater number of veteran soldiers than that of either Wellington or Blücher. They were burning to avenge the defeats of 1814, and longing to return to the excitement of war; while the confidence of the junior officers and men in the genius and star of Napoleon was undiminished.

The weak spot in the army lay, perhaps, in the relations of the marshals and generals to each other, and towards Napoleon himself. The mutual trust between chief and subordinates could not have been what it was in his earlier campaigns.

Colonel Haldane, in a lecture delivered recently at Aldershot, and referring to the Japanese Army in the Russo-Japanese War, says:

> Jealousy and self-seeking did not exist, and co-operation between commanders in the field was a thing assured; the wisdom or unwisdom of orders was unquestioned, and criticism of superiors unknown.

These advantages to any army hardly characterised that of Napoleon at Waterloo.

Some of his higher leaders had taken office under the Bourbon Government when he was sent to Elba. They could scarcely forget entirely that they had seen him return, after crushing reverses, to Paris in 1812 and 1814, for some of which he had blamed his subordinates; and he could scarcely forget that Soult, now his chief of the staff, had declared him to be a madman and adventurer; and Ney, that he would bring him back to Paris in a cage. Nevertheless, their interests and perhaps their lives depended now upon his success; there was no doubt that they would do their best to ensure it, and they were brave men.

As in the Anglo-Allied Army, so with this army, the staff was not a very strong point, as there had been no time to organise it. Only the day before Napoleon crossed the Belgian frontier, Ney, hastily summoned, had joined his command, having only one staff-officer with him, and did not know anything of the regiments which he had the following morning to lead into battle.

The army was divided into six *corps d'armée*, each corps having with it a force of cavalry and artillery. In addition, there was a reserve of about 13,000 cavalry, with horse artillery, under Grouchy; and a further one, of about 18,000 of the Imperial Guard (cavalry, infantry, and artillery), under the personal command of Napoleon.

With regard to the topography of the Franco-Belgian border, and of the boundaries of France, we have already drawn attention to the manner in which this influenced the question of the theatre of war; and need only now add that the particular nature (see earlier mention) of that part of Belgium between the Charleroi-Brussels, and the Charleroi-Sombref, roads, as well as of the districts about the River Dyle between Sombref and Wavre, materially affected the operations of the campaign. A photograph of a portion of this country has been given, taken from the maps of 1797 by Ferraris and Capitaine, which are those said to have been used by Napoleon and the Allies throughout the operations.

★★★★★★

Houssaye writes in *Waterloo, 1815,* that after Napoleon had breakfasted with Soult and others at the farm of Caillou, on the morning of the Battle of Waterloo, "The maps of Ferraris and Capitaine were spread out on the table"; and Lettow-Vorbeck states that the map of Capitaine was used by Napoleon and the chiefs of the Allied Armies.

★★★★★★

With respect to the fortresses and walled or fortified places of Belgium and France, although they were not as a rule at the date of this campaign very formidable strongholds, yet they would have been a danger to the communications of any army which ventured to pass by them without leaving a force sufficient to shut in their garrisons.

As to organisation, between Wellington and his troops there intervened only three great heads to whom his orders had to be conveyed—*i.e.* the leaders of his two corps and of his cavalry; and he kept a large reserve under his own hand.

Between Blücher and his troops there intervened four heads of corps, and he kept no reserve—*i.e.* as a permanent organisation—under his hand.

Between Napoleon and his troops there were six heads of corps (including Grouchy, commanding the reserve cavalry). He kept, like Wellington, a large reserve at his own disposal—the Imperial Guard.

Thus Napoleon had nearly double the number of heads to deal with, and to convey orders to, that Wellington had; and, partly perhaps in consequence, he suddenly modified his organisation—as we shall see—the very morning upon which he went into battle (June 16th) with Wellington and Blücher, placing three of his corps under Ney and four under Grouchy, and completing them with cavalry and artillery.

But a suddenly arranged or temporary organisation is not the same as a more permanent one; and any supersession in command may lead to indecision in action, and perhaps to friction.

It should be also noticed that when writers on this campaign (as, for instance, Siborne, and the German historians) speak of a Prussian brigade, they mean a body of an entirely different strength to that of a French or British brigade.

In England the term "regiment" is used loosely. It may mean one, two, or even four battalions, such as are found in rifle regiments; but on the Continent it answers much to what we term a "brigade," and is a body of some strength. In the Prussian Army the brigades were of exceptional strength, and really corresponded to British or French divisions. Their batteries also, field and horse, had 8 guns; while the French field batteries had 8 guns, the horse 6; the British and Hanoverian, field and horse, only 6; the Dutch-Belgian 8.

If the above is not borne in mind, an incorrect impression of facts may arise. To illustrate this let us turn to the tables in Appendix A.

If we take the 1st Division of the 1st French Army Corps (D'Erlon's), we shall find that it consisted of 8 battalions, each of an *average* strength of about 550 men; and that in this corps, 4 divisions make a total of 17,600 men.

If we take the 1st Brigade of the 1st Prussian Army Corps (Ziethen's), we find it consisted of 9½ battalions, and that 4 brigades make a total of 27,887 men, the battalion *average* being 820.

Thus the Prussian brigade was in certain cases far stronger than the French division, and it was usually more than equal to a division in strength. Therefore, when one reads that a Prussian brigade proceeded to such-and-such a point, it should be viewed as really being a strong division.

Ten British field batteries would mean 60 guns. Ten Prussian or French field batteries, 80 guns—*i.e.* one-third more.

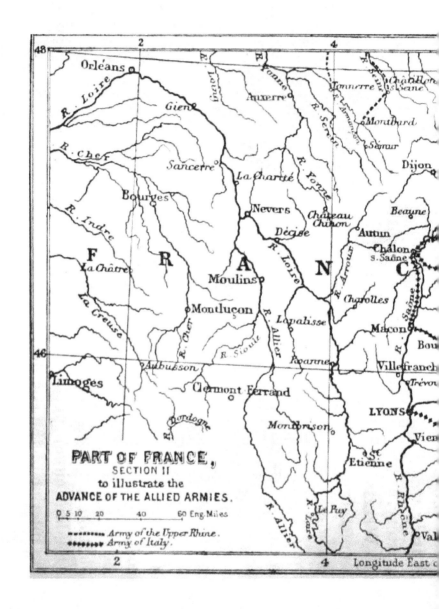

PART OF FRANCE,
SECTION II
to illustrate the
ADVANCE OF THE ALLIED ARMIES.

.... Army of the Upper Rhine.
•••••••• Army of Italy.

6
8
48
46
Remiremont
R. Moselle
Thann
Freiburg
R. Danube
GERMANY
R. Rhine
Langres
Mülhausen
Schaffhausen
R. Saône
Vesoul
Belfort
Hunningen
Constance
Basle
Montbéliard
Gray
R. Ognon
R. Doubs
Baume
Solothurn
R. Aar
Zürich
Besançon
Lucerne
Dôle
R. Doubs
Salins
Neuchâtel
BERNE
SWITZERLAND
Pontarlier
Thun
Freiburg
R. Rhine
E
St. Laurent
Lausanne
Les Rousses
St. Claude
L. of Geneva
Gex
Meillerie
St. Maurice
R. Rhône
Oyonnax
St. Genis
Sion
Brieg
Geneva
Carouge
Bonneville
Nantua
Châtillon
Fort de l'Ecluse
Perte du Rhône
Seyssel
R. Rhône
Aosta
Conflans
Dora Baltea
R. Sesia
R. Ticino
Chambéry
Ivrea
ITALY
Moutiers
Les Echelles
Montmélian
Barraux
Vercelli
R. Po
Isère
Susa
Grenoble
Dora Riparia
TURIN
Briançon
R. Tanaro
R. Po
Mens
reenwich

CHAPTER 2

Events to the 16th of June, 1815

The field army of Wellington, composed of two corps, the reserve, and about 15,000 cavalry, numbered nearly 94,000, with 196 guns.

★★★★★★

The strength of troops throughout these pages is given approximately in round numbers. Exact agreement upon the subject among historians is not obtainable. Siborne, Chesney, and Ropes make the total army of Wellington, however, close upon 106,000, and from this they deduct some 12,000 garrison troops, leaving the field army at about 94,000.

★★★★★★

On June 14th, 1815, it was distributed thus:—

THE 1ST CORPS (PRINCE OF ORANGE)

25,000 with 48 guns, had its headquarters at Braine-le-Comte, and its divisions were posted thus (see map of part of Belgium and the French frontier):—

Troops	Headquarters
1st Division, British Guards (Cooke)	Enghien.
3rd ,, British, German Legion, and Hanoverians, (Alten)	Soignies.
2nd ,, Dutch-Belgians (Perponcher) . . .	Nivelles.
3rd ,, ,, ,, (Chassé)	Near Rœulx.

★★★★★★

The tables in Appendix A show the distribution by divisions, and the composition of the army in fuller detail, and on the map the posts occupied are marked.

★★★★★★

This corps watched the country between the Brussels-Charleroi road and the River Dender to the west. It was the most advanced por-

42

tion of Wellington's army towards the Sambre. Its troops occupied (in addition to those places mentioned as being the headquarters of corps and divisions) Genappe, Quatre Bras, Frasnes, Mons, and Binche.

From the two latter places its posts were pushed out towards the French border; it communicated with the Prussians at Frasnes, Fontaine l'Eveque, and Bonne Espérance; and with the 2nd Corps through Enghien.

The 2nd Corps (Hill)

24,000 with 40 guns, had its headquarters at Ath, and its divisions were thus distributed, (Hooper's Waterloo, however on June 15th, Hill appears to have been at Grammont):—

		Troops	Headquar.ers
2nd Division,		British, German Legion, and Hanoverians (Clinton) . . .	Ath.
4th	,,	British and Hanoverians (Colville) .	Audenarde.
1st	,,	Dutch-Belgians (Stedmann), with a Dutch-Belgian Indian brigade attached (Anthing) . . .	Apparently near Sotteghem.†

This corps watched the country between the Dender and Scheldt, and towards Tournay. It occupied (in addition to those places mentioned above) Renaix, south of Audenarde; Lens, whence it communicated with the 1st Corps at Mons; and also villages bordering the Grammont-Ghent road, or between that road and Alost.

The Reserve (Wellington)

21,000, (exclusive of 12,000 garrison troops), with 64 guns, had its headquarters at Brussels, and its divisions, etc., were thus posted:—

The 5th and 6th Divisions (British and Hanoverians) under Picton and Cole, the Brunswick Corps under the Duke of Brunswick, the Nassau Contingent under Kruse, and the reserve artillery (5 batteries) under Major Drummond—all in, or near, Brussels.

The Cavalry (Uxbridge)

About 15,000 with 44 guns, had its headquarters near Ninove.

It was formed into brigades, there being no cavalry divisional commands, and consisted of the main body of the cavalry, British, German Legion, and Hanoverian; the Brunswick cavalry, near Brussels; and the Dutch-Belgian cavalry, about Mons, Roeulx, Binche, etc. Posts watched the line of the Scheldt and the French border.

The main body (more immediately under Lord Uxbridge) was

posted along the Dender between Ninove and Grammont where the ground was suitable. It was formed into three British brigades, four British and Hanoverian brigades, and one Hanoverian.

The artillery, except the reserve near Brussels, June u, was distributed as a rule in the proportion of two field batteries to each infantry division, and one horse artillery battery to each cavalry brigade.

ARMY OF BLÜCHER—HEADQUARTERS, NAMUR

The Prussian Army under Blücher, (Prince Blücher von Wahlstadt), composed of four corps, numbered about 117,000, (according to Siborne and Chesney. Ropes makes it nearly 121,000), of whom about 12,000 were cavalry, with 312 guns.

Corps						Headquarters
1st Corps (Ziethen)	31,000 with 96 guns .	.	.	Charleroi.
2nd ,, (Pirch I.†)	32,000 ,, 80 ,, .	.	.	Namur.
3rd ,, (Thielemann)	24,000 ,, 48 ,, .	.	.	Ciney.
4th ,, (Bülow)	30,000 ,, 88 ,, .	.	.	Liege.

THE 1ST CORPS (ZIETHEN)

Watched the line of the Sambre from Lobbes and Thuin past Charleroi to Moustier-sur-Sambre. It occupied Bonne Espérance, and slightly overlapped the Dutch-Belgians at this point; also Fontaine l'Eveque, Marchienne-au-Pont, Gerpinnes, and Sossoye (south of the Sambre). The reserve cavalry of this corps was at Sombref; the reserve artillery at Gembloux.

THE 2ND CORPS (PIRCH I.)

Watched the country between Sossoye and Dinant; also the Meuse between Namur and Huy. (Where generals bear the same surname in Prussia they are distinguished by the addition of numerals. General Pirch II. commanded a brigade of this corps). Its reserve cavalry was at Hannut; the reserve artillery on the Namur-Louvain road. Other points occupied are indicated on the map.

THE 3RD CORPS (THIELEMANN)

Watched the country from Dinant along the French border to Rochefort, etc. Its reserve cavalry was between Ciney and Dinant; the reserve artillery at Ciney.

THE 4TH CORPS (BÜLOW)

Watched the Meuse, between Huy and Liege, with the country

behind. Its reserve cavalry was at Tongres, Dalhem, and Looz; the reserve artillery at Gloms and Dalhem.

The French frontier line near Valenciennes and Conde, in the direction of Wellington's right, runs up further to the north than it does near Ciney and Dinant, towards Blücher's left. Therefore, to watch this frontier Blücher's posts had to be pushed some distance south of the Sambre, and of the Meuse east of Namur.

From Brussels, Wellington's line of communications with England lay through Ghent, Bruges, and Ostend, as well as through Antwerp; with Holland through Antwerp; while with Germany he could communicate through Louvain.

Blücher's communications lay through Namur and Liege to Moestricht and Cologne on the Rhine.

In order to ensure prompt communication between the two forces of Blücher and Wellington (a most important matter), Colonel Sir Henry Hardinge was sent as Commissioner to Blücher's headquarters, and the Prussian general, Baron von Müffling, to the headquarters of Wellington.

The latter writes thus, (*Passages from My Life*), as to the arrangements made for him by Wellington:

> I had four *aides-de-camp* with bureau and orderlies; I had as many field *jägers* and letter-carriers, and as many mounted officers as I required at my disposal. I was furnished with far better means for the purpose than Hardinge was.

This shows that all proper attention was given to this point.

It was settled between Blücher and Wellington that their correspondence should be carried on in French, with which language the latter was more familiar than with German, and meetings between them, giving opportunities to discuss their plans, took place on several occasions. Wellington writes on May 3rd, 1815, "I am going to Tirlemont to meet Blücher"; and again, on May 25th, that Blücher and he were going together to Ninove.

Official reports from the Prussian Army would no doubt as a rule reach Brussels through Müffling and Hardinge; but the following letter from Wellington, to the "General Officer commanding the Prussian troops at Charleroi," (written personally by Wellington in French. *Wellington Despatches*, vol. viii.), shows that he also intended to communicate to him all important intelligence (by the Belgian posts). This would be a necessary and natural precaution to take in order to save time, and it may be inferred that he expected to receive it himself through the same channel.

Brussels, May 9th, 1815, 1.30 p.m.:

It is my duty to inform you that all the information I have from the frontier leads me to believe that the French troops are collected between Valenciennes and Maubeuge, and rather about Maubeuge than Valenciennes. . . . I will cause you to be informed through the posts of the troops of the Low Countries, (Belgian posts, communicating with the Prussians, at Binche and Frasnes), of all news that I may obtain.

Correspondence as to the transmission of reports took place with the Prince of Orange, and we read of the establishment of letter posts at certain places.

These details may appear to be matters-of-course and trivial, but they are not so. Their working in war may affect the issue of a campaign. It did affect this campaign materially; and therefore it should be noted that they had at all events engaged the attention of Wellington.

THE ARMY OF NAPOLEON—HEADQUARTERS, BEAUMONT

This was collected by June 14th, 1815, between Maubeuge and Beaumont, and was composed of five corps, the reserve cavalry, and the Imperial Guard. In all it numbered about 123,000, (according to Siborne; Napoleon says 115,000; Chesney, Charras, and Ropes, 128,000; Houssaye, 124,000 and 370 guns), of whom about 22,000 were cavalry, with 350 guns, of these about 116,000 are thus accounted for:—

Troops			Position		
1st Corps (D'Erlon)	20,000 with 46 guns		Near Solre-sur-Sambre.		
2nd ,, (Reille)	23,000 ,, 46 ,,		,, ,, ,,		
3rd ,, (Vandamme)	16,000 ,, 38 ,,	• ,,	Beaumont.		
6th‡ ,, (Lobau)	11,000 ,, 38 ,,	• ,,	,,		
Reserve cavalry (Grouchy)	13,000 ,, 48 ,,	• ,,	,,		
Imperial Guard (Mortier)	18,000 ,, 96 ,,	• ,,	,,		
4th Corps (Gérard)	15,000 ,, 38 ,,	•	Philippeville.		

There was no 5th Corps, this forming a separate force towards the Rhine.

For further particulars see tables, Appendix A. The reserve cavalry consisted of the divisions of Pajol, Expellant, Kellermann (Comte de Valmy), and Milhaud.

Napoleon's plan of attack was to strike from the direction of Charleroi at the centre of the joint forces of Wellington and Blücher. Apparently he was aware of their general position. Charleroi lay near the frontier, on the direct road to Brussels; and the point of junction of any two armies whose troops differ in nationality and language must be usually, to some extent, at all events, a weak one, for there is more probability that there will be confusion and want of cooperation there, than at any other point.

Subsequent events have shown that Napoleon's knowledge of the exact dispositions of the Allies, and his calculation of the time in which they could assemble and unite together, was very imperfect; but he knew that Blücher's army was nearer to him than Wellington's; he therefore expected to meet it first, and also that its fiery leader would stand to fight.

He writes, (Ropes), to his brother Joseph on June 14th from Avesnes:

Tomorrow I go to Charleroi, where the Prussian Army is; that will occasion either a battle or the retreat of the enemy.

It does not appear, from what he himself has written, that he had any intention of breaking through *between* the Allies (*i.e.* in any interval between them); but rather to strike at the Prussians, and then, having defeated them, to drive them back eastward before Wellington could come to their support; and he says (see " Comments," further on) that he did not wish or mean, previous to a battle, to advance as far north as Sombref, for fear that Blücher might retire.

In strength his army was superior to either that of Wellington or Blücher, though inferior to both united, and he anticipated that whatever force he might succeed in defeating would retire along its own line of communications. These were divergent, Wellington's leading to Ostend or Antwerp, and Blücher's to Liege; and thus the retreating army would become separated from its ally.

By demonstrations along the frontier, by movements and counter-movements, and by false reports, he endeavoured to mystify the Allies as to his point of attack; and then, on the night of June 14th, 1815, directed his army to cross the Sambre on the following morning.

His corps were to move off at various hours between 2.30 and 8 a.m., in three columns, Charleroi being the chief objective point.

The situation of the Allied commanders, Wellington and Blücher, was necessarily in no way analogous to that of Napoleon. The latter, assembling behind the French fortresses and his guarded frontier, could choose where he would strike.

The former were for the moment on the defensive; their armies were independent one of the other, and each had separate interests to guard. Wellington was responsible also for the safety of King Louis of France at Ghent, and of the King of the Netherlands at Brussels.

At the same time, consistently with these separate responsibilities, it was of the utmost importance that the two armies should be in a position to act in support of each other when Napoleon did attack.

Their joint line, which we have already described, was greatly extended, being spread over about 100 miles from west to east and 40 from north to south. This was its weak point, but it was deliberately adopted as the best in Wellington's judgment under the circumstances of the case. (*Supplementary Wellington Despatches*, vol. x. "Memorandum upon the Battle of Waterloo," written September 24th, 1842).

It is important, before entering upon the movements of the campaign, to note the respective spheres occupied by the armies of Wellington and Blücher, with the line of demarcation between them.

Müffling states, (*Passages from My Life*), that, previous to Wellington's arrival at Brussels (in April, 1815), at a military conference in Brussels, he (Müffling) laid upon the table a map of Belgium on which was drawn a broad red line from Marchienne, on the Sambre, along the Dyle, by Wavre to Louvain, saying:

> Here you have the strategical line of demarcation prescribed by nature—a westerly, or English, and an easterly, or Prussian, department. We did not get a step further, and on Wellington's arrival all was recorded on the minutes.

Subsequently, as the dispositions of the troops on June 14th, 1815, show, the Prussian sphere towards the Sambre was extended further westward to Fontaine l'Eveque and Bonne Espérance.

★★★★★★

Why this was so arranged does not appear; possibly for considerations of locality or of strength. The Roman road formed a denned boundary, and it may not have been held desirable that the posts of two armies, speaking different languages, should join on the Charleroi road. It should be noticed, though, that if the Prussians retreated on Sombref they must fall back across the Charleroi—Brussels road, leaving it open up to the Belgian post at Frasnes.

✶✶✶✶✶✶

Therefore, ultimately, the line of demarcation became that marked on the map before Appendix A with a broad black line; and any French columns crossing the Sambre to the east of Bonne Espérance would necessarily come into collision in the first instance with the Prussians occupying that ground.

With regard to the point of junction arranged for between the two armies in the event of Napoleon's attack being delivered against their centre, there is some difference of opinion. It does not appear to be established that any precise spot was named, but rather that the *line of junction* was understood to be the road leading from Nivelles, by Quatre Bras, to Sombref, north of Fleurus. (Ligny, where Blücher eventually concentrated to fight, is south of Sombref, and north of Fleurus).

Sombref was a convenient point of assembly for the 1st, 2nd, and 4th Prussian corps, should Napoleon advance to the west of the Meuse; while the 3rd Corps (from Ciney) might act against his flank. Siborne writes:

> Blücher had decided, in the event of a French advance across the line of the Sambre by Charleroi, upon concentrating his army in a position in *front of Sombref*, where Wellington had agreed, in that case, to concentrate as large a force *as time would admit*, in order to check any advance in this direction, or to join Blücher 's right flank, *according to circumstances.*—Siborne, vol. i.

✶✶✶✶✶✶

The words placed in italics above indicate the very general character of the agreement. Charras, among others, implies that there was a more definite promise on Wellington's part to concentrate at Sombref; but Ropes remarks that he gives no authority for this assumption, and considers that there is an absence of any evidence of it.

✶✶✶✶✶✶

Müffling writes, (*Passages from my Life*), that, after Wellington's army had "bivouacked within the triangle Frasnes, Quatre Bras, and Nivelles"—in other words, had assembled on his left—then Gosselies (or, "*en dernier lieu,* between Gosselies and Marchienne") for Wellington, and Ligny for Blücher, would have been excellent points to take up,

49

and were understood to be those from which the two armies could well act in concert.

In front of them they would have had the broken country north of Charleroi; in rear, communication by the Gosselies—Fleurus, and the Roman, roads; and behind, the low swampy district about the Dyle, which would make it difficult for Napoleon to turn their left flank and strike the Brussels road. (See photograph of maps of 1797, by Ferraris and Capitaine).

But to reach such a forward position as Gosselies, not far behind the advanced posts of the Prussians, would only have been practicable if the line of the Sambre had been maintained by the latter much longer than it was probable that it could be, or than it afterwards was.

Of course, in the event of Napoleon attacking Wellington's right or Blücher's left, the concentration of the Allies must have been modified accordingly.

It was Wellington's determination not to move his troops from their cantonments until he had satisfied himself as to the real point of Napoleon's attack. The chief danger of the Allied position was, in his judgment, the possibility of his being deceived as to this. He counted, apparently, (Houssine; Ollech), upon being able to assemble his army upon its left (Nivelles) within less than twenty-four hours from the time when his orders to concentrate went out from Brussels.

The distance from Charleroi to Brussels is but little over 30 miles, (he puts the distance at 18 miles only). Therefore, it was reasonable to suppose that a report of an attack on the Prussians between Bonne Espérance and Charleroi would be received, *via* Binche or Frasnes, where there were Belgian posts, within from five to six hours from the time it was sent off. Siborne considers that an express should have ridden from Binche to Braine-le-Comte in a hour and a half, and from the latter place to Brussels in two more. This would make the report arrive within four hours; but it is fairer to allow a longer time, though the message would be certainly urgent and the *chaussées* leading to Brussels were good.

★★★★★★

Namur is further from Brussels than Charleroi—about 40 miles by the road through Quatre Bras, which would probably be taken; and Müffling, by 5 p.m. on June 15th, had received at Brussels a despatch from Blücher, written at Namur at noon.— Sir F Maurice, *United Service Magazine,* May, 1890.

★★★★★★

Although for some time previous to June 14th, the outposts on the French side of the frontier had been tripled, and no one permitted to pass, Wellington's information as to Napoleon's strength and position appears on the whole to have been very good. He was inclined to expect the attack from the direction of Mons, and perhaps not quite so soon, but was prepared for it wherever it might fall; and his published correspondence, (*Supplementary Despatches, etc.*), indicates undoubtedly that when Napoleon assumed the offensive, it could not have been a surprise.

The following extracts from letters and reports show what he must have known as to the French movements, and we can see from them also what he could not learn:—

May 7th, 1815, Wellington to Sir H. Hardinge:

Communication with foreign countries is forbidden on pain of death, which looks as if an attack was intended.

May 16th, 1815, Wellington to the King of the Netherlands: sends him a detailed memorandum, (also sent to Marshals Blücher, Wrede, and Schwarzenberg), of the strength and organisation by corps of Napoleon's entire force which is very nearly correct, and puts its strength at "not less than 110,000 men"; adding, "There are a great number of troops about Maubeuge, Avesnes, etc."

May 19th, 1815, Wellington to Lord Uxbridge:

I have a most formidable account of the French cavalry. They have now 16,000 *Grosse Cavalerie,* of which 6,000 are *cuirassiers.* They are getting horses to mount 42,000, heavy and light.

It should be noticed that these estimates of *not less* than 110,000 men, of whom 16,000 were cavalry with *more to be added,* come close to the 123,000, (Napoleon says 115,000,—Chesnez, *Waterloo Lectures*), of whom 22,000 were cavalry, at which Siborne places the strength, (as stated earlier).

On June 7th, 1815, instructions were sent to all the governors of the Belgian fortresses to proclaim a state of siege, as soon as the enemy entered the Low Countries.

June 12th, 1815, General Dörnberg writes from Mons to Lord FitzRoy Somerset, for Wellington's information, that he has received intelligence of Bonaparte's being expected every minute at Avesnes; that Soult had passed through Maubeuge; that the forces between Philippeville, Givet, Mezières, (Givet and Mezières are south of Dinant) Guise, and Maubeuge amounted to more than 100,000 troops of the line; and that the general opinion of the French Army was that the arrival of Bonaparte at Avesnes would be the signal for the beginning of hostilities. (This turned out to be the case. Bonaparte reached Avesnes on June 13th.)

June 14th, at 3 p.m., General Dörnberg from Mons informs Wellington that "all the French troops are concentrating on Maubeuge and Beaumont." (*Supplementary Wellington Despatches*, vol. x.).

At 5 p.m. the Prince of Orange reports to Wellington from Braine-le-Comte:

> I have just returned from the front, where all is quiet. . . . . It is said that Bonaparte left Paris on the 11th at night.

(This was practically correct, as he did, so about 2 a.m. on the 12th).

At 10 p.m. Sir H. Hardinge writes from Namur to Wellington:

> The prevalent opinion here seems to be that Bonaparte intends to commence offensive operations.

He also adds that Ziethen had reported that the fires of a body of troops had been seen the night before in the direction of Thimmont (near Beaumont), and also near Merbes-le-Château.

These reports bring down the information sent to Wellington to the night of June 14th. (They do not confirm Oman's statement, "Meanwhile, *i.e.* up to June 14th, nothing save the vaguest reports had reached Wellington."—*Cambridge Modern History*, ch. xx.).

They certainly pointed to a probable attack by Napoleon; but, as to the direction of it, as Sir Frederick Maurice states, ("Waterloo," by Sir F. Maurice, *United Service Magazine*, May, 1890), there was absolutely nothing to indicate that it would be towards Charleroi, rather than towards Mons.

It was not Napoleon's intention that there should be anything.

The position of Maubeuge, Beaumont, and Merbes-le-Château should be especially noted; so also should that of Solre-sur-Sambre, which is between Maubeuge and Beaumont on the road to Mons. The map shows that they lie well to the west of Charleroi, a fact which we shall again refer to.

On the night of the 14th Wellington issued no orders, and made no move, as he had no intelligence to lead him to do so.

Blücher was in a different situation to Wellington. He was nearer the frontier, and received reports more quickly. His left was not in danger, as Wellington's right was, for at all events Napoleon's forces were chiefly between Philippeville and Beaumont—*i.e.* were on the left bank of the Meuse. Therefore, on the night of the 14th, he ordered the 4th Corps (Bülow) from Liege to Hannut; the 2nd (Pirch I.) from Namur to Sombref; the 3rd (Thielemann) from Ciney to Namur; and the 1st (Ziethen) to retreat, if attacked, slowly and contesting every inch of the ground, from Charleroi upon Fleurus. (This order, it is stated, made no reference to any advance of the French. Thus Bülow took it simply as an order to be obeyed on the following day, and did not, unfortunately, move till the next morning;Ropes); but other explanations of the delay are also given).

Thus, by the early morning of June 15th, the French were moving to the attack; the Prussians beginning to concentrate upon Fleurus and Sombref; and Wellington had issued no orders of movement at Brussels. This brings us to the—

Events of June 15th, 1815

Napoleon, having given instructions to his troops to march in three columns early on the 15th, hoped that the greater part would have passed the Sambre by 12 noon; but this they did not accomplish. Reille, with the left column from Solre-sur-Sambre, moved up the right bank, seized Marchienne, and crossed there, followed by D'Erlon, but the latter's flanking parties passed the river at Lobbes, and patrolled towards Mons and Binche. Thus it must have been most difficult for General Chassé, commanding the Dutch-Belgian division in that direction, to feel certain upon what points the French attack would really in the end fall.

The centre column (Vandamme, Lobau, Grouchy, and the Guard) moved upon Charleroi by Ham (sur-Heure). The right (Gérard) upon Châtelet.

Ziethen made a very determined and able resistance during his retreat, which, as an illustration of the skilful handling of a retiring force, has been much commended; and this would have been yet more effective had the bridges over the Sambre been destroyed, which they had not been. (The reason, perhaps, was that the Allies up to the last anticipated the possibility of assuming the offensive themselves, and in that case would have used the bridges. Still, they might have been prepared for demolition).

This resistance retarded the French advance, and there had been also several other causes of delay. Both D'Erlon and Gérard had been slow in starting. General Bourmont, commanding the latter's leading division, deserted to the Allies, and its direction had then to be changed; Vandamme's orders miscarried, owing to the officer bearing them having fallen from his horse and broken his thigh; the roads were bad, and the morning misty and thick.

When the Prussians had been pressed back to Fleurus, night was approaching; so the head of the central column bivouacked two miles south of Fleurus, Napoleon himself passing the night at Charleroi. Ney, coming from Paris, had joined Napoleon near Charleroi before 5 p.m., and was directed to take command of the 2nd and 1st Corps (Reille and D'Erlon), forming the French left. A force of cavalry (Piré's and the light cavalry of the Guard) was also to be sent to him, but he was not to use it without orders.

He was instructed to drive back the enemy along the Charleroi—Quatre Bras road. It has been stated, also, that Napoleon told him verbally on the afternoon of the 15th to occupy Quatre Bras, but no such order appears in writing; it has not been admitted by Ney, and his staff-officer, Heymés, disputes it (Houssaye; Ropes).

With only one staff-officer, Heymés, he galloped off, reaching Reille, near Gosselies, before 6 p.m. (Ropes. The hour varies in different accounts).

After joining Reille he came into contact, near Frasnes, with a small force of Dutch-Belgians, who retired upon Quatre Bras, held by Prince Bernhard of Saxe-Weimar's Dutch-Belgian brigade; Piré's light cavalry, moving along the road, was driven back; and Ney about dusk advanced himself to reconnoitre.

In his front was a wooded country; he was unaware of the strength of Wellington; night was falling; his men had been seventeen hours on foot; and he could hear the guns of Napoleon far behind him, to his right rear, towards Fleurus.

Therefore, Ney halted and bivouacked near Frasnes, rode back to Charleroi to see Napoleon, arrived about midnight, had a conference with him, (the tenor of which is unknown and disputed), remained till about 2 a.m. on the 16th, and then rode back to Frasnes; having been almost continuously in the saddle for many hours. (According to the positive assertion of Colonel Heymés, Ney's A.D.C., strengthened by certain statements of Marshal Grouchy. See Ropes. Houssaye does not allude to the interview).

Blücher in the meantime had moved his headquarters to Sombref. He had ordered here (as mentioned) the 2nd Corps, as well as the 1st; and also the 3rd Corps from Namur. The 4th Corps (Bülow) was directed to move from Hannut to Gembloux; but as it had not yet marched from Liege to Hannut, (as mentioned earlier), it did not receive this order for some hours after it had been expected to do so.

With respect to Wellington's movements, Ziethen has stated (*Waterloo Lectures*, Chesney), that at 4 a.m. on June 15th he despatched a courier to Wellington to say that he was attacked in force, so undoubtedly this information was sent.

Siborne also writes (vol. i.) that the Prussian posts were withdrawn by 5 a.m. from the neighbourhood of Binche, owing to the French advance; thus, at all events, making allowance for errors in time, this information was probably sent off between 4 and 5 a.m.

But, owing to some unexplained cause, no reports reached Wellington at Brussels till 3 p.m. At about that hour he received a report brought in by the Prince of Orange personally, of firing having been heard in the direction of Thuin; and also, at nearly the same time, one from Müffling, just received from Ziethen, to the effect that his outposts were engaged with the French.

It so happened that, early on the morning of the 15th, the Prince of Orange, commanding the 1st Corps, had gone from his headquarters at Braine-le-Comte to visit his outposts; had heard firing in the direction of Thuin and the Prussian posts; and then ridden straight into Brussels, without stopping *en route* at his headquarters. In consequence the following report to him from Baron Behr at Mons remained for some time upon his table at Braine-le-Comte, unattended to (Ollech; Siborne, vol. i., makes the Prince of Orange forward this report himself, but this is apparently incorrect):—

Mons, June 15th, 1815 (no hour given):
I acquaint your Royal Highness with a report which has just been sent me from Major-General van Merlen (commanding a brigade of Dutch-Belgian cavalry to the east of Mons), that General Steinmetz, commanding at Fontaine l'Eveque, has just sent an officer to warn him that the 2nd Prussian Brigade has been attacked this morning, and that the alarm guns have been fired along the whole line. It appears that the attack is upon Charleroi, where the infantry fire was very sharp. At the outposts of General van Merlen all is quiet.
P.S. The advanced posts in front of Mons are also quiet.

Eventually the above was forwarded from Braine-le-Comte by Sir G. Berkeley, to Brussels, together with an explanation, *dated 2 p.m.*, of the Prince of Orange's absence; and also a report from General Dörnberg at Mons to Lord FitzRoy Somerset for Wellington's information, which appears to have been the following:—

Mons, June 15th, 1815, *9.30 a.m*:

To Lord FitzRoy Somerset:

A man who was yesterday at Maubeuge says all the troops march towards Beaumont and Philippeville, and that no other troops but National Guards remain at Maubeuge. I just hear the Prussians were attacked.

★★★★★★

Oman says, "General Dörnberg failed to send any reports as to matters in his front till night," and attributes neglect to him.— *Cambridge Modern History.* But see, as to what is stated above, *Supplementary Wellington Despatches*, vol. x.

★★★★★★

In enclosing these reports Sir G. Berkeley stated that he had heard from other quarters that the Prussians had been attacked at Charleroi and had evacuated Binche.

Thus these extremely important reports from Mons, indicating as they do that Napoleon's attack was not in that direction, but that his columns had moved to their right from Maubeuge towards Charleroi, were not sent off till after 2 p.m. from Braine-le-Comte; and they did not for some reason reach Brussels till late in the evening, apparently after 9 p.m.

But although he had no news from Mons, Wellington, upon the information given him, as mentioned, by Müffling and the Prince of Orange, determined to direct his corps to assemble in readiness to march, and some, especially towards his extreme right, to actually march eastward.

His remark to Müffling, (*Passages from My Life*), who had told him that Blücher would now concentrate at Ligny, near Sombref, was:

If all is as General von Ziethen supposes, I will concentrate on my left wing—*i.e.* the corps of the Prince of Orange. I shall then be à *portée* to fight in conjunction with the Prussian army. Should, however, a portion of the enemy's forces come by Mons, I must concentrate more towards my centre. For this reason, I must positively wait for news from Mons, before I fix my rendezvous.

His orders, dated 5 p.m., were despatched apparently between 5 and 7; some possibly a little later.

******

Müffling; Ropes. Interesting details as to their despatch are given in Lady De Lancey's *A Week at Waterloo in* 1815, edited by Major D. Ward; and in *Notes and Reminiscences of a Staff-Officer*, by Lieutenant-Colonel Basil Jackson, edited by R. C. Seaton, both republished by Leonaur. To ensure safe arrival they were despatched in duplicate, one copy by a steady mounted orderly, given instructions as to pace, and to bring back a receipt; the other by an officer of the Royal Staff Corps attached to the Quartermaster-General's Department. Sir William De Lancey, having sent them and transacted other business, returned to his house at about 9 p.m.

******

The troops of the Prince of Orange were to assemble at Enghien, Braine-le-Comte, and Nivelles, and, from the two former places, to move on to Nivelles, if it was certain that the attack was on Wellington's left or the Prussian right.

The cavalry along the Dender were "to collect this night at Ninove," the 2nd Hussars remaining out, however, beyond the Scheldt. One brigade and the Cumberland Hussars were ordered to Vilvorde (north of Brussels).

Of Hill's corps, the 2nd Division was to assemble at Ath; the bulk of the 4th Division to move from Audenarde to Grammont; and the Dutch-Belgians beyond the Scheldt to collect at Sotteghem.

The reserve in and near Brussels was to be held in readiness to march, and a brigade at Ghent was ordered to Brussels. (Some further details are given in the tables, Appendix A).

Late in the evening the reports sent by Sir G. Berkeley from Mons arrived; and Müffling had heard that Blücher was certainly concentrating on Sombref.

Then Wellington issued orders to concentrate to his left, these being dated 10 p.m. (They are termed "Additional Instructions," and probably went out between 10 and 11 p.m.).

The 3rd Division was to move from Braine-le-Comte to Nivelles; the 1st from Enghien to Braine-le-Comte; the 2nd from Ath, the 4th from Grammont and Audenarde, and the cavalry from Ninove, all to

Enghien. The reserve from Brussels was to march when assembled, followed by the Cumberland Hussars and some other cavalry, "by the road of Namur to the point where the road to Nivelles separates."

★★★★★★

This means, apparently, when the reserve assembled the following morning, as had been previously ordered. Ropes says that no orders were issued to the reserves, but these appear in the *Wellington Despatches*, vol. x.

★★★★★★

Having despatched these last instructions, Wellington, in order to impart confidence to the people of Brussels, determined to go, as had been arranged, to the Duchess of Richmond's ball, which has since become historical, and where also he would meet the leaders of his army. He remained there some little time, proceeding to the front early the next morning. To sum up what we have said, the position of the armies on the night of June 15th, 1815, was this:—

FRENCH ARMY

The left column, under Ney, had its advanced posts at Frasnes, but its rear stretched back 14 miles through Marchienne-au-Pont, which was occupied by D'Erlon, one-fourth of whose troops were still on the right bank of the river.

Gosselies was held by two divisions of Reille's corps, the 3rd Division keeping touch with Napoleon near Heppignies. (Some accounts say near Wagnée (or Wangenies), a village between Heppignies and Fleurus).

The centre column, under Napoleon, had its head about two miles south of Fleurus; its rear at Charleroi, some nine miles behind.

The right (Gérard) was near Châtelet.

Napoleon himself returned to Charleroi for the night. His troops on this day had in some instances been 18 hours on foot, and had marched distances varying from 18 to 25 miles.

PRUSSIAN ARMY

Blücher had collected the 1st Corps about Fleurus and Bry; the 2nd at Mazy, four miles from Sombref; the 3rd at Namur; but the 4th (Bülow) was still only on the road from Liege to Hannut, owing to the misunderstanding as to orders sent.

ANGLO-ALLIED ARMY

Of Wellington's army, a brigade of Dutch-Belgians with a battery of horse artillery held Quatre Bras; the Dutch-Belgian generals, be-tween Braine-le-Comte and Mons, were collecting their brigades, and from Brussels orders had gone out from Wellington to concentrate towards his left. Only one-half of the Prussian Army (two corps) were in front of Napoleon at Ligny, and but a small force of Dutch-Belgians before Ney; while the rest of Wellington's troops were miles away in their cantonments.

Could Napoleon and Ney have known at this moment the exact situation of their opponents, they would doubtless have strained every nerve to complete the advantage they had obtained.

But the fog of war does not lift at one's pleasure. Napoleon's blow had been delivered, to a great extent, in the dark; neither he nor Ney knew with certainty the position or strength of the Allied armies; their men were weary and hungry; the campaign was but commencing, and next day heavy demands might be made upon the troops; their col-umns were not closed up: and so, when darkness came on, they halted.

The Nivelles—Sombref road, therefore, did not fall that night into the hands of the French.

COMMENTS

With regard to Napoleon's plan of action, it was, of course, open to him to have adopted others. He might have advanced against the Prussian left, but this would have been less likely to cut off Blücher from Wellington, and the ground was not very favourable.

He might have attacked Wellington's right, with either all or a por-tion of his force, a plan which Wellington's dispositions were, as we shall see, designed to guard against; but this would not have cut off Wellington from Blücher. He might even have acted on the defensive near Paris, but this course, even if it had been advantageous, would have been too unpopular with the army, and in France generally, to be adopted.

In attacking the Allied centre, he had, as the event proved, many chances in his favour. His plan was so successful at the outset that, could he have pushed it more actively on the night of June 15th, or at dawn the next day, he might have seized the Nivelles—Sombref road, forming the line of junction of the two Allied armies.

Many writers (Jomini and Charras among them) have held that Napoleon's success on June 15th was really incomplete, because he failed to seize that road. They do not admit the force of what he him-self has written, that he took good care *not* to occupy it on the night of the 15th, for the reason that:

> Marshal Blücher would then have been obliged to make Wavre the place of concentration of his army; the Battle of Ligny would not have been fought, and the Prussian Army forced to give battle in its then unconcentrated condition, and not supported by the English Army.—*Correspondance de Napoleon*, vol. xxxi.

It has been also contended that this assertion is inconsistent with Napoleon's statement that he gave a verbal order to Ney on the afternoon of the 15th to occupy Quatre Bras, because the seizure of that place might equally have led Blücher to fall back on Wavre.

But there is little profit in pursuing this topic further. Napoleon had at all events gained a great advantage by the night of June 15th. His uncertainty as to the position and strength of the Allies, the fact that his columns were not closed up, the exertions which his troops had already made, and the approach of darkness, formed strong reasons in themselves for his refraining as he did from pushing beyond Fleurus.

Criticisms against the Allied operations have been directed less than might have been expected against the defective transmission of reports from the front after the French had actually attacked. As to this, Wellington has censured no one in his despatches; and probably a want of military experience (not zeal), misunderstandings between men of different armies, and the fact that orderlies or officers had met with accidents, been wounded, or killed, were the causes of what happened, and made him abstain from awarding official blame.

Nevertheless, he writes in referring to Müffling's *Passages of my Life*, "There was certainly something out of order in the communication between the two armies in the middle of June"; and that this was so is shown by what we have already said.

★★★★★★

Letter to Lord Ellesmere Walmer, September 25th, 1851—*Personal Reminiscences of the Duke of Wellington* (1903), p. 185. Müffling's *Passages from my Life* came out in Berlin in 1851, before the duke's death, and was translated into English by Colonel Yorke in 1853.

★★★★★★

A despatch from Charleroi to Brussels, sent at 4 a.m., (Chesney, *Waterloo Lectures*, some accounts say it was sent later; but in any case its delivery was very slow), it arrived at 3 p.m.—a distance of 35 miles.

One from Mons, dated 9.30 a.m., took nearly the same time to traverse about 38 miles, arriving at Brussels late in the evening.

In alluding to this Wellington says, "Nobody can say whether there was any misconduct in anybody, for the failure of early communication" ("Memorandum upon the Battle of Waterloo"); and misconduct has not been imputed to any individual of any rank, whether British, Belgian, or Prussian: but certainly the transmission of the reports on June 15th, 1815, was very unsatisfactory, and seriously affected Wellington's plans.

Some have held the view that Wellington and Blücher, when Charleroi was first attacked, should have concentrated at once in the position they afterwards did take up at Waterloo, or that Wellington should have fallen back behind Brussels.

The latter was partially General von Kleist's plan (as mentioned earlier), but it would have permitted Napoleon to occupy unopposed a considerable district of Belgium, which, for political reasons and in the interest of the King of the Netherlands, was regarded by both Wellington and Blücher as undesirable.

After the Prussian defeat at Ligny, it did become necessary to retire to Waterloo; but to fall back after a lost and very closely contested battle is a different thing from doing so before it has been fought.

The criticisms most frequently advanced against Wellington's dispositions are:—

1st, That he should have realised, before Napoleon attacked, that he would do so in the direction of Charleroi.

2nd, That the disposition of his troops in cantonments was unnecessarily extended—merely for an alleged convenience of supply.

3rd, That a more central and compact disposition would equally have effected Wellington's object.

Let us take these in their order:—

The answer to the 1st must be that we know as a fact that, on the night of June 14th (as mentioned), Napoleon had 43,000 men near Solre-sur-Sambre, eight miles east of Maubeuge, 58,000 at Beaumont, and but 15,000 at Philippeville.

All the above places, except Philippeville, lie some miles to the west of Charleroi. Maubeuge is only 13 miles from Mons, and nearly 30 from Charleroi; Beaumont is 13 miles from Maubeuge, and over 16 from Charleroi.

A march of 13 miles after dark on June 14th from Beaumont to Maubeuge (and only eight from Solre-sur-Sambre to Maubeuge), would have assembled at Maubeuge by the morning of the 15th a force of 100,000 men, which would then have been twice as close to Mons as to Charleroi, and in a position from which they could advance, past Mons, either against Brussels or Wellington's right.

With respect to a mere "convenience as to supplies" having dictated the extension of the troops, we have Wellington's statement that military reasons, not convenience only, demanded it; and further, we know that the supply question was one which had caused him no little worry. As far as was safe it was desirable in the public interests to make the burden of the troops fall as lightly as might be upon the country occupied.

With regard to the 3rd criticism, perhaps General Sir James Shaw-Kennedy may be taken as putting it in the plainest and most direct manner; and he also states (what others usually have abstained from) the dispositions which he would have preferred himself. Moreover, no one's opinion as to the Waterloo campaign has a greater claim to attention, for he served throughout it, and was in a position to know many important details. (He was in charge of the Quartermaster-General's Department, 3rd Division, and had also seen much service in the Peninsula).

Colonel Chesney alludes to him as one possessing "that faculty of judicial criticism which makes history valuable." (*Waterloo Lectures*).

Sir James Shaw-Kennedy writes (*Notes on the Battle of Waterloo*):

> It is necessary to go into the question of what ought to have been their (*i.e.* the Allied Armies') line of cantonments, as soon as it was known that Napoleon had a large organised army ready to take the field, and what position they should have taken up when it became known that the French Army was in motion, so as to render it certain that Napoleon could not bring a portion of the Allied Army into action with his concentrated force, and that he could only reach Brussels after an overthrow of the whole of the Allied Army when in junction in a general action.

★★★★★★

Hooper states that for seven days previous to June 14th, "troops of all arms flowed into the country between the Sombre and Meuse," so that they were in motion a week before the attack.

Meaning apparently the joint armies of Wellington and Blücher.

★★★★★★

He then expresses the view that the disposition should have been this:—

Blücher's headquarters at Genappe, his army cantoned between Louvain and Gosselies, with strong bodies of cavalry along the Sambre and advanced posts along the frontier.

Wellington's headquarters at Brussels, his army cantoned from Brussels to Soignies, with cavalry posts along the frontier from the right of Blücher's outposts to the Scheldt, and thence down that river to Audenarde.

It can be seen that the above disposition would have left no infantry divisions to the west of the Brussels—Soignies road; and it appears designed to provide only against Napoleon bringing his entire concentrated force against a portion of the Allied Army. But Wellington had to protect Ghent and his line of communications from every description of French attack; and the damage, disturbance, and sense of insecurity which even a partially successful raid against it would have caused must have been most serious.

Comparatively recently a paper under Wellington's hand has been published, written in 1842, which bears upon the danger of such a central position as is above suggested.

★★★★★★

This memorandum is enclosed in a letter to Mr. Arbuthnot, dated October 10th, 1842, and is given in *Personal Reminiscences of the Earl of Ellesmere*, Notes on Waterloo. I am not aware of its having been published before, but possibly it may have been so.

★★★★★★

The following is an extract from this:—

A common inspection of the map will show this. Place our right at Ostend, and the left at Namur on the Meuse, and take any central position you please. Then take the French position, with its right at Givet and Charleroi, by Le Quesnoi, Valenciennes, Courtray, Lille, and Dunkirk to the sea, and the folly and danger of a central position will be seen—we being, par force, on the defensive.—(Signed) Wellington.

Let us then apply the above test, which Wellington suggests, to the dispositions preferred by Sir James Shaw-Kennedy.

If we turn to the map of part of Belgium and the French frontier, made to extend to the west as far as Ostend, it will be seen that a line drawn from thence to Namur passes as nearly as possible through Ninove and Hal.

The French position, which Wellington alludes to, from Givet to Dunkirk, is given practically by the Franco-Belgian frontier line of 1815, marked upon the map, behind which at any point Napoleon could collect his troops.

A semicircle (CBD) has been drawn on the map with Ghent as a centre, the circumference of which passes by Brussels and mainly to the west of the Brussels—Hal—Soignies road.

This shows that any French force striking up north, from Condé or Lille, at Wellington's line of communications, would, could it gain a point a little north of Ath, or south of Courtray, be as close or closer to Ghent than any Allied force at Brussels, or between Brussels and Soignies; also that if it could pass Audenarde, it would gain some of the roads by which Wellington's right communicated with Ostend and Ghent, although his main line of communications lay through Ghent and Bruges, more to the north. It can be seen also that the French frontier north of Condé is only about five miles further from Ghent than Soignies is, and from it the road to Ghent is rather more direct.

Napoleon, as we know, assembled the bulk of his army very rapidly on the night of June 14th between Maubeuge and Beaumont, and D'Erlon's patrols easily passed the Sambre at Lobbes. What was to have debarred Napoleon, at any time after "the French Army was in motion," (see quotation from Sir James Shaw-Kennedy, given earlier), massing instead a large body at Valenciennes and Condé, and making a powerful raid with mounted troops against Wellington's communications, then sweeping round and falling back to France, well to the westward? The roads were good, and the fortresses could be turned.

He had with him 13,000 reserve cavalry under Grouchy, besides the cavalry with each corps. Why also could not a march from Maubeuge, made after dusk even on June 14th—such as that of Marmont to his left along the Douro from Toro to Tordesillas in 1812—have brought the French into a position from which a successful raid at daylight was possible? Could cavalry posts along the frontier and the Scheldt, with infantry from Brussels to Soignies, have repelled such a raid?

★★★★★★

Had Napoleon seen an opening for such a raid he pretty certainly would have attempted it. Success would have increased his military prestige with the army and people of Belgium, and might have led to political changes in England, which he based his hopes upon.

★★★★★★

Those who consider that they could, will hold that Wellington was over-prudent in keeping a considerable infantry force at Audenarde, Renaix, etc., as well as one of cavalry on the Dender; others will not, and here we may leave this question. Wellington held that it would be dangerous not to have infantry at these posts; and the test which he has suggested in order to prove this appears to do so.

Whether there was ground for the expectation that Wellington's troops could be concentrated to their left in time to act effectively with the Prussians, can be better discussed in the next chapter.

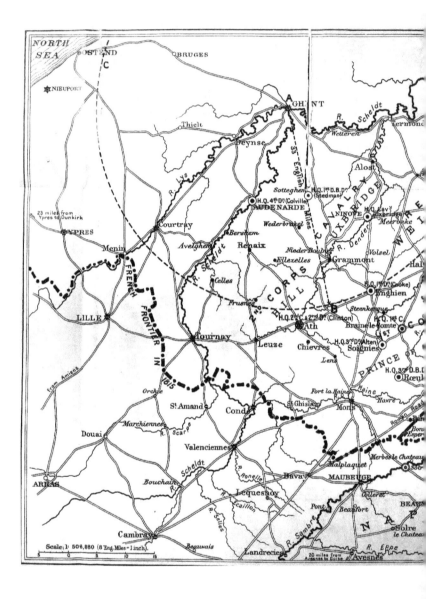

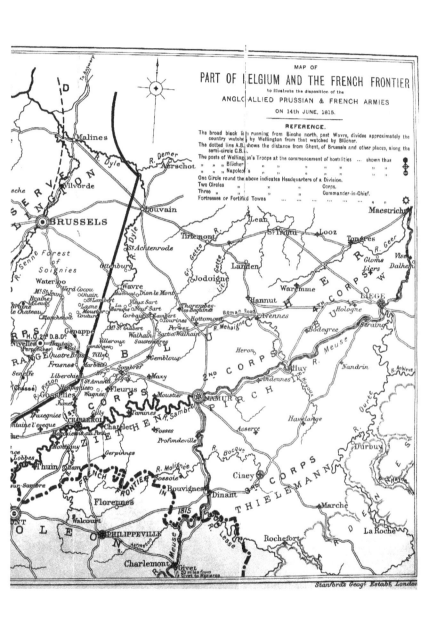

MAP OF

PART OF BELGIUM AND THE FRENCH FRONTIER

to illustrate the disposition of the

ANGLO ALLIED PRUSSIAN & FRENCH ARMIES

ON 14th JUNE, 1815.

REFERENCE.

The broad black line running from Binche north, past Wavre, divides approximately the country watched by Wellington from that watched by Blücher.

The dotted line A.B. shows the distance from Ghent, of Brussels and other places, along the semi-circle C.B.D.

The posts of Wellington's Troops at the commencement of hostilities ... shown thus

"   "   Blücher's   "   "   "   "   "   "

"   "   Napoleon's   "   "   "   "   "   "

One Circle round the above indicates Headquarters of a Division.

Two Circles   "   "   "   Corps.

Three   "   "   "   "   Commander-in-Chief.

Fortresses or Fortified Towns   ...   .

Stanford's Geog¹ Estab¹, London

Chapter 3

The Battles of Ligny & Quatre Bras, June 16th, 1815

At dawn on June 16th the French columns awaited the orders of Napoleon, to whom Grouchy had reported that the Prussians were massing near Fleurus. At about eight the emperor resolved to organise his army into two wings, the left under Ney, the right under Grouchy; while he himself, with the Imperial Guard as a reserve (15,000, with 96 guns), was to support either wing as might be required, and at first to accompany the right.

Ney's command was to consist of the corps of Reille and D'Erlon (Girard's division near Heppignies excepted), Kellermann's cavalry, and the light cavalry of the Guard (42,000, with 96 guns); Grouchy's of the corps of Vandamme, Gérard, and Lobau, with three corps of reserve cavalry (about 58,000, with 144 guns).

During the morning and afternoon, several orders or instructions were sent to Ney; and as his action with respect to these has been much criticised, we give them in the original French in Appendix B.

The first (no reply to this appears to be forthcoming, Appendix B, I), from Soult, Chief of the Staff, was received by Ney about 6 a.m. It desired him to report the exact position of Reille and D'Erlon's corps, as well as what he had ascertained of the enemy. No allusion was made in it as to advancing on Quatre Bras.

The next (Appendix B, II.), sent off at about 9 and received between 10 and 11 a.m., was in the form of a letter from the emperor, brought by his *aide-de-camp*, Colonel Flahaut. In it Napoleon writes to Ney in detail with respect to the orders which he will receive from Soult; and tells him that he himself is going to Fleurus—"I will," he says, "attack the enemy there *if I encounter him*" (the italics in this and following orders are ours); he informs him that, after what took place, he would decide upon his plan'

He writes:

I shall adopt my course, perhaps at three in the afternoon, perhaps this evening; my intention is that, after I have chosen my course, you should be ready to march on Brussels. You will march this evening if I form my plan early enough. . . . If there is any skirmish (*echauffourée* translated as scuffle or skirmish) with the English, it is preferable that it should fall upon the line rather than on the Guard.

In addition, he announces his intention of taking away the light cavalry of the Guard, and replacing it by Kellermann. "You can," he writes, "dispose your troops thus": one division two leagues in advance of Quatre Bras ("*les Quatre Chemins*"), "*s'il n'ya pas d'inconvénient*," (if there is no difficulty); six divisions round Quatre Bras; one division at Marbais—"so that I may draw them to me if I want them"; Kellermann's, (he is frequently called "Comte de Valmy."), cavalry at the intersection of the Roman road with that to Brussels—"in order that I may draw it to me if I require it."

The next was the order from Soult (Appendix B, III.), alluded to in the above letter, and reached Ney at about 11 a.m. In its tenor it was, on the whole, much the same as the letter. It directed him to march the 2nd and 1st Corps, (these two corps would give the six divisions Napoleon mentions, including Girard's division near Heppignies), with Kellermann's cavalry, to "*les Trois Bras*," (in many old maps "Quatre Bras" is termed "*les Trois Bras*"), and thence reconnoitre the roads to Brussels and Nivelles, "from whence the enemy has probably retired"; also to place one division at Marbais, which was to reconnoitre towards Gembloux and Wavre, and one division with some cavalry at Genappe, (Genappe would roughly be "two leagues in advance of Quatre Bras," as in the emperor's letter), "*s'il n'y a pas d'inconvénient.*"

The points to be more especially noticed in the above letter and order are that Napoleon had scarcely realised the serious resistance he would meet with beyond Fleurus or at Quatre Bras. The expressions, "*If I encounter the enemy*" and "If there is any *skirmish with the English*," also the order to occupy Genappe "*s'il ny a pas d'inconvénient*" all indicate this. Seemingly he expected that the Allies, especially Wellington, would not make any determined opposition so far south. There is also this to note, that by Soult's order Kellermann's cavalry was to be posted at Quatre Bras; but by the emperor's letter it was to be placed further south, and to be at Napoleon's disposition.

Moreover, Ney, after he had occupied Quatre Bras, was to await instructions as to Napoleon's further plans, which might not be decided till 3 p.m., or even before the evening.

A reconnaissance on the morning of the 16th had shown Ney that the Allied force holding Quatre Bras had been strengthened; the wood of Bossu, and the villages south of it, were lined with Dutch-Belgian troops; and he knew, from experience, that Wellington never showed his strength unnecessarily.

On receiving Napoleon's orders, he informed Reille and D'Erlon of them, directing them to move to the front and concentrate. D'Erlon, in rear of Reille, was to come up to Frasnes, detaching one division with some cavalry to Marbais, and Kellermann to move to Frasnes and Liberchies. (Liberchies was near the intersection of the Roman road with that to Brussels (see Napoleon's letter, Appendix B, II.).

D'Erlon delayed in closing to the front, partly because, having received a report from Girard that the Prussians were massing at St. Amand, near Ligny, he thought it necessary to ask for further instructions. He was told to move up at once, but it was 11.45 before he began his march.

In the meantime an order (Appendix B, IV.) came from Soult, telling Ney to "unite the corps of Reille and D'Erlon with Kellermann's cavalry," with which he ought to be able to " destroy all the enemy's corps " who could oppose him.

Then, at about 1.30 p.m., as soon as Reille's column arrived at Frasnes, before it had closed up, and before D'Erlon had appeared at all, Ney made preparations to attack Quatre Bras, moving forward at about 2 p.m. This brought on the Battle of Quatre Bras.

To turn now to Napoleon's movements.

At about 1 p.m. he arrived at the front beyond Fleurus, from which point the Prussians had fallen back, and here found Grouchy, who, seeing the enemy in force, had halted. Napoleon, having reconnoitred, considered that there was only one Prussian corps opposed to him; and this he determined to attack in front, while Ney came upon its right flank.

In accordance with this plan, he (at 2 p.m.) sent an order (Appendix B, V.) to Ney, telling him that at 2.30 Grouchy would attack this Prussian corps between Bry and Sombref, and that he (Ney), having "pressed the enemy vigorously," should manoeuvre towards him and "aid in enveloping" it.

Between 2.30 and 3 Grouchy advanced as directed, and this brought on the Battle of Ligny.

Thus, at about the same hour, the Allies, under Wellington and Blücher, their inner flanks being (see plan) little over three miles apart, were attacked at Quatre Bras and Ligny under Napoleon's orders.

But the situation of the Allies was not altogether that which Napoleon believed. There were three Prussian corps, not one only, in front of him at Ligny—Pirch I. and Thielemann having joined Ziethen; while General Constant de Rebecque, Chief of the Staff to the Prince of Orange, had, in the latter's absence at Brussels, assembled the divisions of Perponcher and Chassé; and Perponcher had reinforced Prince Bernhart's brigade at Quatre Bras. (With Bylandt's Brigade. Perponche himself reached Quatre Bras at 3 a.m).

Wellington's troops were now moving up from Brussels and the west. He himself had left Brussels at about 8 a.m.

★★★★★★

Various hours are named between 6 and 8 a.m., but 8 is the hour given by Lord FitzRoy Somerset, Military Secretary. Very possibly Wellington, however, was in the saddle at Brussels a little time before 8, and left between 7.30 and 8).

★★★★★★

Before this, at about 7, he had ordered Lord Hill (Ropes says that no time is mentioned on the orders to Hill; but see, as to one order, *Wellington Despatches*, vol. viii. it is there dated 7 a.m.), to march the 2nd Division from Enghien to Braine-le-Comte, (whence by some order received it moved on to Nivelles and was afterwards diverted to Waterloo); directed the cavalry to Braine-le-Comte; instructed the 1st Dutch-Belgian Division to move from Sutterheim to Enghien (leaving 500 men at Audenarde); and given orders, either verbally or in writing, for the great mass of the army to march on Nivelles and Quatre Bras. (See "Dispositions of the Army at 7 a.m. on June 16th," given further on. When these orders reached the troops is not very clear, but officers' letters allude to their reception on the line of march).

Exceptions being that the 4th Division was only to close in as far as Braine-le-Comte, (further movements of this division is mentioned further on), and that the Dutch troops at Sutterheim were to remain at Enghien. These exceptions were troops on the extreme right of the army.

After leaving Brussels, Wellington reached Quatre Bras at a little after 10 a.m.; saw the Prince of Orange, who had arrived at 6 a.m. from Brussels; and then rode to the front to observe the country in the direction of Frasnes. From this point he wrote a letter in French, and no doubt in haste, to Blücher at 10.30 a.m., a photograph of which is given further on. Almost immediately afterwards, however, deciding that he had time, he galloped off to Bry (about five miles) to see Blücher personally; and there, at the windmill of Bry, they had an interview. From this point the French columns were seen moving on St. Amand; and the Prussian troops were formed up to receive their attack.

Müffling, who was present at this interview with Blücher at Bry, has left us an interesting account of it. (*Passages from My Life*). Wellington promised to come to the assistance of the Prussians, if possible, at about 4 p.m., "provided" he was not attacked himself; but this proviso is all-important, as he was attacked, and attacked heavily.

It appeared to him that the manner in which the Prussian troops were posted, exposed to view and artillery fire, was injudicious. It was entirely contrary to his own practice, but on his venturing to draw attention to this, Gneisenau (he writes) gave him "an angry answer"— something to the effect that the "Prussians liked to see their enemy." (*Personal Reminiscences of the Duke of Wellington,* by Lord Ellesmere, edited by the Countess of Strafford). At the end of the interview he rode back to Quatre Bras, where he arrived between 2 and 3 p.m., shortly after Ney's attack had commenced.

Battle of Ligny
June 16th, 1815

In this battle Napoleon's troops numbered about 68,000, of whom over 13,000 were cavalry, with 210 guns. But this does not include the corps of Lobau, in reserve, which did not arrive till towards the close of the battle. (These numbers are taken from Ropes. There is much discrepancy in the strength given by different historians, partly depending upon whether the corps of Lobau is, or is not, included). The Prussians (Bülow's corps not being present) numbered about 87,000, of whom over 8,000 were cavalry, with 224 guns.

The Prussian position covered the Nivelles—Namur road, from near Marbais to Tongrines, and was somewhat in the form of a crescent. In front of it ran the streamlet of Ligny, and there were also in advance several hamlets and villages which lent themselves to defence, though some were rather far in advance of the main line.

On their right the 1st Corps (Ziethen) occupied the village of Bry, with high ground adjacent to it; and also Ligny, St. Amand, St. Amand la Haye, St. Amand le Hameau, and Wagnelée.

On their left the 3rd Corps (Thielemann), which arrived about noon, extended from Sombref to Point du Jour, occupying in front Tongrines, Tongrenelle, Boignée, and Balâtre. The 2nd Corps (Pirch I.), having arrived about 11 a.m., formed up between Bry and Sombref.

The cavalry was posted mainly behind Ligny, Wagnelée and the Nivelles-Namur road; and the ground, sloping down both from the north and south towards the Ligny stream, afforded some good positions for artillery to both armies.

Napoleon determined to force the Prussian centre, while also attacking their flanks, hoping that Ney would co-operate with him in enveloping their right. Vandamme moved upon St. Amand, Gérard upon Ligny, and Grouchy himself upon Tongrines.

The French soon became committed to a fierce contest for the various villages held by the Prussians. Ligny, St. Amand, and other hamlets were taken and retaken, or partially retaken, more than once; Hameau St. Amand four times. The Prussian resistance was desperate, but at 5.30 they had lost St. Amand, though still holding Ligny; and had fallen back from Boignée and Balâtre, though still holding Tongrines and Tongrenelle.

At 3.15 Napoleon sent through Soult an order to Ney (Appendix B, VI.) to send D'Erlon's corps at once to envelop the Prussian right:

Make for the heights of Bry and St. Amand. The fate of France is in your hands.

The part which the corps of D'Erlon took upon June 16th in connection with the Battles of Ligny and Quatre Bras is very singular, and was briefly this:—

MOVEMENTS OF D'ERLON'S CORPS

The bearer of the order to Ney, General Labedoyère, (Heymés, Ney's *aide-de-camp*, says Colonel Laurent was the bearer; but D'Erlon that it was Labedoyère) went first to D'Erlon, then close to Frasnes, urging him to act immediately on Napoleon's orders. The latter did so in anticipation of Ney's sanction, and arrived from the north westward of Wagnelée, moving towards Fleurus at about 7 p.m.

★★★★★★

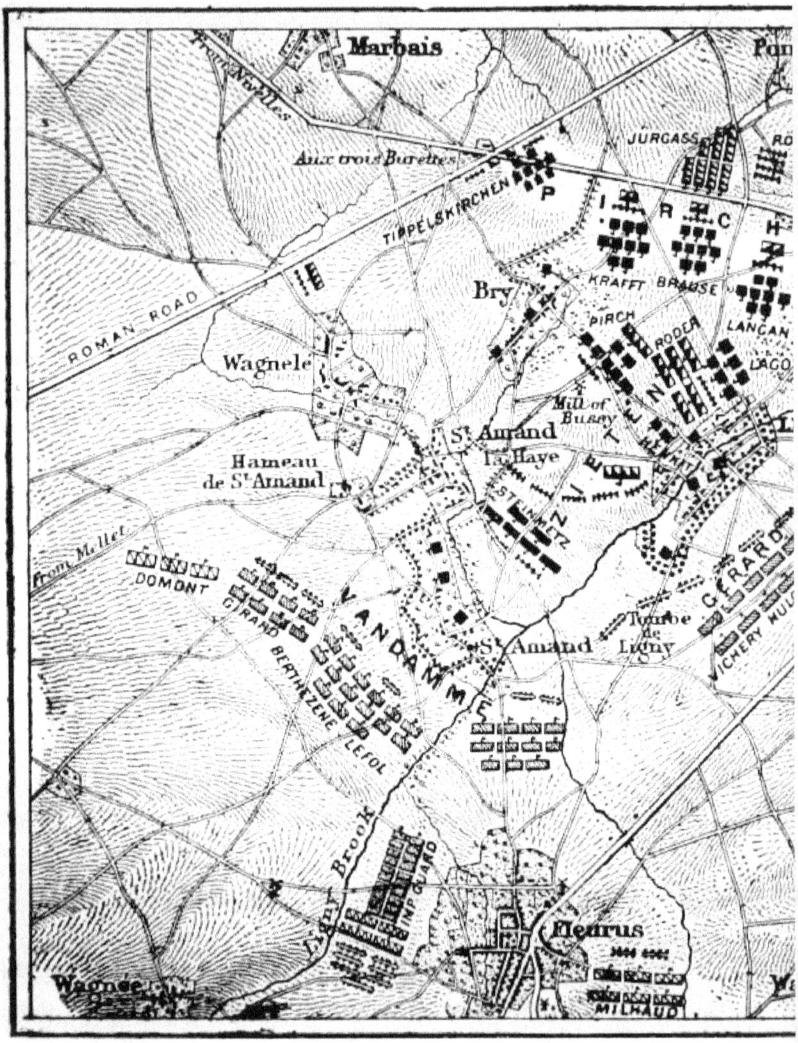
Marbais
From Nivelles
Aux trois Burettes
JURGASS
TIPPELSKIRCHEN
P
I
R
C
H
KRAFFT
BRAUSE
Bry
ROMAN ROAD
PIRCH
RODER
LANGAN
Wagnelé
Mill of Bussy
St. Amand
la Haye
Hameau de St. Amand
STEINMETZ
from Mellet
DOMONT
GIRARD
VANDAMME
BERTHEZENE
LEFOL
St. Amand
Tombe de Ligny
GERARD
VICHERY
Ligny Brook
IMP. GUARD
Fleurus
MILHAUD
Wagnée

BATTLE OF LIGNY

at ¾ past 2 o'clock, p.m.

SCALE

0   ¼   ½   ¾   1 Mile

Prussians
French

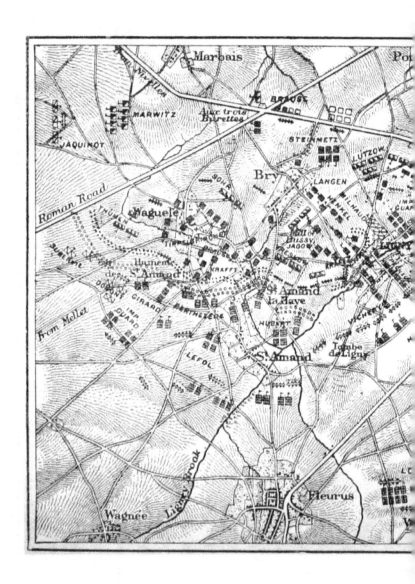

Vieille Maison

Hunrée

Old Castle

Sombref

Botey

Le Pont du Jour

To Namur

BOUCHE

FLOTTUM

LUCK

Mott Potriaux

Ligny Br.

Tongrines

IMP GUARD

KAMPFEN

Tongrenelles

Ligny

Balatre

Boignée

MARCHAND

PAJOL

Old Road to Namur

Velaine sur sel Terpes

BATTLE OF LIGNY
at ½ past 8 o'clock p.m.

SCALE

0 ¼ ½ ¾ 1 Mile

Prussians

French

He had, it is said, read the words scrawled in pencil, "*Dirigez-vous sur les hauteurs de Bry et de St. Amand* (*i.e.* on to the heights of Bry, etc.), as "*Dirigez-vous a la hauteur,*" etc. (*i.e.* in the line of Bry, etc.), which led him further south; but there is controversy as to the wording, as well as the delivery, of this order (see Houssaye).

✶✶✶✶✶✶

Napoleon, seeing D'Erlon's column approaching in the distance, and doubtful if it was that of an enemy or a friend, delayed an attack which he was about to make against the Prussian centre until he could ascertain this with certainty, thus losing nearly an hour of valuable daylight. Ney, at Quatre Bras, requiring D'Erlon there, and furious at his having left his command, sent him an imperative order to return. He received this just as he neared Wagnelée, and marched back, but arrived too late to save Ney from defeat. Thus D'Erlon's corps of over 20,000 strong wandered to and fro on June 16th, between Quatre Bras and Ligny, without firing a shot, and exercised no influence upon either field, beyond the fact that its approach gave confidence to the French, and possibly caused anxiety to the Prussians.

In the meantime, Lobau was approaching Fleurus; and Blücher, from continually reinforcing his troops at the villages, had expended his reserves.

This was the decisive moment of the battle. Napoleon, with 18,000 foot, 5,000 horse, and 100 guns, now fell upon the Prussian centre with an onslaught which carried everything before it. Ligny was taken. Blücher, leading a last charge of cavalry, had his horse killed, and was left under it till rescued by his *aide-de-camp*; and at 9.30 the French had gained a complete victory. But it was simply a victory, not a rout: there was no flight, and no active pursuit.

The Prussians held Bry and Sombref for a time, and at about 1 a.m. withdrew towards Tilly, Gentinnes, and Gembloux, while the French bivouacked about St. Amand, Ligny, and other points close to but south of Bry and Sombref, Napoleon returning for the night to Fleurus.

The Prussians lost about 12,000 men and 21 guns. The French about 11,000 men.

Battle of Quatre Bras
June 16th, 1815

There was no special strength in the position of Quatre Bras in it-self. Its importance lay mainly in the fact that the road by which Wellington was to concentrate with Blücher, and also that from Charleroi to Brussels, passed through this point.

The force with which Ney first attacked was about 16,000 infantry, 1,700 cavalry, and 38 guns (Hooper makes Ney's force 9,000 infantry, 1,865 cavalry, and 22 guns; but this does not include Jerome's division, about 8,000, which came into action close in rear); while opposed to him at that time was Perponcher's division of Dutch-Belgians, under the Prince of Orange, with only about 7,000 infantry, 16 guns, and no cavalry.

The force of the Prince of Orange was boldly and intentionally much distributed, so as to give the appearance of strength, and delay the French advance till reinforcements could arrive. It held a portion of the extensive wood of Bossu (about a mile and a half in length, by half a mile in width—this wood has been since cut down; Houssaye); and to the east of this and south of Quatre Bras, where the ground was open and undulating, occupied the farm buildings of Gemioncourt; the villages of Pierpont and Piermont (or Pieraumont), and the outskirts of La Thile, on the Nivelle-Namur road. A reserve with some guns was at Quatre Bras.

From high ground around Quatre Bras itself, troops upon the field of Ligny could be seen with a glass. A stream rising in the wood of Bossu flowed past Gemioncourt, widening into a pond between that and La Thile, and this stream was bordered by a thick hedge difficult to pass. To the south of the stream the ground rose so that the French, from that side, could see the general character of the position which they were about to attack; but the tall rye grass covering much of the plateau, and which was as high as the men's shoulders, greatly concealed the Allied troops. (*Cavalry in the Waterloo Campaign*, by Sir Evelyn Wood).

It was about 2 p.m. when Ney attacked. The division of Bachelu was on the right, that of Foy on the left, and Jerome's soon afterwards came up in support. The Dutch-Belgians were being fast pressed back, when Wellington came up from Bry. Picton's division was now seen approaching from Brussels, followed by the Brunswick corps and Nassau contingent; some Dutch-Belgian cavalry also appeared from Nivelles.

Ney, opening a heavy cannonade, endeavoured to carry the position before the reinforcements could arrive. He gained the south edge of the wood of Bossu, Pierpont, the ground up to Gemioncourt (but not the farm), and the village of Pieraumont, while his skirmishers reached the Nivelles-Namur road near La Thile. This was the first crisis of the battle.

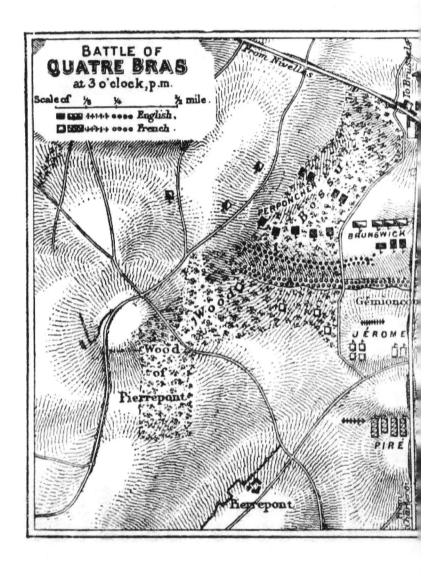

BATTLE OF
QUATRE BRAS
at 3 o'clock, p.m.

Scale of ⅛ ¼ ½ mile.

English.
French.

From Nivelles

To Brussels

PERPONCHER
BOSSU
BRUNSWICK

Gémioncourt

JÉROME

WOOD

Wood
of
Pierrepont

PIRÉ

Pierrepont

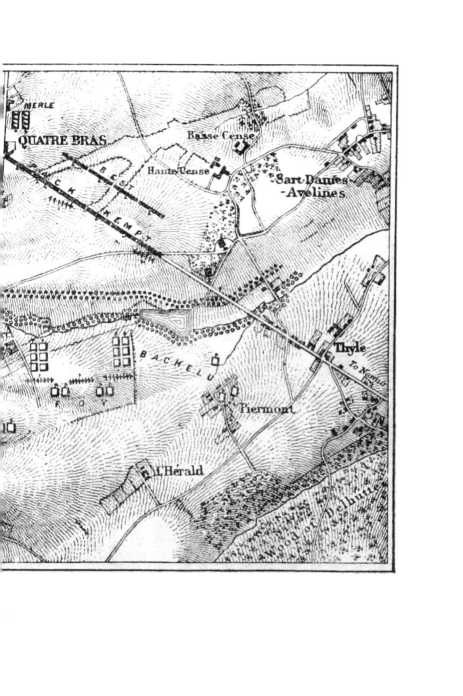

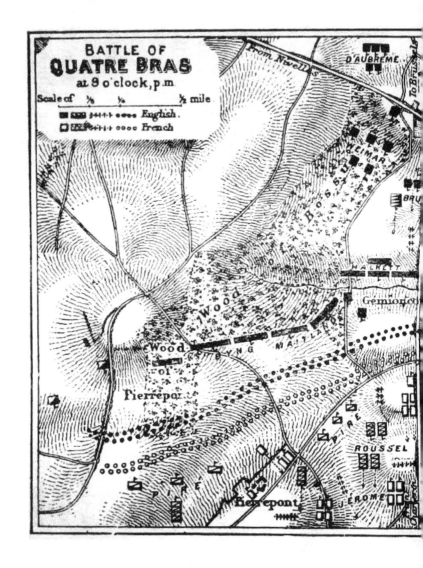

BATTLE OF
QUATRE BRAS
at 9 o'clock, p.m.

Scale of ⅛   ¼   ½ mile

English.
French.

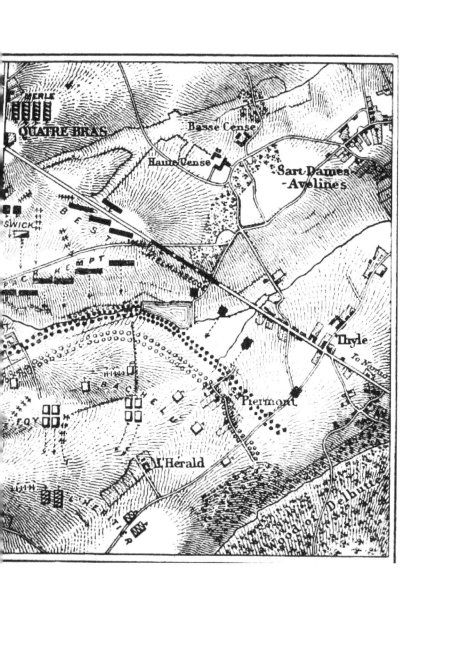

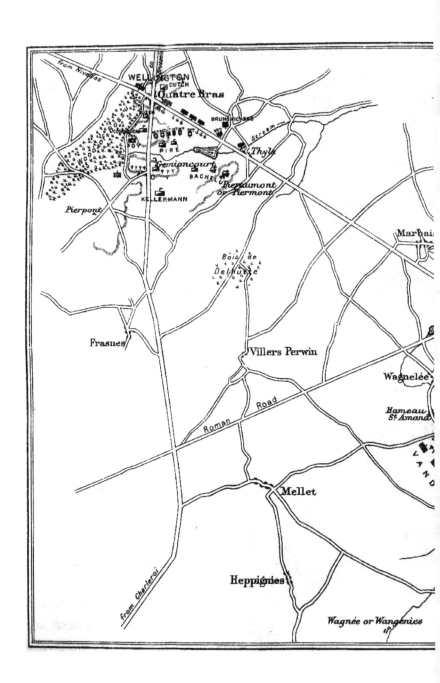

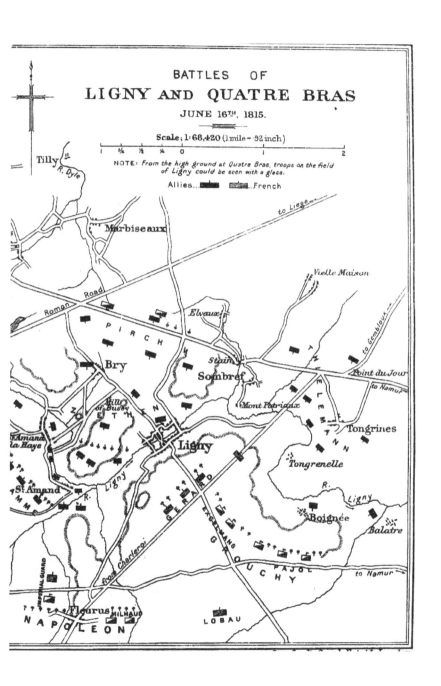

BATTLES OF
LIGNY AND QUATRE BRAS
JUNE 16TH, 1815.

Scale: 1:68,420 (1 mile = .92 inch)

¾ ½ ¼ 0   1   2

NOTE: From the high ground at Quatre Bras, troops on the field
of Ligny could be seen with a glass.

Allies..........   ....French

But at this juncture Picton with the troops from Brussels arriving, lined the Nivelles-Namur road, and the 95th Rifles drove back the French skirmishers towards Pieraumont.

From this time until the evening, the battle fluctuated as reinforcements came up on either side. The struggle was so sustained that it is impossible to do justice to it in a brief description; but its general character was this:—

Ney, being superior in artillery, and having towards the close of the day 5,000 good cavalry, which had repulsed the Dutch-Belgian and Brunswick horse, made more than one resolute effort to destroy the British infantry on the plateau above Gemioncourt, who were unsupported by mounted troops; as well as to carry the wood of Bossu.

A most determined onset: was met halfway by Wellington, who, in a counter-attack with Picton's force, gradually bore the assailants back to Gemioncourt; but the French efforts were again and again renewed.

The cavalry repeatedly charged Wellington's squares through the long rye grass, while the supporting fire of the French artillery caused them very heavy loss; but not even at Waterloo was the steadfast courage of the British infantry more brilliantly illustrated than at Quatre Bras, and Ney's utmost efforts failed to make them yield. The Brunswick troops fought gallantly at the outset, but their leader, the Duke of Brunswick, being killed, they dispersed; the Belgians were driven back, and the wood of Bossu was temporarily carried to its northern edge.

At this juncture, about 5 p.m., the 3rd (Alten's) Division arrived from Braine-le-Comte; and Ney then ordered up D'Erlon's corps, but found that it had gone off towards Ligny. At 6.30 the 1st (Cooke's) Division (the Guards) reached the field, driving the French from the wood of Bossu, and this decided the battle.

Wellington being now stronger than Ney, advanced with his whole line; the French were driven back to Frasnes, and the Anglo-Allied army bivouacked along the southern edge of the wood of Bossu, and about Gemioncourt and Pieraumont, Wellington proceeding for the night to Genappe.

The Allied loss in this battle was about 5,000, that of the French over 4,000. In his despatch Wellington especially mentions the 28th, 42nd, 79th, and 92nd Regiments, whose squares suffered heavily, but the gallantry of many other corps also was conspicuous.

Events of June 17th

During the morning of June 17th, after the Battle of Ligny, Napoleon made no movement. He spent it in riding over the field of battle, and in general conversation with his staff. Pajol's cavalry had captured a Prussian battery, which it is said had lost its way upon the Namur road; and this circumstance, together with the belief that the Prussians would fall back along their line of communications, appears to have confirmed Napoleon in the conviction that they had done so.

At noon he directed Grouchy, with about 33,000 men, to follow up the Prussians and complete their defeat. But it was 2 p.m. before Grouchy got off; it began to rain in torrents, and just as he was starting he received orders to proceed to Gembloux, "and explore in the direction of Namur and Moestricht," ascertaining what the enemy was intending to do—*i.e.* whether to separate themselves from the English or not. Grouchy's subsequent movements we shall touch upon later, merely saying here that they did not attain their main objects.

By daylight all the Prussian corps, the 4th (Bülow's) from Hannut included, were in full retreat, not towards Namur, but in the direction of Tilly and Wavre, and at nightfall on the 17th were concentrated in and about the latter town.

About 12 o'clock Napoleon, in addition to detaching Grouchy, wrote to Ney to again attack Quatre Bras, telling him that he would support him from Marbais, which he proceeded to do.

With respect to Wellington, the cavalry from about Ninove had joined him at Quatre Bras on the evening of the 16th and morning of the 17th, the first regiment (11th Hussars) having arrived at about 8 p.m. on the 16th.

He writes, (letter from Walmer, *Personal Reminiscences of the Duke of Wellington*, by Lord Ellesmere):

On the 16th (the day of the Battles of Quatre Bras and Ligny) we saw, (meaning with a glass from Quatre Bras), what passed on the Prussian field of battle, and the failure of the charge of cavalry made by Blücher; we were certain that the Prussians did not possess the whole of it; we were doubtful what they did possess.

Again, "Memorandum upon the Battle of Waterloo:"

On the morning of the 17th we saw all the movements on the Prussian field of battle (at Ligny), the detachment of Grouchy's corps towards Wavre, and the march of the great body of French cavalry along the road from Sombref. . . . As soon as we could see, I sent my *aide-de-camp*, Colonel Alexander Gordon, with two squadrons of the 10th Hussars, to patrol up to the Prussian Army, and to communicate with its commanding officer. He had been with us at the mill of Bry the preceding day. He found French vedettes on the field of battle, (These he drove in; *Personal Reminiscences of the Duke of Wellington*, by Lord Ellesmere. Colonel Gordon, it is stated, brought back positive accounts of the state and position of the Prussian Army after his interview with Ziethen).

The French troops were in possession of all the villages on the rivulet which the Prussians had occupied the previous day. He communicated with Ziethen at Sombref, and came back and reported that Blücher had retired upon Wavre, and that Ziethen was ordered to retire in the same direction. I determined to take up the position at Waterloo, with which I was well acquainted.

It should be mentioned also that on the night of the 16th, an officer had been sent by Blücher to Wellington; but having been wounded, he did not reach him. Another officer did reach him at about 9 a.m. on the 17th, and by him Wellington sent back a message to Blücher that he would fall back himself and fight at Waterloo, if he (Blücher) would join him there with one corps. (Ropes; Müffling's *Passages from My Life*. Some accounts say "with one or two corps." Blücher says "with two corps"—*Wellington Despatches*, vol. viii.)

Wellington's arrangements to retire from Quatre Bras were very skilfully made. First, baggage and all impedimenta were moved to the rear; then the main body quietly withdrew; then the outposts, which had remained out, rapidly fell back behind a screen of cavalry, Ney not realising the intended retirement until they were gone. Lastly, the cavalry and horse artillery galloped off. Beyond a sharp encounter of cavalry at Genappe there was little fighting, for rain, falling in torrents, hampered the French pursuit.

From Genappe, on the 16th, the reserve artillery, and also the 2nd Division (from Nivelles), had been ordered on Quatre Bras; the 4th Division towards Nivelles; and Lambert's Brigade (6th Division) from Assche on Genappe. But on falling back from Quatre Bras on the 17th all were directed towards Waterloo, except those brigades, (see note following), 4th Division still at Braine-le-Comte or *on the road* to Nivelles, and Prince Frederic's Dutch-Belgians (Wellington *Despatches*, vol. xii.). Towards night Wellington formed on a position south of Waterloo. Napoleon followed closely, and both armies bivouacked opposite each other.

★★★★★★

Note: These brigades were directed to collect and halt at Braine-le-Comte. With Prince Frederic's Dutch-Belgians, they were posted near Hal on June 18th. One brigade, 4th Division, however (Mitchell's), having reached Nivelles, went on with the 2nd Division to Waterloo.

★★★★★★

COMMENTS

Many writers have blamed Ney, Reille, and D'Erlon for inactivity on the morning of June 16th in not having more rapidly closed the French columns to the front; and Ney especially for not having seized Quatre Bras, which at dawn was so weakly occupied by the Allies. (See Chesney's *Waterloo Lectures*). As far as possibility goes, they doubtless could have closed and advanced sooner; nevertheless, it does not appear that any charge of wilful inactivity can be justly imputed.

It must not be forgotten that the statement that Ney received a verbal order from Napoleon, at any time on the 15th, to occupy Quatre Bras is disputed; and in the first order Ney received from Soult (Appendix B, I.) no allusion to Quatre Bras is made.

Though the troops had gone through a trying day on the 15th, Reille is said to have been formed up on the road awaiting orders before 7 a.m. on the 16th; but there was apparently uncertainty as to what Napoleon's instructions to the army would finally be. We know that it was not until 8 a.m. that he determined to organise it, as he did, into two wings and a reserve; Ney had to work in with his plans; and D'Erlon's corps might have been withdrawn from him by the emperor, as it was later.

Moreover, as soon as Ney did get an explicit order to take possession of Quatre Bras (Appendix B, III.) he prepared to do so, and advanced before his force was entirely closed up.

Colonel Flahaut, Napoleon's *aide-de-camp*, who took the emperor's letter (Appendix B, II.) writes to Ney's son in 1829:

The infantry made us wait a long time for it; but as soon as your father had rejoined us, (Colonel Flahaut had ridden to the front), and before it had come up, he ordered the English to be attacked.

The following considerations also probably weighed with Ney. He knew what Napoleon did not know—*viz.* that Quatre Bras was oc-

89

cupied by Wellington's troops, though in what strength the woods of Bossu, and the undulating ground covered with tall rye, made it difficult for him to be certain. The letters and orders he received (Appendix B, I., II., and III.,) were not worded so as to imply special urgency, or that Quatre Bras was to be attacked at any cost.

Also a weak and unsuccessful attack might have rendered him unable to support Napoleon in his plans, and these plans were not to be formed until 3 p.m., or perhaps until the evening of the 16th. Henry Houssaye writes, (1815, *Waterloo*, Leonaur 2010), upon the authority of the diary of Foy and letters of Reille, that when Ney urged Reille to attack, he remonstrated, he said:

> It may turn out to be one of those Spanish battles, in which the English never appear till their own time has come. . . . This remark made him (Ney) ponder, and he delayed the attack till the arrival of Bachelu's 2nd Brigade and Foy's division.

Houssaye explains that Reille referred:

> . . . .to the ordinary tactics of the English in the Spanish Wars (*i.e.* the Peninsular War), when Wellington never unmasked his forces until the moment of the enemy's decisive attack.

As Colonel Henderson says (*Some Notes on Wellington*, by Lieutenant-Colonel G. F. R. Henderson, a lecture read before the Military Society of Ireland, 1897):

> That there were very few troops to be seen was, in the judgment both of himself (Ney) and his subordinates, no proof whatever that the whole English Army was not hidden away in the woods and valleys, and the opportunity was suffered to escape.

Thus the French experience in the Peninsula affected the day at Quatre Bras.

The remarks of Sir Edward Hamley, (*Operations of War*), with respect to Ney not having endeavoured to reach Genappe (beyond Quatre Bras), (see Appendix B, III., as to Napoleon's instructions), appear just:

> It would have been extremely rash, for Ney to have advanced beyond the Nivelles-Namur road till Napoleon had reached it with the main body, for he would have been exposing his flanks to the British from Nivelles and to the Prussians from

Sombref, and had Napoleon been defeated at Ligny his retreat would have been cut off. Nothing but an explicit order from Napoleon to advance at all hazards would have justified him in making the attempt.

Moreover, Napoleon had attached to his orders the condition:

If there should be no hindrance to their execution. (*S'il n'y a pas d'inconvénient*).

Napoleon's inactivity on the morning of June 17th marked a turning point in the campaign.

Had he driven Blücher's army eastward away from Wellington it would, of course, have been of inestimable advantage to him, and increased materially his prospects of success.

This want of energy has been attributed by many to a physical and mental failure which others do not admit, for though he could scarcely now, after years of exhausting strain, have been physically the Napoleon of Marengo and Austerlitz, yet he had never shown greater energy than between his return from Elba and June 16th. Possibly a simpler reason may account for his having passed the morning after Ligny in going over the field and discussing general topics with his staff—*viz.* that he was but following his habitual practice.

Müffling writes that Wellington doubted on June 17th whether he could with safety, before falling back from Quatre Bras, allow his men to cook their dinners, (*Passages from My Life*, the order was given to cook, and the men were not disturbed during the meal), and adds:

I could not share this apprehension. The enemy had only bivouacked on the 16th in the dusk of the evening, and in such cases it *always* was Napoleon's custom in his wars in Germany, to allow his troops first to cook, and to break up at ten the next morning.

Also Alison has, in his *History of Europe*, these allusions to this custom of Napoleon's:—

Referring to Marengo (1800):

There appears to have been no hot pursuit; after his victory he returned to Milan, and discoursed there much upon peace, religion, literature, and the sciences.

Referring to Eylau (1807):

The next day, after his usual custom, Napoleon rode over the battlefield, accompanied by his generals and staff.

Referring to Wagram (1809):

So exhausted were the French that they displayed very little vigour in the pursuit; neither cannon nor provisions were taken. The day after the battle, Napoleon, according to his usual custom, rode over the field of battle.

Referring to Lutzen (1813):

At daybreak on the following morning Napoleon left Lutzen, and, according to his usual custom, rode over the field of battle.

Referring to Dresden (1813):

Early in the morning of the 28th Napoleon, according to his usual custom, visited the field of battle.

The above extracts are sufficient to show that it was his ordinary custom. This, in addition to the facts that he felt confident that the Prussians were retreating eastwards, that his troops were much fatigued, that the supply of ammunition, the care of the wounded, and other matters required to be looked to, may account for what it is difficult on good military grounds to explain.

The Prince of Orange, and the generals under him, in assembling at Quatre Bras instead of Nivelles, early on June 16th, pending the arrival of Wellington, showed a resolution and acceptance of responsibility for which they deserve, and have gained, credit; but it is not to be inferred, because Wellington afterwards approved of their decision and directed the army upon Quatre Bras, that a concentration on Nivelles, had it been carried out, would have proved an error. Once a position was occupied in face of an enemy, Wellington would naturally be most unwilling to withdraw unnecessarily.

Nevertheless, Nivelles would have been both a quicker and therefore safer point of assembly for Wellington's troops. (Sir F. Maurice touches upon this subject—*United Service Magazine*, July, 1890).

It is true that to have yielded up Quatre Bras would have left the road towards Brussels open at that point; but had Ney advanced upon that road, Picton and the reserve would have been in his front; Wellington from a flanking position, (Moltke, *Essays on Flank Positions*, dwells much on the advantages such a position confers on the holder; *Development of Strategical Science during the 19th Century*, Lieutenant-

General von Caemmerer; translated Karl von Donat), threatening his left and line of retreat; and Napoleon miles away to his right rear.

Under these circumstances, would Ney have advanced? Had he done so, would he probably have got far? and had he met with a repulse, would it not have been more crushing than that at Quatre Bras? These are, perhaps, valueless conjectures, for there are no certain answers to them; but they naturally arise.

In connection with the Battles of Ligny and Quatre Bras, the following facts should be noticed:—

At Ligny the Prussian right was much advanced, and liable to be turned; Blücher's troops on the right and centre had all become engaged, while Napoleon had still a strong reserve in hand; the Prussian soldiers much exposed to artillery had suffered heavily, and yet the battle was very closely contested; and there was practically no pursuit.

At Quatre Bras the want of cavalry to oppose the French cavalry was what most hampered Wellington and caused the Allied loss. Wellington's advance, after Picton's arrival, to meet Ney's attack, although he was then much inferior to Ney in strength, is termed by Müffling "a resolution, at a critical moment, worthy of a great commander." (*Passages from My Life*). It completely succeeded, as the weakness of the Allies was concealed by the nature of the ground.

Another point, which should receive attention is this: that Ligny and Quatre Bras, though they may be technically, and are usually, spoken of as two battles, were in their character essentially one. Von Ollech justly calls his plan of them in *Geschichte des Feldzuges von 1815*, "*Schlachtfeld von Ligny und Quatre Bras*"—*i.e.* the battlefield (not battlefields) of "Ligny and Quatre Bras."

Ney was throughout acting under Napoleon's orders, and was attacking the two co-operating Allied Armies, with the French left; but that was all—he had no command which can be fittingly termed "independent," and at a critical moment D'Erlon was withdrawn from him.

The two fields of battle were so close together (see plan Pieraumont, Wellington's left, is little over three miles from Wagnelée, Blücher's right), that Wellington could ride from one to the other field and confer with Blücher, and ride back again, in less than three hours; and with a glass could see from Quatre Bras the troops at Ligny, he writes:

I positively saw the principal events on the field of Ligny. I was besides frequently informed by reports from Hardinge (at

Ligny), the last brought by his brother after he was wounded.

And Lord FitzRoy Somerset makes the same statement also. ("Memorandum upon the Battle of Waterloo," *Personal Reminiscences of the Duke of Wellington*, by Lord Ellesmere).

The distance which, at the opening of the battle, separated Napoleon near Fleurus from Ney near Frasnes, was about that between Wellington's right and left in his first position before the Battle of Salamanca; under that between Hill and Graham at Vittoria; and much under that between Wellington's right and left at the passage of the Bidassoa. D'Erlon's whole corps of 20,000 men marched from Ney to join Napoleon, and back again to Ney, between 4 p.m. and 9 p.m.

Thus Wellington's army, though not actually in touch with that of Blücher, co-operated with it closely; and, though it could not prevent Napoleon from being successful with his right against Blücher, it occupied and finally defeated his left, of over 40,000 men, under Ney.

On June 16th, as well as on the days to follow, the two armies acted in close concert, and Napoleon failed to separate them.

The influence which the character of a country—in other words its topography—exercises upon a campaign is forcibly brought out. Had there been a good high road from Charleroi between the two *chaussées* leading thence to Quatre Bras and Fleurus respectively, (see photo of map of Ferraris and Capitaine), and good cross communication, then Napoleon could have advanced from Charleroi in three columns, of which the centre could have readily reinforced either the right or left, and he would then have quickly learnt what was going on at these points; but as it was he was more or less tied to roads with difficult communication between them, and endeavoured to direct the left (Ney) at Quatre Bras from his extreme right at Fleurus, which was difficult to do, especially while acting upon a somewhat incorrect conjecture as to the position and strength of his enemy.

Ney, in one of the last official letters written by him before his execution, dated June 26th, 1815, and addressed to the President of the Provisional Government in Paris, says: "How did the emperor conceive it possible to fight two battles on the same day?" and considers that he should have "led all his forces against Wellington."

Others hold that it would have been the emperor's best policy to have observed, without attacking, Wellington, and to have fallen heavily (as he did) upon Blücher, who was his nearest opponent, and the one whose army could most quickly concentrate.

For the latter view there is much to be said; but, in any case, it was not Napoleon's plan of attack that told most against him on June 16th, but rather the late hour at which its execution was commenced; and the fact that he allowed the Prussians to withdraw unobserved, even by pursuing cavalry, and deceived himself as to the tenacity, energy, and skill of the two Allied commanders.

In considering the concentration of Wellington's troops upon Quatre Bras, the question of the way in which this was retarded by the distribution in cantonments of the army on June 15th (when the attack was delivered) must be kept distinct in the mind from that of how far it was retarded by other circumstances.

We have seen on what grounds the Anglo-Allied troops were kept in their cantonments until the point of real attack was reported, and why these cantonments were taken up; also, that it was expected that the bulk of the army could be concentrated on its left (*i.e.* Nivelles) within twenty-four hours; and lastly, that owing to the defective transmission of reports from the Prussian and Belgian outposts on June 15th, Wellington only heard at Brussels at 3 p.m. what he should have heard at 10 a.m.; and at 8 or 9 p.m. what he should have heard at 2 p.m.

This not only entailed a loss of valuable time, but it adversely affected the execution of the concentration in other respects. The orderlies who took out the 5 and 10 p.m. orders from Brussels on June 15th had to carry them at night. The weather was fine and the roads fairly good; but still, riding by night is not riding by day. Wrong turnings can be more easily taken, the pace will be slower, and accidents are more likely to happen. On this occasion, had the reports of the French attack (which took place at 4 a.m.) been duly transmitted, the orders both to assemble and to march would have gone out by day and not by night. As it was, these orders, even those to assemble dated 5 p.m., must have been delivered to most of the troops after sunset, and the 10 p.m. orders when they were in bed. Necessarily, this would materially delay the preparations for the march, as well as the march itself. Had the 10 p.m. orders been issued from Brussels at 3 p.m. on the 15th, certain of the troops could have marched some distance that night (for instance, the reserve at Brussels), and all got off at dawn, or before dawn, on the 16th.

Instead of this, all the troops had to march when more or less tired from a sleepless night of preparation, and during the worst part of the heat and dust of June 16th.

Thus, owing to reports from the front not having been promptly sent on to Brussels, some six or seven hours' fully were lost; and by the orderlies having to ride at night, some further time was lost. Had these causes of delay been avoided, Picton's division, with the reserve, might have reached Quatre Bras early on the 16th; Alten's division at 9 a.m. instead of 5 p.m.; Cooke's (the Guards) before noon instead of at 6.30 p.m.; and the cavalry in good time for the battle. But, as we shall see, there were other causes of delay upon the line of march.

It is difficult to establish now the exact time at which the 5 and 10 p.m. orders of June 15th reached the headquarters of each of Wellington's *corps d'armée*; and after that, through the leaders of corps, the various divisions, brigades, and regiments.

What we are able to do, however, is to give certain statements from officers of different divisions, brigades, etc., which show when the troops to which they belonged did receive them, and then draw what conclusions seem reasonable.

At the risk of being tedious we quote from several of these statements, because they bring out facts which bear with importance upon the question of the time occupied in completing the concentration. It is clear from them that, in addition to the delay caused by the defective transmission of reports, and by the conveyance of orders after dark, there were other delays on the line of march. Therefore, they are instructive.

Let us take the 1st Division at Enghien. Captain Powell, 1st Foot Guards, writes in his journal:—

June 15th, 1815: "8 p.m., dragoon arrived with intelligence that the Prussians had been forced across the Sambre (he also mentions that his regiment had been before this warned to be in readiness). 1.30 a.m. (the 16th), *drums beat to arms.*"—*Waterloo Letters*, by Major-General H. T. Siborne. The originals are in the British Museum. In this and following extracts from these letters the italics are ours; and the substance is given, though the wording is occasionally shortened).

At 3 a.m. an order came for the brigade to assemble at Hove (a little south of Enghien); "4 a.m., *order given to move* by Steenkerque on Braine-le-Comte." Here it arrived at 9 a.m., and was joined by the 2nd Brigade. "Great difficulty experienced in getting through the town, crowded with vehicles. Moved on at 12 noon. At 3 arrived near Nivelles." The brigade was scarcely halted when "an *aide-de-camp* brought the order to advance immediately to Quatre Bras."

Other accounts substantially agree with this, but Captain Batty, Grenadier Guards, writes on June 21st, 1815, that the troops "marched"—not assembled—at 3 a.m.

We see, then, that the 10 p.m. orders of June 15th to march reached the 1st Division at Enghien probably before 1.30 a.m. on the 16th, when the drums beat to arms; but certainly before 3 a.m. Enghien is about 21 miles from Brussels.

We see, also, that there was a three hours' delay at Braine-le-Comte, and that the order to go on to Quatre Bras was delivered on arrival at Nivelles.

With regard to the 2nd Division (Clinton), headquarters at Ath, something appears to have delayed the orders, which is not clearly explained. Lord Hill, commanding the corps in which this division was, though his headquarters are stated to have been at Ath, (as mentioned earlier), seems when he received his orders to have been at Grammont, where one of his brigades (Mitchell's) was posted. Apparently the 5 p.m. orders from Brussels, if not later ones, had reached him at Grammont before 3 a.m. on the 16th: but the 52nd Light Infantry, of the 2nd Division, probably because they were at Quevre-au-Camp, camp south of Ath and west of Mons received orders to move only at 10 a.m. on the 16th. (*Life of Lord Hill*, by the Rev. E. Sydney; also Records of 51st Light Infantry and 52nd Light Infantry),

As to their march the Rev. Mr. Leake, then in the 52nd, writes, in his *History of Lord Seaton's Regiment*, that they reached Enghien a little after 2 p.m., marched " a considerable distance" on the Hal road, then *countermarched* back again towards Enghien, and by a cross-road got to Braine-le-Comte at midnight.

Next let us take the cavalry at and near Ninove. Lieutenant-Colonel Basil Jackson, on the Quartermaster-General's staff under Sir William De Lancey, writes, (*Notes and Reminiscences of a Staff Officer*, by Lieutenant-Colonel Basil Jackson, edited by R. C. Seaton (1903). Colonel Jackson died in 1889, aged 94), that he was sent himself to Ninove, at some time after 10 p.m. on the 15th, with a letter to Colonel Cathcart, Assistant Quartermaster-General of the cavalry; and that as he approached the place he "found lights in the adjacent villages and men stirring about, indicating that the order for marching had been issued." (This may mean to Ninove, the place of assembly). Taking his way back "at a leisurely pace," he reached Brussels " about 4 a.m.," in time to see Picton's division march out past the Hotel Bellevue.

We have also the orders from the Assistant Quartermaster-General of Cavalry at Ninove to Sir William Ponsonby, commanding a cavalry brigade, dated 1.30 a.m., June 16th. They direct the brigade to be assembled with the utmost expedition, and to form up on the high road to the west of Ninove. (*Supplementary Wellington Despatches* (1863), vol. x.).

Colonel Clark Kennedy, then Captain Clark, Royal Dragoons, in this brigade, writes that after having been aroused at about 4 a.m. they were "put in motion," as soon as biscuits, etc., for three days had been issued; that the direction of their march was "changed three or four times" in the day; that there were "several halts"; and that, after marching somewhere about 50 miles, they arrived at Quatre Bras about dusk. (*Waterloo Letters*. Captain Clark, afterwards Sir A. Clark Kennedy, captured one of the two French eagles taken, and which now hang in the chapel of the Royal Hospital at Chelsea).

It should be noticed that Colonel Jackson rode from Brussels to Ninove and back (30 miles), returning at a "leisurely pace," between 10 p.m. and 4 a.m., from which we may gather that the night of the 15th was not very dark nor the road bad.

Sir Hussey Vivian, commanding Vivian's cavalry brigade, writes on June 23rd, 1815, that he received orders at Nieder Boulner (near Grammont) to march at daylight to Enghien, and he makes the distance from Grammont to Nivelles 36 miles. (*Waterloo Letters*, and *Memoir of Lord Vivian*, by the Hon. Claud Vivian, 1897).

Lieutenant-Colonel Taylor, 10th Hussars, in this brigade, writes (in 1829) that the brigade assembled between Vivorde, (*Waterloo Letters*. "Vivorde" or "Voorde" is a small place west of Ninove), and Grammont, and thence *marched at about 7 a.m.*, through Grammont and Enghien towards Braine-le-Comte. Beyond Enghien they halted and fed, etc.; beyond Braine-le-Comte an order came from Lord Uxbridge, (who had on the march ridden on to Quatre Bras, where he arrived between 2 and 3 p.m), to throw away their hay-nets, and trot at nine miles an hour towards Nivelles. From Nivelles they were hurried on to Quatre Bras, he says:

Our horses, in spite of the long march—between 30 and 40 miles, I should think for some of the corps—were very fresh.

Captain W. B. Ingleby, Royal Horse Artillery, writes, April 25th, 1838, (*Waterloo Letters*), that he joined Vivian's brigade of cavalry near Enghien on June 16th—at what hour is not stated—having come from a station between Ninove and Alost. His battery bivouacked towards night near Braine-le-Comte, but he states that "some of the cavalry regiments pushed on" to the field (Quatre Bras).

We must have marched this day between 50 and 60 miles, by a most irregular and circuitous route. (This appears an excessive estimate, according to other accounts).

An officer of the 2nd Life Guards, in Somerset's cavalry brigade, writes that his regiment marched from Meerbeke (near Ninove) *at 7 a.m.* on June 16th, and after a long march through Braine-le-Comte and Nivelles, halted for the night in a wheatfield. (*Battle of Waterloo*, by a Near Observer, published shortly after the battle).

Captain William Hay, C.B., 12th Light Dragoons, in Vandeleur's cavalry brigade, writes, (*Reminiscences,* 1808-15, edited by his daughter, Mrs. S. C. I. Wood, 1901):

We marched from our quarters at Volsel, (or Volzel, is east of Grammont), at about 6 *a.m.* (on the 16th), with directions to assemble in brigade at Enghien . . . arrived there about 9 a.m. . . . remained till nearly 12 awaiting orders; the road literally choked with troops, artillery, and ammunition.

The brigade was directed to separate, to be led through unfrequented paths by the commanding officer of each regiment, and to meet at a rendezvous fixed on by the quartermaster-general.

From the above statements we are able, apart from the question of the exact time at which the orders from Brussels were received, to arrive at this—that the Guards got off in brigade about 4 a.m.; and the cavalry from points near Ninove and Grammont, not later than 7 a.m. on the 16th, some possibly earlier; that the march was then continued towards Quatre Bras; that during it there was great jamming and crowding in the villages and on the road; some loss of time through misdirection; and that the last few miles, from Nivelles on, were done at a quick trot.

The 11th Hussars are mentioned by Lord Uxbridge as being the first regiment to reach Quatre Bras, "at about 8 p.m.," and as the last few miles were done at a trot, this regiment probably passed through Nivelles (seven miles short of Quatre Bras) at about 7 p.m. (*Waterloo Letters*. Lord Uxbridge writes in 1842, being then Marquis of Anglesey).

Lord Uxbridge places the distance from " Ninove and environs" to Quatre Bras at "between 30 and 40 miles"; Sir Hussey Vivian, that from Grammont to Nivelles—7 miles short of Quatre Bras—at 36 miles. We cannot therefore be far wrong in placing the average distance marched by the cavalry between their cantonments and Nivelles at about 36 miles. (We consider the distance to *Nivelles* in connection with Wellington's letter to Blücher, shown further on).

The time taken to cover this by the regiment first to pass through Nivelles seems to have been about twelve hours, including halts; that by other regiments rather more.

In the *Cavalry Journal* for January, 1906, ("Horsemanship for Long Distance Riding," by W. Paget Tomlinson), the rate of march, including all halts to feed, etc., is placed for a long distance ride (such as 60 miles) at about five miles an hour—the pace kept up while on the move being about six miles an hour. But in this march from the Dender, made when time was an object, and the distance under 40 miles, the rate of march, including halts, was at, or under, three miles an hour. Such a pace is wearisome to men and horses on the march; it is never adopted from choice.

The question then arises—What was the cause of this?

The chief cause could scarcely have been the heat of the day, the heavy state of the roads deep in dust, or the weight carried; for although all these may have been very trying, the horses are said to have arrived fresh.

★★★★★★

Sir Hussey Vivian, in his journal (June 3rd, 1815), expresses his disapproval of the order that shabraques (weight 7 lbs.) were to be carried on the march (*Life of Lord Vivian*, by the Hon. Claud Vivian, 1897).

★★★★★★

Their condition, by what was accomplished on the 17th and 18th, seems to have been good; they had been accustomed to marching, for it is mentioned that Lord Uxbridge assembled the whole of the cavalry frequently for exercise, when they sometimes covered, in going, drilling, and returning, 30 miles; and the Foot Guards, carrying packs, marched 27 miles over the same roads on the same day in fifteen hours. All ranks also must have been keen to push on, for they were concentrating with the possibility of meeting the enemy.

It seems that one great cause of delay was the jamming in the streets of villages, and the blocking of the roads by guns, troops, and vehicles. The cavalry, in short, and other arms as well, were perpetually checked, and could not get on.

It need not be a matter of much surprise that in the mixed Anglo-Allied Army, hastily got together, this delay should not have been guarded against by staff supervision, and the arrangement of routes, etc., beforehand. The direction which the army might have to march in was uncertain, and the move in the end sudden.

So far as Wellington and his quartermaster-general (De Lancey) are concerned, no one can read the detailed instructions for the marches of columns in the Peninsula—at Vittoria, the Bidassoa, Nivelles, etc.—without seeing that they, at all events, were thoroughly alive to the importance of the supervision of details on the march of troops; but it is sometimes overlooked that, in the British portion of the force, what was practically a new organisation—*viz.* that of "*corps d'armée*"—had been introduced. In the Peninsula, between Wellington and his divisional commanders there was no intervening head, except when divisions were put together for a temporary purpose (as they were under Hill or Beresford). In this campaign, however, there were permanent leaders of corps, with a corps staff, and the cavalry was massed together in a large body of several brigades.

Thus many details, which in the Peninsula would have naturally fallen within the province of the headquarter staff, here fell within that of the corps staff. With a hastily improvised army, a new staff, and a new staff system, there can never be perfection. (From this not being realised, the British Army has on some occasions been placed in positions of difficulty and danger). This is one lesson this campaign teaches. Another is that the detailed arrangements for the march of all large bodies in the field are of much consequence, and concern not only the headquarter staff, but also the staff of the whole army—that is, of corps, divisions, and brigades.

It is a very difficult matter to organise the march of large bodies of infantry, cavalry, and artillery, all moving at a different pace, without clashing and delays upon the road; and especially so where there are few roads, and some villages to pass with narrow streets. It requires experience and training, as all know who have had much to do even with the conduct of peace manoeuvres on a large scale.

But why we more especially allude here to the delay which took place upon the march is to show that it added to the loss of time caused by the defective transmission of reports from the front; by the bridges over the Sambre not having been blown up; and by the orders from Brussels on June 15th having to be sent out at night.

In spite of these many drawbacks to the execution of his plans, Wellington assembled a sufficient force at Quatre Bras on the 16th to defeat Ney; but had the cavalry arrived earlier the battle would have ended sooner, the victory been more complete, and the Allied loss less.

In connection with the disposition of his troops in cantonments, it must be taken into account that, had the delays we have mentioned not happened, a sufficient force (including cavalry) could have been at Quatre Bras in time to oppose Ney, even had the latter closed up his extended columns early on the morning of the 16th. These were scattered 14 miles from front to rear on the night of the 15th.

It is reasonable to consider that in any expectation that the greater part of the Anglo-Allied army could be assembled on its left within twenty-four hours, Wellington did not include his out-lying infantry on (and some beyond), the Scheldt, such as the 4th Division (Colville) at Audenarde, and the Belgians between Grammont and Ghent. These certainly were to be closed in from the right; but the distance (about 40 miles) made it impracticable that they could reach Nivelles in 24 hours, much less Quatre Bras. Again, by the 10 p.m. orders from Brussels of June 15th, the 4th Division was directed to Enghien only, and by the 7 a.m. orders of the 16th merely to Braine-le-Comte. (See "Disposition of the Army at 7 a.m. on June 16th"). From thence, when it could have brought to Waterloo, it was sent to Hal. (From Genappe, after the Battle of Quatre Bras, it was directed on Nivelles; but the bulk of it, next day, was ordered back to Braine-le-Comte as mentioned earlier).

Some have held that headquarters should have been moved from Brussels to Nivelles on June 15th, so as to be nearer the front; but it must not be forgotten that, up to the evening of the 14th, Napoleon had not crossed the frontier; that there might have been many reasons why Wellington's presence at Brussels up to the last was desirable; and that, as Sir F. Maurice points out, moving the headquarters of a large army without previous arrangement is apt to cause confusion and delay, both in the reception of news and the issuing of orders. ("Waterloo," *United Service Magazine*, September, 1890).

An examination into all that took place on June 15th and 16th, 1815, tends, it is submitted, to this conclusion,—that it was not the disposition of the Anglo-Allied troops in their cantonments on June 14th which of itself, or necessarily, made the army so late in concentrating at Quatre Bras; and that what has been spoken of as a "surprise" on the part of Napoleon, did not arise from Napoleon's movements having been unforeseen and unprovided for, or from false information credited by Wellington, or mainly from the strategical plans of either Wellington or Napoleon, but from occurrences in the defending armies unconnected with those plans, and which we have described.

With respect to Wellington's letter to Blücher, which has been the subject of much comment in Germany, (see before), we give a facsimile of it further on, taken from the photograph in *Geschichte des Feldzuges von* 1815, by General von Ollech (1876).

The translation is as follows:—

> Upon the heights behind Frasnes,
> June 16th, 1815, at half-past ten.

My dear Prince,—

My army is situated as follows. Of the corps of the Prince of Orange, one division is here and at Quatre Bras, the remainder at Nivelles. The reserve is on the march from Waterloo to Genappe, where it will arrive at noon. The English cavalry will be at the same hour at Nivelles. Lord Hill's corps is at Braine-le-Comte.

I do not see any great force of the enemy in front of us, and I await news from Your Royal Highness, and the arrival of troops to decide upon my operations for the day.

Nothing has appeared in the direction of Binche, nor on our right.

> Your very obedient servant,
>
> Wellington.

When Wellington left Brussels at between 7 and 8 a.m. on the morning of June 16th, he could not possibly have known the exact position on the line of march of troops miles away, moving under orders sent out between 10 p.m. and midnight of the 15th; but he knew what those orders were.

Let us consider the above letter paragraph by paragraph. The first paragraph is, "Of the corps of the Prince of Orange one division is here, (*i.e.* north of Frasnes), and at Quatre Bras, the remainder at Nivelles."

Now of this corps, the Dutch-Belgian divisions were as stated, except that Chassé's division, though no doubt momentarily expected at Nivelles, did not actually march in till an hour or so later—"nearly noon," (*i.e.* shortly after Blücher must have received the letter). It had been ordered (from Roeulx, etc.) to Nivelles by the 5 p.m. orders of June 15th.

The 1st Division (Guards) were, by orders of 10 p.m. on June 15th, to march from Enghien to Braine-le-Comte, and were afterwards moved on to Nivelles. The distance is, in all, about 18 miles by Steenkerque.

Wellington might well have anticipated that, marching early in the morning, they would have been approaching Nivelles by 10.30 a.m. As a matter of fact they did march at between 3 and 4 a.m., and were within half a mile of Nivelles at 3 p.m., having had many delays, and one halt of three hours near Braine-le-Comte, where the road was crowded with "numberless waggons and baggage confusedly huddled together in the street." (*Waterloo Letters*).

The 3rd Division (Alten) had been directed by the 5 p.m. orders on the 15th to assemble that night (from Soignies, etc.) at Braine-le-Comte, and by the 10 p.m. orders to move to Nivelles. From Braine-le-Comte to Nivelles is under ten miles. This division, by 10.30 a.m. on the 16th, might well have been at Nivelles. It did arrive at noon. (Shortly after Blücher must have received the letter).

The next paragraph is, "The reserve is on the march from Waterloo to Genappe, where it will arrive at noon."

We know that Picton's division left Brussels at about 4 a.m. (almost all accounts say 4 a.m., but some 5); and that Wellington rode past it when it was halted near the village of Waterloo.

★★★★★★

Account of Major Forbes, 79th Highlanders, and Major Winchester, 92nd Highlanders. *Waterloo Letters.* The historical records of the 79th (Cameron) Highlanders (1887) say that they halted at Waterloo at 8 a.m., having left Brussels at 4 a.m.

★★★★★★

As Wellington was certainly at Quatre Bras before 10.30 a.m., he probably passed this division at about 9 a.m. or a little later.

Field-Marshal Sir W. Gomm, then assistant quartermaster-general of the 5th (Picton's) Division, writes, (*Waterloo Letters*, Major-General H. T. Siborne), that the reserve, after it had halted at Waterloo, "moved on at 1 p.m. through Genappe to Quatre Bras." This has been frequently interpreted, (Houssaye; Ropes), to mean that it moved on from *Waterloo* at 1 p.m.; but Quatre Bras is 10 or 11 miles from Waterloo (*i.e.* a march of some four hours), and the head of Picton's division, had it left Waterloo at 1 o'clock, could not possibly have reached Quatre Bras when it did (about 2.30). The explanation, perhaps, is that Sir William Gomm really means that, from a later halt than that at Waterloo—and we know from the accounts of other officers that there was one near Genappe—they "moved on at 1 p.m. through Genappe."

But, however this may be, there is no doubt that it was not Wellington's understanding that the reserve was to halt as long as it did at Waterloo.

★★★★★★

See "Memorandum upon the Battle of Waterloo," *Supplementary Despatches* (1863). There was evidently a misunderstanding in some way. The 10 p.m. order from Brussels directed the reserve to march by the road to Namur to the point where the road to Nivelles separates. This would be to Waterloo. But on the other hand, in the "Disposition of the Army at 7 a.m. on June 16th," the reserve appears as ordered on to Genappe; and General Lettow-Vorbeck, on the authority of General Dörnberg's manuscript, states that he (General Dörnberg), on returning from Brussels to Mons at 4 or 5 a.m. on the 16th, was desired by Wellington to order it on towards Quatre Bras,

★★★★★★

Had it moved on soon after he passed it, it would have been on the march to Genappe when he wrote this letter; and as the distance to Genappe is between eight and nine miles, it would have been nearing the latter place, at all events, by noon.

The next paragraph is, "The English cavalry will be at the same hour at Nivelles" (*i.e.* by 12 noon).

The duke probably expected the cavalry to get off on its march before 7 a.m. As we have said earlier, the march to Nivelles was about 36 miles. Had they got off at 5 a.m., a rate of march of five miles an hour, including halts, would have brought them to Nivelles at about noon.

There seems nothing over-sanguine in the supposition that they would be there at noon, nor any ground for the duke to anticipate that their rate of march (including halts) would be three miles an hour.

The last paragraph is, "Lord Hills corps is at Braine-le-Comte."

Of course, Hill's entire infantry corps could by no possibility be at Braine-le-Comte at 10.30 a.m. on the 16th; for the distance (about 40 miles) precluded that the 4th Division (though ordered to Braine-le-Comte), and the Dutch-Belgians towards the Scheldt, should, under any circumstances, be there until hours later. Wellington wrote this letter hurriedly in the field, and in the most general terms; but for reasons which we have already touched upon, it is improbable that Hill's troops towards the Scheldt were in his mind.

The 2nd Division of this corps (Clinton's), about Ath, Lens, etc., had been directed by the 5 p.m. orders of June 15th to assemble at

105

Ath; by the 10 p.m. orders to move to Enghien; and by written order at 7 a.m. to Braine-le-Comte. From Ath to Braine-le-Comte is about 20 miles. Had this division marched from Ath at 3 a.m., it would have been nearing Braine-le-Comte at 10.30 when the duke wrote, but something went wrong with its orders as mentioned earlier.

The above details have occupied more space than the matter perhaps calls for, since no one in England doubts the good faith in which any letter of Wellington's would be written; but without giving them it is impossible to show on what an incomplete knowledge of actual circumstances, and what unsubstantial grounds, certain Continental writers, mentioned previously, have made the imputations which they have; and on this account it maybe well to place them before British officers.

With regard to the letter above discussed having induced Blücher to fight at Ligny, an assertion made of recent years, the official report of the operations of the Prussian Army of the Lower Rhine, signed by General Gneisenau, by order of Field-Marshal Blücher, runs thus:

> On June 16th only three corps of the army had joined; nevertheless, Field-Marshal Blücher resolved to give battle; Lord Wellington had already put in motion to support him a strong division of his army, as well as his whole reserve stationed in the environs of Brussels; and the 4th Corps of the Prussians being also on the point of arriving.

There is nothing here to indicate that Blücher was misled into fighting at Ligny by imperfect information as to the position of Hill's corps, the cavalry, or other portions of Wellington's army; and with regard to the "strong division" and "reserve" which it is mentioned that the duke had "put in motion," a greater force than this did support the Prussians by sustaining the attack of, or occupying, 40,000 men of Napoleon's force under Ney, at Quatre Bras—though it did not take part in the fighting three miles beyond at Ligny.

Before Wellington's letter could have reached Blücher the Prussian troops were forming up at Ligny, and the French columns advancing; it was also anticipated that Bülow's corps was approaching. Blücher (writes Ropes; also Siborne), had long since fixed upon Sombref as the point of concentration for his army, and:

> Had even chosen the line of the brook of Ligny as a possible battlefield. To say that his decision to receive the attack of the French at Ligny was based upon any promise of support made by Wellington is entirely contrary to the evidence.

Sur les hauteurs derrière
Frasne le 16me juin 815
à 10 heures et demi

Mon Cher Prince
 Mon Armée est située comme il
suit.
 Le corps d'Armée du Prince d'Orange
a une Division ici et à quatre Bras;
et le reste à Nivelles.
 La Réserve est en marche de Waterloo
sur Genappe; où elle arrivera à Midi.
 La Cavalerie Anglaise sera à la
même heure à Nivelles.
 Le corps de Lord Hill est à Braine
le Comte.
 Je ne vois pas beaucoup de
l'ennemi en avant de nous;

et j'attends les Nouvelles de
votre Attaque; et l'arrivée
des bombes pour décider mes
Operations pour la Journée.

Rien de nouveau du côté de
Bench; ni sur votre Bord.

Votre très obéissant serviteur
Wellington

Horsburgh also says:

> Where are the documents to support such a contention (*viz.* that a definite promise unfulfilled induced Blücher to fight at Ligny)? this letter (that of Wellington which we have been discussing) not being sufficient. (*Waterloo, a Narrative and a Criticism*, by E. L. S. Horsburgh, 1900).

Let us now turn to the paper, "Disposition of the British Army at 7 a.m. on June 16th."

It has perhaps attracted more notice and comment than would otherwise have been the case, because some have considered that it probably misled Wellington to write the letter to Blücher above discussed. (From his possibly supposing that the troops were at, or very close to, the places named in the second column). The duke may, of course, have seen it before he wrote to Blücher, but there can be no certainty that he did. With his excellent memory, he could have written the letter from a recollection of his own orders, and it is couched in very general terms. This memorandum has been also condemned as an unintelligible as well as confusing document, not very creditable, as an official paper, to the staff of the army. But its real object and intention have been most probably misunderstood, and an importance has been assigned to it, which it would not have possessed at the time in the eyes of those by whom, or for whom, it was drawn up.

It is signed by no one; it is not in any respect of the character of an instruction for the movement of the army; it is made out without headings to the top of the columns, and the place where, or date when, it was put together are not mentioned. It did not appear in the first edition of the *Wellington Despatches*, but was apparently found by Sir De Lacy Evans at a subsequent period, among his papers, and sent by him as of interest, with an explanation of it, to Colonel Gurwood, the editor of those *despatches*. (See *Wellington Despatches* (ed. 1852), vol. viii. The memorandum, a copy and suggested explanation of which is given further on, is not among the archives at Apley House, but Sir De Lacey Evans copied several of Sir W. De Lancey's papers).

It is necessary to mention the above points because in the edition of the *Wellington Despatches* of 1852, vol. viii.—though not in the supplementary ones (1863)—it is placed between instructions for the movements of the army which are signed by Sir W. De Lancey, deputy quartermaster-general. Probably from this circumstance it has been occasionally assumed to be of the nature of one of these signed instructions; but it is in reality merely an unsigned—or copy of an unsigned—Q.M.G.'s memorandum.

Sir De Lacy Evans was most likely the only person living, when he sent it to Colonel Gurwood, years after Waterloo, who really knew what its purpose was, and he appended to it the explanation of its columns which appears at its foot, signed by him. Therefore, it should not, in justice to Sir W. De Lancey, be discussed apart from that explanation, or as if it meant that the troops in the left column were all at the places named in the central one. (Sir De Lacy Evans says, "At," or "moving on"—an important distinction. See copy of the memorandum with Sir De Lacy's statement upon it, given further on).

Sir De Lacy Evans states that the paper was "written out for the information of the commander of the forces by Colonel Sir W. De Lancey." It may be accepted, therefore, that it was so; but it is probable that, had Sir De Lacy imagined when he sent it to Colonel Gurwood, that it would have been criticised as it has been, he would have added to it some more particulars, such as the place and time at which it was drawn up, whether the Duke of Wellington ever saw it, and the date at which his own explanation was inserted upon it. As matters stand, and without even the original paper to refer to, much respecting it must be simply conjecture.

It is scarcely conceivable, however, that Sir William De Lancey would have put together for Wellington's information any paper which, for its purpose, was a confusing and misleading one. Though a young man for his position—for he was only thirty-four when killed at Waterloo—he was one of the most experienced staff-officers in Wellington's Army, and had been in the Quartermaster-General's Department for ten years. Wellington thought so highly of him that he successfully pressed his appointment to his staff again in 1815. From Corunna to Vittoria he had gained much credit in the field, having the gold cross for nine general actions up to 1814.

Sir Augustus Fraser, (*Letters of Sir Augustus Fraser*), writes of his death at Waterloo, "This is our greatest loss; none can be greater, public or private." Sir Harry Smith, (*Autobiography of Sir Harry Smith*, vol. i.), speaks of him as "that gallant fellow De Lancey"; and the Duke of Wellington, "This officer is a serious loss to His Majesty's service; and to me at this moment." (*Wellington Despatches*, ed. 1852, vol. viii).

Again, Sir De Lacy Evans, who sends the memorandum, or a copy of it, to Colonel Gurwood, would scarcely have added his "explanation" to the paper without a certainty that it was correct. How he came to be in possession of the copies of the "Instructions to the Army" for June 15th, 16th, and 17th sent out by Colonel De Lancey, and the originals of which were lost, appears clearly in the notes to the *Wellington Despatches*, ed. 1852, vol. x. He was with Colonel De Lancey when these instructions were issued and despatched, and took copies of them, and probably of this paper of dispositions as well.

Ropes says:

> Evans, who became afterwards a distinguished general officer, (he commanded a division in the Crimean War), was in 1815 a major, and was serving as an extra *aide-de-camp* to Major-General Ponsonby, who commanded the 2nd Brigade of Cavalry. His attestation to the memorandum, therefore, can hardly have been made at the time.

There seems to be a misapprehension here. Sir De Lacy Evans appears certainly, by the *Waterloo Letters*, (edited by Major-General H. T. Siborne, see also Siborne's *History of the Waterloo Campaign),* to have served on the staff of the cavalry upon and *after* the retreat from Quatre Bras on June 17th; but he distinctly says himself that he was with Colonel De Lancey when the orders for June 15th, 16th, and 17th were issued. In the *Dictionary of National Biography* he is stated to have "returned to Europe (from America) just in time to join Wellington's army in Belgium, and was at once attached to the staff of Picton's division (quartered in Brussels) as Deputy Quartermaster-General"— probably the correct term would be Deputy Assistant Quartermaster-General. He had been employed in the Quartermaster-General's Department in the Peninsula, and in the subsequent war with America; and after Waterloo was continued in it as a lieutenant-colonel and assistant quartermaster-general with the army of occupation.

On this account it is unlikely that he was serving in the post of extra *aide-de-camp* to Sir W. Ponsonby for more than some very temporary purpose; but it would be probable that, when the pressure of work in issuing the orders for concentration occurred, he would be employed by Sir William De Lancey, and under circumstances which would enable him to know, at the time when the paper was made out, what its meaning was, whether he entered his explanation upon it then or afterwards.

It may help us in a consideration of this memorandum, and towards its solution, to note that it was at all events put together *after* 7 a.m. on June 16th. At that hour the troops had left Brussels for good for Quatre Bras, and Wellington was just setting out. According to the Oldfield manuscripts, (Ropes; The *Oldfield MSS.* were written by Major John Oldfield, Brigade-Major R.E., during the Waterloo Campaign), Sir W. De Lancey did not accompany the Duke out of Brussels, and may have preceded or followed him. He is not mentioned as being with him at the interview with Blücher at Bry.

The paper was apparently either jotted down most hastily in Brussels, just before the duke left for the front, (he rode quickly to Quatre Bras, and, almost at once, on to Bry), or, which is also possible, made out subsequently and hastily by De Lancey in the field, at some point south of Waterloo, to give to the duke when they met, or send to him; its purpose being to show Wellington, out in the field, the whereabouts generally of the troops at a certain hour (7 a.m.), and where they would be marching to under some particular orders issued at that hour. Possibly, too, it was—or was meant to be—supplemented by word of mouth.

The expression which occurs in the paper four times, of "Beyond Waterloo," and which has been viewed as clearly incorrect, (Houssaye; Ropes), would, to anyone south of Waterloo, mean north of that point; and, so understood, would be correct. It is noteworthy, also, that in the right-hand column of the paper we find the troops entered as marching to places, such as Genappe and Quatre Bras, to which they had not been directed under the orders or instructions of which we have written copies—*viz.* those of 5 p.m. and 10 p.m. of June 15th, and to Hill of 7 a.m. on the 16th; but everything entered in the central column is provided for under those orders, of which we do possess written copies signed by Sir W. De Lancey. (*See Wellington Despatches*, ed. 1852, vol. viii.). Why the columns were kept distinct we cannot now say with certainty, but can understand that it was considered at the time convenient.

Doubtless, wherever this memorandum was jotted down, there was no time for its compiler to make detailed calculations of times, distances, and so on. Most of the troops were miles away, and all was hurry. Hence the very general character of the entries in the central column, explained by Sir De Lacy Evans to mean "at" a place, *or* "moving on" it.

What is said above is put forward solely as a possible explanation of the paper; and we place, opposite the memorandum, further on, a table showing how it would read if the columns were headed as Sir De Lacy Evans says they should be—certain notes being added.

DISPOSITION OF THE ARMY AT 7 O'CLOCK A.M., JUNE 16th *

1st Division . . .	Braine-le-Comte.	Marching to Nivelles and Quatre Bras.
2nd ,, . .	,, ,, .	,, to Nivelles.
3rd ,, . .	Nivelles . .	,, to Quatre Bras.
4th ,, . .	Audenarde . .	,, to Braine-le-Comte.
5th ,, . .	Beyond Waterloo	,, to Genappe.
6th ,, . .	Assche . .	,, to Genappe and Quatre Bras.
5th Hanoverian Brigade .	Hal . . .	,, to Genappe and Quatre Bras.
4th ,, ,, .	Beyond Waterloo	,, to Genappe and Quatre Bras.

2nd Division ⎧ Army of the ⎫
3rd   ,,   ⎨   Low   ⎬ . . . ⎧ At Nivelles and Quatre
            ⎩ Countries ⎭   ⎩ Bras.

1st Division ⎫
Indian   ⎬   ,,   Sotteghem, marching to Enghien.
Brigade   ⎭

Major-General Dörnberg's ⎫
Brigade and Cumber- ⎬ Beyond Waterloo ⎧ Marching to Genappe
land Hussars   ⎭   ⎩ and Quatre Bras.

Remainder of the cavalry Braine-le-Comte. Marching to Nivelles and Quatre Bras.

Duke of Brunswick's Corps Beyond Waterloo Marching to Genappe.
Nassau Corps . . . ,, ,, ,, ,,

The above disposition written out for the information of the commander of the forces by Colonel Sir W. De Lancey. The centre column of names indicates the places at which the troops had arrived, or were moving on. The column on the right of the paper indicates the places the troops were ordered to proceed to at 7 o'clock a.m., June 16th, previous to any attack on the British.

(Signed) DE LACY EVANS.

* Given in the *Supplementary Wellington Despatches* (Ed. 1863), vol. x. p. 496; and in *Wellington Despatches* (Ed. 1852), vol. viii. p. 143.

Columns being headed according to the postscript signed by Sir De Lacy Evans, and notes added

Troops.	Places at which the troops had arrived, or were moving on.	Places the troops were ordered to proceed to at 7 a.m. on June 15th.
1st Division [1] . .	Braine-le-Comte .	Marching to Nivelles and Quatre Bras.
2nd ,, [2] . .	,, ,,	Marching to Nivelles.
3rd ,, [3] . .	Nivelles . .	,, Quatre Bras.
4th ,, [4] . .	Audenarde . .	Marching to Braine-le-Comte.
5th ,, [5] . .	Beyond Waterloo	Marching to Genappe.
6th ,, [6] . .	Assche . .	Marching to Genappe and Quatre Bras.
5th Hanoverian Brigade [7]	Hal . . .	Marching to Genappe and Quatre Bras.
4th ,, ,, [8]	Beyond Waterloo	Marching to Genappe and Quatre Bras.
2nd Division { Army of 3rd ,, { the Low { Countries } [9]	. . . .	{ At Nivelles and Quatre { Bras.
1st Division } Indian ,, } [10] Brigade }	Sotteghem . .	Marching to Enghien.
Major-General Dörnberg's Brigade and Cumberland Hussars [11]	Beyond Waterloo	{ Marching to Genappe { and Quatre Bras.
Remainder of cavalry [12]	Braine-le-Comte .	Marching to Nivelles and Quatre Bras.
Duke of Brunswick's Corps [13] . . .	Beyond Waterloo	Marching to Genappe.
Nassau Corps [13] . .	,, ,,	,, ,,

[1] Moving on Braine-le-Comte, by 10 p.m. order, June 15th.

[2] Moving on Braine-le-Comte by written order to Hill, 7 a.m., June 16th.

[3] Moving on Nivelles by 10 p.m. order, June 15th.

[4] Directed to move on Enghien from Audenarde by 10 p.m. order, June 15th, but probably still (7 a.m.) at Audenarde.

[5] It was "Beyond Waterloo," if "beyond" means north of; marching from Brussels, under 10 p.m. order of June 15th (Picton's division).

[6] Was near Assche. By orders of 5 p.m. of June 15th, placed "in readiness to march." See also orders to Lambert at Assche (page 535).

[7] Ordered to Hal by 5 p.m. order of June 15th (Siborne, vol. i. App. and 446). It was in the 5th (Picton's) Division, with the reserve.

[8] It was "Beyond Waterloo," if "beyond" means north of, with the reserve.

[9] Were to assemble at Nivelles by order of 5 p.m. of June 15th; and were, on the morning of the 16th, assembling there and at Quatre Bras.

[10] Moving to Sotteghem by 5 p.m. order of June 15th, and to Enghien by written order to Hill on morning of June 16th.

[11] It was "Beyond [i.e. north of] Waterloo," following reserve by 10 p.m. order of June 15th.

[12] Moving on Braine-le-Comte (so stated in 7 a.m. written order to Hill, June 16th).

[13] They were "Beyond [i.e. north of] Waterloo," following reserve by 10 p.m. order of June 15th.

P.S. With reference to Notes 5, 8, 11, and 13, it should be noticed that, according to the right-hand column of this paper, Picton's Division (the 5th), as well as the rest of the reserve, had, at 7 a.m. on June 16th, been ordered to march past Waterloo to Genappe. Thus Sir William De Lancey did not consider that the reserve was to remain halted at Waterloo.

CHAPTER 4

The Battle of Waterloo, June 18th, 1815

Wellington, in taking up a defensive position south of Waterloo in order to give battle to Napoleon, did so in the full expectation that Blücher would respond to the request which he had made to him from Quatre Bras, on the morning of June 17th, that he would come to his support from Wavre.

His troops occupying this position numbered about 68,000, of whom 12,000 were cavalry, with 156 guns. (This does not include 17,000 men placed near Hal to watch the right. Charras makes it about 70,000, with over 13,000 cavalry and 159 guns). Little more than one-third of this force were British.

Napoleon's army, not including the corps of Grouchy (33,000), which had been detached from Ligny to follow the Prussians, was about 72,000 strong, of whom about 16,000 were cavalry, with 246 guns. (Charras says 240 guns).

Thus, even without Grouchy, upon whose absence from the field Wellington could not count, Napoleon was rather stronger than his adversary in each of the three arms, but especially in artillery. With Grouchy he would have been far superior in infantry also; and in its composition and organisation, his army, for reasons which we have already explained, was more formidable.

******

See *ante. Notes on the Battle of Waterloo*, estimates the force with which Wellington fought as far from *equivalent* to one of 68,000 British troops. Against it Napoleon fought up to 6 p.m. with about 61,000 French troops, not including those with which he opposed the Prussians towards Planchinoit. After 6 p.m., as the Prussians came closer, the preponderance against Napoleon became great.

★★★★★★

From the very first Wellington's plan was to fight in conjunction with Blücher; but at the same time, no positive information that the Prussians would or could come to his support appears to have been received by him before the early morning of June 18th. Thus, in awaiting Napoleon's attack instead of falling back towards Brussels, he showed great resolution, and confidence both in himself and in his ally.

Blücher could not give any assurance as to what he could do until his ammunition columns had joined him at Wavre; and his various corps, after the retreat from Ligny, had been put into a condition to fight again. But at between midnight on the 17th and 2 a.m on the 18th, (Von Lettow-Vorbeck, in *Napoleon's Untergang* (1904), says 2 a.m.; other accounts earlier), he wrote as follows to Müffling, for the information of Wellington:—

> I have made the following dispositions for the movements of my troops. The corps of Bülow will march at the break of day from Dion le Mont, by Wavre, upon St. Lambert, to attack the enemy's right flank. The 2nd Corps will follow it immediately. The 1st and 3rd Corps will hold themselves in readiness to continue the movement.
>
> The exhausted condition of the troops, of which a portion, especially the rear of the 4th Corps, has not yet arrived, will not permit me to commence the movement sooner.

It will be noticed that the above letter completely meets the request of Wellington to the extent of two corps—the remainder being "held in readiness." But the gallant Blücher, shaken though he was from his fall at Ligny, chafed at the thought that a great battle might be fought with Napoleon south of Waterloo, at which he and a large portion of his army were not present; so that, at about 9.30 a.m. on the 18th, he ordered his *aide-de-camp*, Count Nostitz, to write further from him to Müffling in the following words, which have become famous wherever the story of Waterloo is told:—

> I have the honour to beg you to say in my name to the Duke of Wellington, that, ill as I am, I will march at the head of my army to attack at once the right wing of the enemy, if Napoleon attempts anything against the duke. In case the enemy should

attempt nothing today, I am of opinion that we should together attack the French Army tomorrow. I charge you to communicate this to the duke, as the result of my heart-felt conviction. I consider this plan as the best, and most adapted towards the end in view in our present situation.

We know now that Count Nostitz, before despatching this letter, showed it to Gneisenau, the chief of the staff, who, with a perfectly proper regard for the safety of the Prussian Army, desired him to add this postscript:—

General Gneisenau agrees in the views expressed in this letter. He has the honour to beg that you will carefully examine whether it is the duke's real intention to fight in his position; or if it is a question of a mere demonstration which might become very dangerous to our army. I beg of you to give me your opinion with respect to this; for it is of the most extreme importance that our movements should be based upon what the duke will really do.

★★★★★★

Napoleon's Untergang, Von Lettow-Vorbeck, Berlin (1904). Siborne, vol. i., makes this letter reach Wellington on the evening of June 17th; but it is generally considered that this is owing to some confusion between the above letter and the first one despatched, stating that Blücher would send two corps (Ropes). Siborne states that the Prussian officer bearing the letter was met and brought to headquarters by an escort of Vivian's cavalry, which was patrolling towards Ohain.

★★★★★★

The above letter and postscript are very interesting. They show Blücher determined to join Wellington with his main army; but also that his chief of the staff, while concurring, was keenly alive to the danger in which the Prussian Army might be placed, should Wellington retreat towards Brussels; and Napoleon attack it as it emerged from the broken country bordering the Dyle.

As the Prussians advanced towards the Lasne, they reconnoitred most carefully, in order to ascertain the true position of the troops, both of Wellington and Napoleon; and this, together with the difficult character of the ground they had to traverse and other accidental causes of delay, much retarded their arrival upon the battlefield.

Under Blücher's orders the Prussian Army was, on the morning of

June 18th, moving as follows:—

The 4th Corps (Bülow)—the one furthest off, unfortunately—was, as the least fatigued, appointed to lead, and a portion of it passed through Wavre about 7 a.m., making for St. Lambert; but the remainder, followed by the 2nd Corps (Pirch I.), were much delayed by a fire in the town, and by a report that Grouchy had attacked the Prussian outposts.

The 1st Corps (Ziethen) did not get off till nearly noon, and then marched towards Ohain.

In the account of the battle we shall see how they all came upon the scene.

Blücher joined Bülow's corps upon the march; the 3rd Corps (Thielemann) was left to defend Wavre; and the baggage was sent to Louvain.

On the night of the 17-18th Wellington had communicated by patrols through Ohain with the Prussians at Wavre; and writes, ("Memorandum upon the Battle of Waterloo"), that on the morning of the 18th he saw Prussian cavalry collected on the high ground on the Waterloo side of the defile of St. Lambert, at least one hour before the battle had commenced—*i.e.* about 10 a.m.

★★★★★★

This was no doubt the advance-guard of Bülow's corps, which had passed through Wavre before the fire broke out; but a long delay occurred before the main body came up. There is a story that Wellington rode himself to Wavre, having only an orderly with him, to confer personally with Blücher on the night of the 17th; but this is now generally considered to be unfounded (see Ropes; Horsburgh).

★★★★★★

Thus, early upon this eventful day, Wellington no doubt felt confident that in the battle he would have effective Prussian support, and probably earlier than he actually received it.

Napoleon's chief fear was that Wellington would retire and not give battle. He appears to have entertained little or no apprehension that the Prussians could intervene, believing that their defeat at Ligny had been too complete; and he looked to Grouchy to occupy them, should they attempt to do so.

His plan of attack was to force the Anglo-Allied centre and left, and thus interpose his army between Wellington and Blücher.

The rain had ceased towards daylight; but the ground had become so spongy and wet, that guns could not readily move over it.

Napoleon therefore postponed his attack until the sun had slightly hardened the surface of the fields; and, pending this, held, with much pomp, a parade of his army—possibly with the object of impressing his opponents with a sense of its power. Wellington, during this pause, visited the entire Anglo-Allied position (see plan), making careful dispositions for its defence, and he thus describes it, (Despatch to Lord Bathurst—Waterloo, June 19th, 1815):—

> The position which I took up in front of Waterloo crossed the high roads from Charleroi and Nivelles, and had its right thrown back to a ravine near Merbe-Braine, which was occupied, and its left extended to a height above the hamlet Ter la Haye, (appears to be north of the village of La Haye, which was occupied), which was likewise occupied. In front of the right centre, and near the Nivelles road, we occupied the house and gardens of Hougoumont, which covered the return of that flank; and in front of the left centre we occupied the farm of La Haye Sainte. By our left we communicated with Prince Blücher at Wavre, through Ohain; and the marshal had promised me that, in case we should be attacked, he would support me with one or more corps as might be necessary.

(Sir James Shaw-Kennedy, Assistant Quartermaster-General to the 3rd Division at Waterloo, considers, *Notes on Waterloo*, that the Belgian map of Craan best shows the details of the ground; and the plans of Siborne the position of the troops. In this account these have been usually followed). We may supplement the above brief description with the following details. The position, which barred the approach to Brussels, was in many respects an excellent one. It ran along the crest of a low ridge close to the road from Wavre to Merbe-Braine, which road, sunken in parts and bordered by hedges, offered in itself defensive advantages. The ridge, though of no great width, was practicable for all arms. Towards the south it descended gradually, affording the defenders a good field of fire; while its northern slopes and undulations gave concealment and cover to Wellington's troops, and particularly those in reserve—a point to which he carefully looked in all his defensive battles, for it enabled him both to protect his men from the enemy's artillery, and also to make unexpected counter-attacks.

The right was strongly posted behind the steep ravine of Merbe-Braine. The left was less so, but it rested on the edge of the bro-

GROUND-PLAN OF THE FARM OF LA HAYE SAINTE.

(Not drawn to scale.)

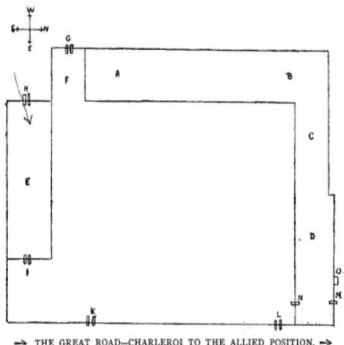

→ THE GREAT ROAD—CHARLEROI TO THE ALLIED POSITION. →

A, B, C, D, Dwelling-house, stables, and cow-house, of which D is the dwelling-house.

E, A barn.

F, A passage.

G, A great gate.

H, A great gate.

I, A door.

K, A great gate.

L, M, N, Doors.

O, A well, being a square building, with loopholes flanking the door and wall.

The interior measure of the yard, from the building C, D to the building E, is 40 yards, and 45 yards from the building A, B to the wall K, L.

The buildings are very strongly roofed and built. The passage F has the same roofing as the houses.

THE CHATEAU OF HOUGOMONT.

Taken chiefly from Kennedy's 'Notes on the Battle of Waterloo.'

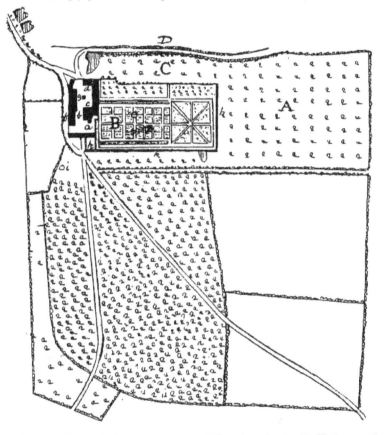

A, Great orchard. B, Kitchen-garden. C, Small orchard. D, Hollow road. *a*, Chapel. *b*, Chateau. *c*, Farm buildings. *d*, Cowshed. *e*, Gardener's house. *f* and *g*, Barns. *h*, Small garden. *i*, Haystack. *k*, *k*, Wall loopholed by British troops.

ken country towards Ohain, from which direction the support of the Prussians was looked for.

In front the villages of Hougoumont, La Haye Sainte, and La Haye (south of Ter la Haye) were well adapted to the purposes of advanced posts, as they were close to the main position, which overlooked them, and so could be readily reinforced. Hougoumont was of special importance. It consisted of a *château* with outbuildings, a walled garden, and orchard; and to the south a thick wood, screening the occupants from observation and fire.

A glance at the plan shows that, from the ridge north of Hougoumont (which bulges out to the south) and the enclosures of the *château*, a flanking fire could be brought against an enemy attacking the right and centre of the position to the west of the Charleroi road.

As far as the very limited time would allow, Hougoumont and La Haye Sainte were placed in a state of defence—loopholes were made; platforms from which to fire through them erected; and abattis placed across the Nivelles and Charleroi roads; while on the extreme left, Papelotte and Smohain, as well as La Haye, were occupied.

Behind the position, between Mont St. Jean and Brussels, stretched the extensive forest of Soignies; but this was open in character, free from underwood, and traversed by fairly good roads, passable for all arms.

Wellington, having on the 17th sent into Brussels for a plan of this ground, which had been made by Colonel Carmichael Smyth and other officers, drew up his troops as follows.

The first line was of infantry, with cavalry upon the flanks, and was thus posted:—

On the right, Cooke's division (Guards)—brigades of Byng and Maitland—having to their right rear and right front, watching the ground between Hougoumont and Braine-le-Leud, (sometimes spelt Braine-l'Alleud), Mitchell's brigade, (the only brigade of the 4th, Colville's Division present at Waterloo, the remainder having been directed to Hal), and a squadron of cavalry (15th Hussars).

Hougoumont was occupied by the light companies of Cooke's division, under Colonel Macdonell and Lord Saltoun, together with a regiment of Nassau troops and two companies of Hanoverian sharpshooters.

Behind this portion of the line, thrown back between Merbe-Braine and the Nivelles road, was Clinton's division—brigades of Adam, Du Plat, and Hugh Halkett.

Next to Cooke's division came Alten's—brigades of Colin Halkett,

Kielmansegge, and Ompteda, the last occupying La Haye Sainte, with Kruse's Nassau contingent in rear.

Next Picton's division—brigades of Kempt and Pack—the 95th Rifles, of Kempt's brigade, occupying a sandpit and broken ground near La Haye Sainte. In advance, exposed upon the slope, (why this brigade was so exposed does not seem clear), was Bylandt's Dutch-Belgian brigade.

Next Best's brigade, of the 6th (Cole's) Division; next Vincke's, of Picton's division (both Best's and Vincke's brigades, belonging to different divisions, were Hanoverians, and for some reason were placed together in the first line); and beyond this the cavalry brigades of Vandeleur and Vivian, the patrols of the latter being pushed out towards Ohain and Frischermont.

The whole of the front from beyond Hougoumont to Smohain was covered by a line of skirmishers or vedettes; and to the right, beyond the main position, Chassé's Dutch-Belgian division occupied Braine-le-Leud, keeping up communication with the troops towards Hal. (The troops at Hal, 10 miles north-west of Braine-le-Leud, and at Tubize near it, consisted of Dutch-Belgians under Prince Frederic of Orange, and two brigades of the 4th Colville's Division—in all between 17,000 and 18,000 men).

The second line was composed chiefly of cavalry, in the following order from the right: to the west of the Charleroi road, the brigades of Grant, Dörnberg, and Somerset, with, in rear, Arentsschildt's Hussars of the German Legion; to the east of the road, Ponsonby's brigade. (Termed the "Union Brigade," because it consisted of an English, Scotch, and Irish regiment—*viz.* the 1st Royals, the Scots Greys, and the Enniskillen Dragoons).

The reserves were in rear of the right and right centre, and consisted of the Brunswick corps—cavalry and infantry—near Merbe-Braine; the Dutch-Belgian cavalry under Collaert, of which the brigade of Ghigny was near the Charleroi road; and Lambert's infantry brigade of the 6th (Cole's) Division, (just arrived from America), which was posted near the farm of Mont St. Jean.

The artillery was distributed along the main ridge—30 guns to the west of the Charleroi road, 26 to the east, and the rest in reserve; but all the batteries became more or less engaged in the course of the battle.

The French position was nearly parallel to that occupied by Wellington, and was under a mile distant from it. From the right, near Frischermont, it ran along a ridge to the village of La Belle Alliance

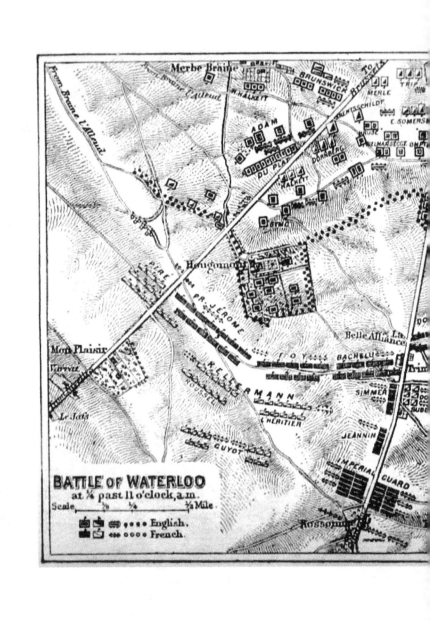

BATTLE OF WATERLOO
at ¼ past 11 o'clock, a.m.
Scale, ⅛ ¼   ½ Mile

●● ●●● ●●●● English.
■● ●●● ●●●● ○○○● French.

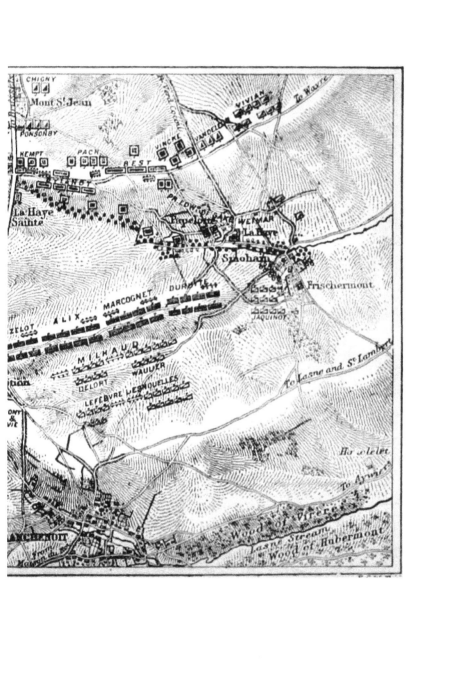

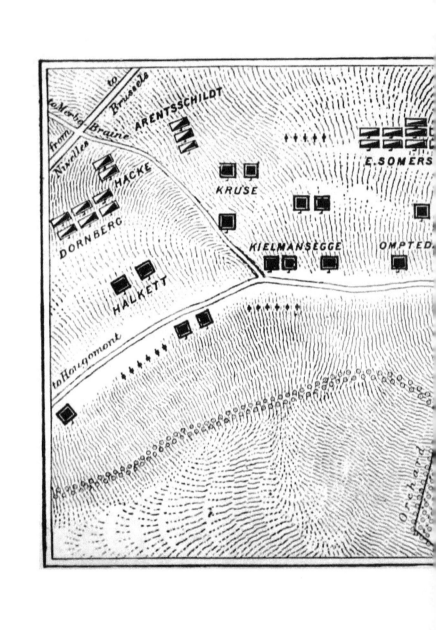

LA HAYE SAINTE

Scale.

¼ Mile.

Allies.

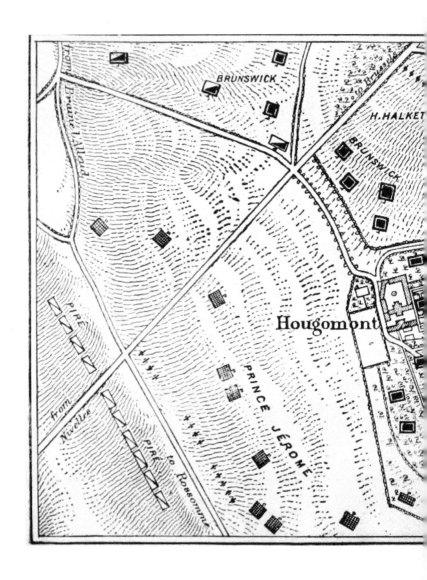

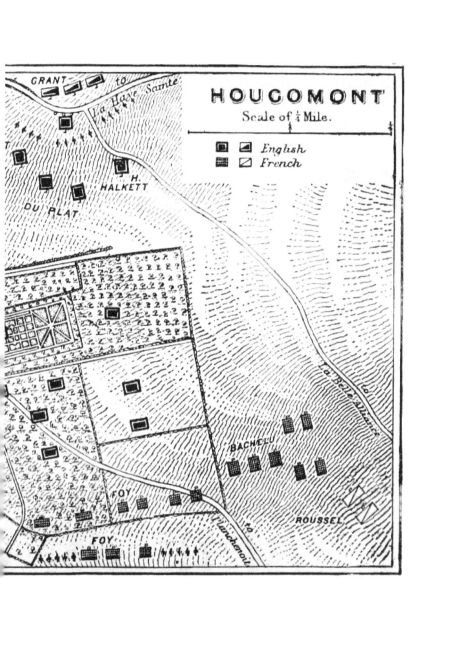

HOUGOMONT

Scale of ¼ Mile.

☐ ◪ English
▦ ▨ French

GRANT to
La Haye Sainte
H. HALKETT
DU PLAT
BACHELU
FOY
ROUSSEL
to Planchenoit
FOY
La Belle Alliance

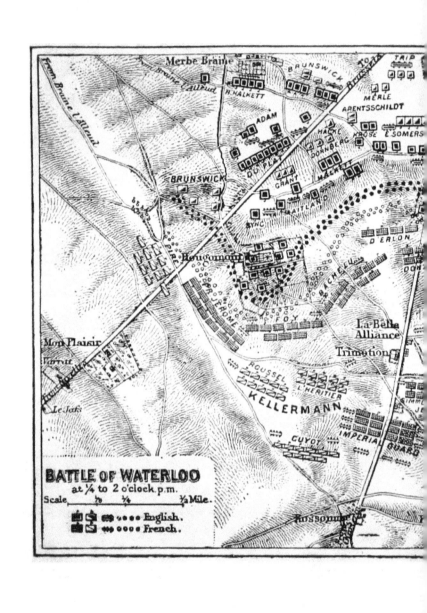

BATTLE OF WATERLOO
at ¼ to 2 o'clock p.m.

Scale ⅛ ¼ ½ Mile.

☐☒ ⇔ ••• English.
☐☒ ⇔ ••• French.

Mont St Jean
To Wavre
PONSONBY
BYLARDT VINCKE
VIVIAN
KEMPT PACK BEST VANDELEUR CHIGNY
FIELD OF SAXE WEIMAR
La Haye
Sainte
Papelotte
La Haye
ALIX
DURUTTE
Smohain
MARCOGNET
Frischermont
JAQUINOT
DELORT WAULIER
To Lasne and St Lambert
MILHAUD
DONONT
LEFEBVRE DESNOUELLES
SUBERVIE
Boulelet
To Aywiers
Wood of Virere
ANCHENOIT
Lasne Stream
Wood of Hubermont
From
Maison du Roi

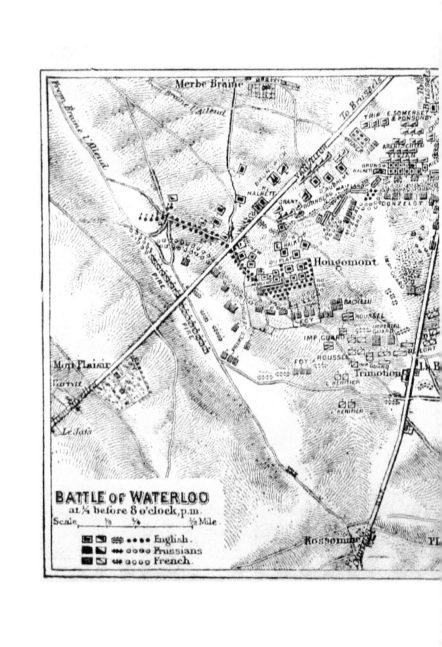

BATTLE OF WATERLOO
at ¼ before 8 o'clock, p.m.

Scale ⅛ ¼ ½ Mile

English.
Prussians.
French.

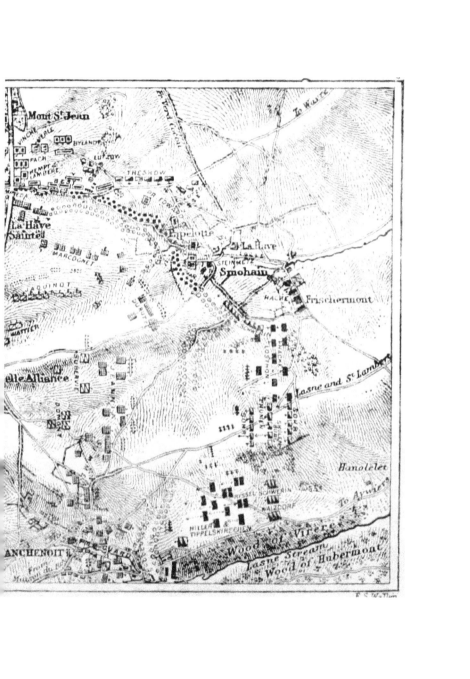

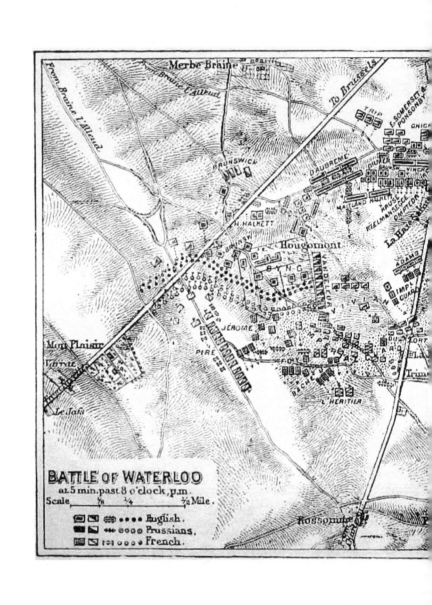

BATTLE OF WATERLOO
at 5 min. past 8 o'clock, p.m.
Scale ⅛ ¼ ½ Mile.

English.
Prussians.
French.

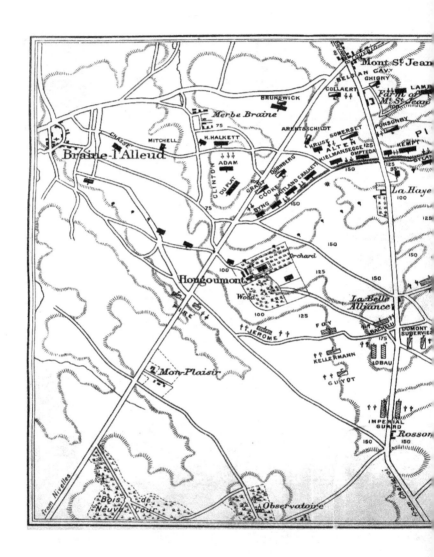

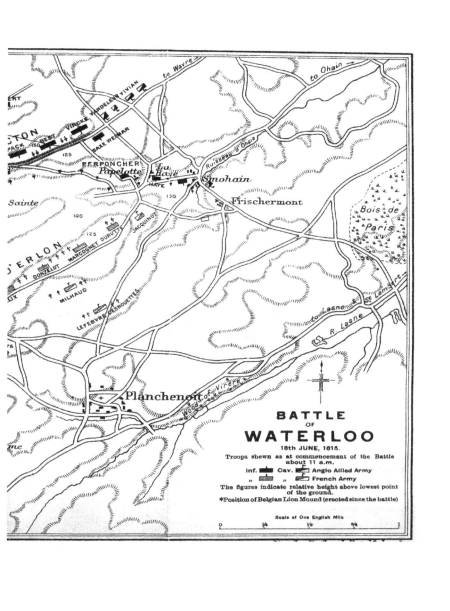

BATTLE
OF
WAATERLOO

18th JUNE, 1815.

Troops shewn as at commencement of the Battle
about 11 a.m.

Inf. ▬ Cav. ▬ Anglo Allied Army
  „ ▬ „ ▬ French Army

The figures indicate relative height above lowest point
of the ground.

*Position of Belgian Lion Mound (erected since the battle)

Scale of One English Mile

0   ¼   ½   ¾

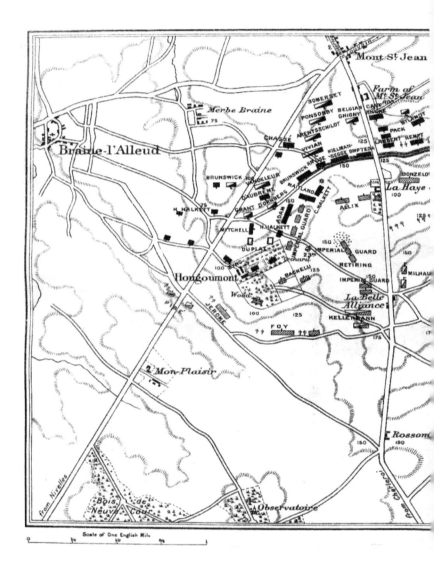

Scale of One English Mile.

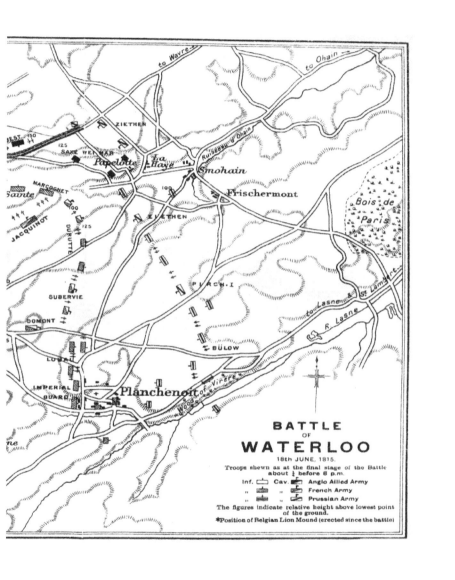

BATTLE
OF
WATERLOO
18th JUNE, 1815.
Troops shewn as at the final stage of the Battle
about ½ before 8 p.m.
Inf.☐ Cav.◼ Anglo Allied Army
„ ▬ „ ◼ French Army
„ ▬ „ ◻ Prussian Army
The figures indicate relative height above lowest point
of the ground.
✱Position of Belgian Lion Mound (erected since the battle)

on the Charleroi road, and thence over some ridges south of the wood of Hougoumont to the Nivelles road. Napoleon disposed his troops thus:—

In front line, beginning from the right, the corps of D'Erlon—divisions of Durutte, Marcognet, Allix, and Donzelot. (Houssaye and Lettow-Vorbeck have been followed here. They place Donzelot's division to the right of Allix; but Siborne, Ropes, and several others, place it to the left). Next, to the west of the Charleroi road, the corps of Reille—divisions of Bachelu, Foy, and Jerome. (Jerome was wounded early in the battle, and his place taken by Guillemenot). To the right of the whole line was the cavalry of Jacquinot; to the left that of Piré, each throwing out vedettes to their outer flank.

In second line, to the east of the Charleroi road, was the cavalry of Milhaud; in the centre, south of La Belle Alliance, the corps of Lobau, with the cavalry of Domont and Subervie; to the west of the Charleroi road, the cavalry of Kellermann. (Ropes speaks of Kellermann and Milhaud, not as in the second line but as in the reserve; but Houssaye, and Siborne, i., place them in the second line. In any case, the cavalry and infantry of the Guard were in reserve behind).

The reserves, in third line, consisted of the cavalry and infantry of the Imperial Guard—the light cavalry (Lefebvre Desnouettes) being in rear of Milhaud, the heavy cavalry (Guyot) in rear of Kellermann. The infantry, in front of the farm of Rossomme, consisted of 24 battalions, formed in four deep columns.

★★★★★★

Eight battalions (Grenadiers and *Chasseurs*) formed the Old Guard under Count Friant; eight battalions (Grenadiers and *Chasseurs*) the Middle Guard under Count Morand; eight battalions (*Voltigeurs* and *Tirailleurs*) the Young Guard under General Duhesme. The whole were under General Drouot, in the absence of Marshal Mortier, left sick at Beaumont (Siborne, vol. i.). The Young Guard were men of at least 4 years' service; the Middle of 8; and the Old of 12, with distinguished service.

★★★★★★

The artillery of D'Erlon and Reille were in the front line. The remainder of the guns were with the various corps and the reserves.

BATTLE OF WATERLOO
June 18th, 1815

The conflict opened with an attack by Napoleon, at about 11.30 a.m.

★★★★★★

There is much discrepancy in the times given for the commencement of the battle. By the stop-watch of Lord Hill it was 11.50 a.m.; Wellington says in one letter 10, in another 11; Kennedy, 11.30; Napoleon, 12. This is perhaps to be accounted for in part by one person considering the battle to commence from the first gun fired; another from the first serious attack upon some particular part of the position; or another from the first advance of skirmishers, and so on.

★★★★★★

Wellington writes thus from Paris on August 17th, 1815:

> It is impossible to say when each important occurrence took place, or in what order. We were attacked first with infantry only; then with cavalry only; lastly and principally with cavalry and infantry mixed.

Sir James Shaw-Kennedy divides Napoleon's attacks, throughout the battle, into five chief phases, (*Notes on the Battle of Waterloo*, 1865), *viz.*:—

> 1. The preliminary attack upon Hougoumont (about 11.30 a.m.).
>
> 2. The infantry attack upon the centre and left (commencing at about 1.30 p.m.).
>
> 3. The great cavalry attacks upon the right centre to the west of the Charleroi road (from 4 to 6 p.m.).
>
> 4. The renewed infantry attack upon the centre at La Haye Sainte; also partial attacks by cavalry and infantry between the Charleroi and Nivelles roads (6 to 7.30 p.m.).
>
> 5. The combined and final attack of both infantry and cavalry, supported by a powerful artillery, upon the whole line.

He adds also:

> All the published accounts of the Battle of Waterloo have, in my opinion, the defect of not separating the important portions of the action from each other. Without doing so, it cannot, I conceive, be understood. The Battle of Waterloo had this distinctive character, that it was divided into five separate attacks, four of which were isolated attacks, and one only (*i.e.* the last) was general on the whole Anglo-Allied line; these five attacks

141

were distinct, and clearly separated from each other by periods of suspension of any close attacks. (The 4th phase, or attack, however, began before the 3rd cavalry attack was entirely over-though they were distinct in character) . . . The battle was a great drama in five acts, with distinct and well-defined intervals.

We propose in the following brief description of the battle to consider it under the five successive phases indicated above, as they tend to keep the sequence of the main attacks clear in the mind, and should be of assistance to those who desire to follow the tactical details of the battle in larger works relating to them.

But it should be understood, in addition, that throughout the entire day the attacks upon Hougoumont were more or less continuous; that during the 4th and 5th phases the pressure of the Prussians upon Napoleon's right, which before that had caused him anxiety, had become severely felt, obliging him to detach largely from his reserve to meet it; and lastly, that a general advance by Wellington of his whole line, at the conclusion of the 5th phase, together with a most vigorous Prussian pursuit, turned the French defeat into one of the most irretrievable and disastrous routs recorded in history.

1ST PHASE: HOUGOUMONT

The preliminary attack upon Hougoumont (about 11.30 a.m.)

The object of this was partly to gain possession of this important post previous to an advance on the main position, but chiefly to divert the attention of Wellington from his centre and left, against which a serious attack was being prepared.

Under cover of a general cannonade and a cloud of skirmishers, the division of Jerome, supported by Foy and Bachelu, attacked the *château* and enclosures of Hougoumont. After repeated onsets they gained possession of the wood, part of the orchard, and the avenue leading to the Nivelles road, but, though the gate of the *château* was for a moment entered, they could not carry the *château* itself, nor the walled garden.

Probably the gallantry of the defenders of this post has never been surpassed on any battlefield. (Within half an hour 1,000 men fell in the orchard of Hougoumont; and throughout the day, including both armies, some 10,000 men). They consisted chiefly of Guards, reinforced from the ridge by Wellington, who withdrew the Nassau troops. (These showed unsteadiness, and their sympathies were possibly with Napoleon. The same troops had behaved extremely well when fighting on the side of the French at Vittoria; *Conversations with the Duke of Wellington*, by Earl Stanhope).

At one time the artillery from the main position shelled the wood, over the heads of the garrison, and cleared it of the French; the outbuildings were repeatedly set on fire, but the flames as often extinguished; and it may be said at this point that, throughout the day, the garrison of Hougoumont, in spite of every effort made to take the post, held it with the greatest gallantry.

2ND PHASE: THE INFANTRY ATTACK

The infantry attack upon the centre and left (commencing at about 1.30 p.m.)

(Although this was almost entirely an infantry attack, it was supported on the left by a body of cavalry. It commenced, possibly, nearer 2 p.m.)

The object of this was to pierce Wellington's line, gain possession of the road through Mont St. Jean to Brussels, and separate Wellington from Blücher.

With no little exertion D'Erlon, under the supervision of Ney, had massed nearly 80 (many accounts say 80 guns; Ropes, 78 guns; Kennedy, 74 guns), guns upon a ridge in front of the French position, which at about 600 yards from Wellington's line runs out east of the Charleroi road, south of La Haye Sainte; formed his columns of attack behind it; and awaited Napoleon's signal to advance.

This was for some time delayed because—a point to be noticed—the appearance, at about 1 p.m., of some troops at a distance, beyond the wood of Paris towards St. Lambert, had disturbed Napoleon. First of all, he thought they might be Grouchy's, but from an intercepted despatch he learnt that they were certainly Prussians. He then detached the cavalry of Domont and Subervie to observe them, and subsequently the corps of Lobau (two divisions), and also wrote to Grouchy (Appendix B, XI. PS.) in the hope that he might intercept them.

★★★★★★

This letter did not reach Grouchy (see "Movements of Grouchy," further on) till too late for him to be of any service. He had despatched a previous one to him (Appendix B, X.) at 10 a. m. We shall refer to these in the "Movements of Grouchy," but need not enter into them here.

★★★★★★

Having done this, he directed D'Erlon to attack. But in the meantime, Wellington, having observed the preparations made, had proceeded from his right towards the centre. Lord Uxbridge also had warned the cavalry to be on the alert; and, as the French advanced, prepared for a counterstroke with the brigades of Somerset and Ponsonby.

D'Erlon, under cover of his massed guns, to which the Allied artillery replied, moved forward with the divisions of Durutte, Marconi, Allix, Donzelot, (Allix's Division was commanded by Quiot apparently), supported to the west of the Charleroi road by Bachelu's division of the corps of Reille and a body of cavalry from Milhaud's Corps.

As he drew near there was, according to the French accounts:

Something weird in the appearance of the British position; for except Picton's skirmishers and Bylandt's Belgian brigade, no infantry was to be seen, and the guns appeared to be entirely unsupported. (*Cavalry in the Waterloo Campaign*, by Sir Evelyn Wood, 1895).

As the French got closer, however, they were met with a heavy fire, and a hard contest began. With great bravery Quiots' troops gained possession of the orchard and garden of La Haye Sainte, and twice set the farmhouse itself in flames; the French also carried the village of Papelotte, and pushed up to the crest of the ridge.

★★★★★★

Charras, Hooper, and Ropes make the farmhouse itself fall also before 4 p.m. but Kennedy, Siborne, Chesney, and Houssaye at about 6 p.m. or later. It is impossible to obtain agreement as to this point; and probably the smoke and flames of the farmhouse, and the capture of the garden and orchard, led to the contradictory opinions formed.

★★★★★★

Bylandt fell back, but the deadly volleys of Kempt and Pack's brigades broke the steadiness of the French columns; and then Ponsonby, with the "Union Brigade," passing through the infantry, swept down upon the shaken troops in one of the most brilliant and successful charges recorded in the annals of cavalry. (It was at his moment, as the Scots Greys passed through the 92nd Highlanders, that the cry of "Scotland for ever" was raised—the subject of the well-known picture).

The French fell into great confusion. The whole valley between

Papelotte and La Haye Sainte was filled with fighting, struggling men. Nearly 3,000 of D'Erlon's divisions were killed or wounded, 3,000 were made prisoners, and two eagles were captured.

★★★★★★

One by Captain Clark—afterwards Sir James Clark Kennedy—of the Royals; and one by Sergeant Ewart, of the Scots Greys. These, with their standards, now hang in the chapel of the Royal Hospital at Chelsea. The capture of the eagle by the Scots Greys is the subject of the picture, "The Fight for the Standard." Shaw, the Life Guardsman, having, it is said, killed seven of his opponents, died on the field from his wounds after this charge.

★★★★★★

In the meantime, to the west of the Charleroi road, Alten's division, formed in squares, had received the *cuirassiers* as they appeared upon the ridge with a very telling fire; and Somerset's heavy cavalry, taking them suddenly in flank, drove them in disorder down the slope.

Then Somerset's brigade, crossing the Charleroi road to the east, mingled with Ponsonby's, and all dashed at D'Erlon's 80 guns massed upon the ridge (see earlier). Killing the gunners and horses and cutting the traces, they rendered nearly half the guns useless. But this impetuous attack had carried them too far; and the cavalry of Milhaud and Jacquinot, coming up when they were scattered and not properly supported, inflicted severe loss upon them.

★★★★★★

Lord Uxbridge's candid criticism of himself in later years is valuable. "I committed," he writes, "a great mistake in having myself led the attack." (apparently with Somerset's brigade). He considered that he had been with even a weak second line in hand, some loss would have been avoided and the guns probably secured (*Waterloo Letters*, Siborne, 1891).

★★★★★★

Picton, Sir W. Ponsonby, and many valuable officers and men were killed at this period of the battle. Throughout the attack efforts were unsuccessfully made to carry Hougoumont; a heavy cannonade had also been kept up against the right, but the character of the ground greatly protected those troops of Wellington's not closely engaged from its effects.

After this there was rather a prolonged pause. The corps of D'Erlon had completely failed in its attack, and been terribly cut up. The Prussians, also, though still at a distance, were evidently approaching in force; and Napoleon hesitated for a time as to the best course to be followed. It was 4 p.m. before he commenced the—

3RD PHASE: THE CAVALRY ATTACKS

Cavalry attacks against the right centre to the west of the Charleroi road (from 4 to 6 p.m.)

The first of these was made under Ney's direction by the whole corps of Milhaud, followed by Lefebvre Desnouettes—in all 40 squadrons of cavalry. Crossing the Charleroi road from east to west, they then advanced up the space between La Haye Sainte and Hougoumont in many lines against the right centre—Alten's division and the Guards—who, as they approached, formed squares, or what Sir James Kennedy termed "oblongs," to receive them.

It contributes to a correct understanding of the cavalry attacks in the battle, to say, at this stage, that the French squadrons, in closing with infantry, did not usually do so at any great speed; also that the Allied position gave the defenders the advantage of the ground. The French had to move up the ridge, while the Allied cavalry as a rule charged down it, with a momentum both from the slope and pace.

Wellington says that Napoleon, in his cavalry attacks, came forward:

Not fast, but in great masses, the object being to occupy a position till the infantry came up afterwards. They received attacks standing still, and with a volley of carbines. (*Personal Reminiscences of the Duke of Wellington,* by Lord Ellesmere, 1903).

Lord Uxbridge also writes (as to Waterloo):

No heavy mass having a well-formed front actually came collectively against our bayonets. Constantly a few devoted fellows did clash with them, and some pressed between the squares. They were always in column, and they never charged at speed. (*Waterloo Letters*).

Describing Milhaud's advance Sir James Shaw-Kennedy writes:

They did not gallop on to the infantry, but made every other effort to enter the oblongs, by firing into them, cutting aside the bayonets, and surrounding them to obtain a point of entrance. (*Notes on Waterloo*).

When the above is borne in mind, and also that Wellington had given orders to the artillery to leave their guns at the last moment and take refuge in the infantry squares, opening fire again when the cavalry were driven off, one can better understand the onset and repulse of the French squadrons, which, when retiring in disorder, were usually charged and broken by the Allied horse.

★★★★★★

Wellington, it is said, had given instructions to take off a rear wheel of each gun and roll it into the square. The French cavalry carried ropes to throw round captured guns and drag them away, and this was to prevent that (H. R. Clinton, 1878, *War in the Peninsula, France, and Belgium*). They never spiked the guns, which would perhaps have involved dismounting.

★★★★★★

As Milhaud's cavalry approached, rounds of grape and canister made havoc in their ranks, and the Allied gunners took refuge in the squares; then the volleys of the infantry threw them into disorder; then, as they turned to escape, Grant's, and the remnant of Somerset's, cavalry charged and routed them; lastly, as they were retiring, scattered and broken, the artillery once more opened upon them.

But Milhaud was not quickly discouraged. Again he returned to the charge, and again fell back discomfited before Wellington's immovable infantry. Foy is said to have exclaimed:

These children of Albion, stood as if they had taken root in the ground. (*The War in the Peninsula, France, and Belgium*, by H. R. Clinton 1878).

Then a further and supreme effort was made. Once more what remained of Milhaud's and Lefebvre Desnouettes' cavalry, together with that of Kellermann and Guyot, (77 squadrons in all, about 12,000 strong, in twelve lines), attempted to break through the Allied infantry. (It is said that part of the cavalry joined in this charge without he orders of Napoleon).

Kennedy (who witnessed the attack), writes:

The whole ground between La Haye Sainte and Hougoumont was covered with this splendid array of horsemen. Their advance, made in a manner that showed the highest discipline, was majestic and imposing . . . it was one of the most powerful efforts ever made by cavalry against infantry in the history of war.

A heavy fire of artillery supported this attack; but though carried through with much enthusiasm and obstinacy, it completely failed, and in the end was overthrown in exactly the same way as had been the previous ones. It was renewed once more for the last time, with the same results: so that by about 5.30 or 6 p.m. almost the whole of Napoleon's heavy cavalry (and most of Wellington's also) had been rendered practically ineffective for the remainder of the battle. The Cumberland Hussars and some of the Belgian cavalry had shown a very poor spirit in these attacks, the former regiment galloping off to Brussels.

Throughout these cavalry efforts Wellington's close supervision of the battle was constant; he was much exposed to fire, and was forced occasionally to enter a square for safety.

During them—to turn now to the Prussians—Bülow, with the 4th Corps, had debouched (at about 4.30 p.m.) from the wood of Paris; and by the time of their termination (about 6 p.m.), 30,000 Prussians, advancing between Frischermont and the stream of the Lasne, had driven the French back to Planchenoit, their near approach having produced this important effect, that Napoleon, to oppose them, reinforced Lobau with 12 battalions of the Imperial Guards, thus greatly weakening his reserve.

Throughout the march from Wavre, Blücher—Marshal Vorwärts ("Forwards"), as his soldiers called him—had urged the Prussians on.

> The roads were so narrow, and so deep in mud, that the rate of marching was terribly slow, and the toil excessive; the guns sank axle-deep in the mire, and the tired horses could not extricate them. The men took their places. 'We cannot get on,' they exclaimed, as they tugged in vain at the traces. 'But you *must* get on,' said loyal old Blücher, riding alongside the labouring teams. 'I have pledged my word to Wellington; you will not let me break it.' (*The Story of Waterloo*, by Major-General H. D. Hutchinson., C.S.I. 1890).

Thus by 1 p.m. a large portion (three brigades) of Bülow's corps had reached St. Lambert, although the rear-guard had not entirely closed up till 3 p.m.

At St. Lambert there was, however, a delay; and so, as we have said, it was half-past four before the Prussians had issued from the wood of Paris.

The anxiety of Gneisenau, the chief of the staff, for the safety of the Prussian Army, should Wellington retreat, and his distrust of the latter, (see Ropes; Ollech; Rose, *Napoleonic Studies*; also *ante*), may, as some hold, have partly occasioned this; but in any case the Prussian march had been a most arduous one, and a certain delay was necessary before moving into battle.

In a comparatively recent Life of General von Grolman, who was Quartermaster-General of Blücher's army, some light is thrown upon the halt at St. Lambert by General E. von Conrady. (*Life and Works— Leben und Wirken—of Carl von Grolman,* by General E. von Conrady, Berlin, 1895).

He writes that Major von Lützow, of the general staff, having for some time waited impatiently in the wood of Frischermont for the troops, rode back to St. Lambert, where he found Blücher and Gneisenau. (The wood of Paris, east of Frischermont, is sometimes spoken of, apparently, as the wood of Frischermont).

He urged an immediate advance, mentioning the heavy attacks being then made on Wellington, but no decision was arrived at. Then Grolman, coming up just at this moment from Wavre, and hearing what was said, cut the matter short with the words:

> March, march, in the field-marshal's name I order you to cross the defile at once. (*Aber Marsch, Marsch, in des Feldmarschall's namen befehle ich, so fort über das Defilée zu gehen.* Colonel F. N. Maude, C.B. (late R.E.), in *Evolution of Modern Strategy,* 1905, draws attention to this passage in Conrady's *Life of Grolman*).

And Blücher concurring, the troops advanced.

If this story is accurately told, it is probable that General von Grolman very clearly saw that he was expressing Blücher's wishes, restrained perhaps by the not-unnatural prudence of Gneisenau.

As Blücher approached the field, information reached him from Thielemann at Wavre that he was attacked by Grouchy, and asking for support; but Blücher replied that he must do his best with his own corps, as the contest would that day be decided, not at Wavre, but at Mont St. Jean.

Before the cavalry efforts had failed, Napoleon, despairing of their success, had directed what may be termed the—

4TH PHASE: LA HAYE SAINT

Renewed infantry attacks upon the centre at La Haye Sainte; also partial attacks by cavalry and infantry between the Charleroi and Nivelles roads (6 to 7.30 p.m.)

The French advance was now made against portions of the position by the remains of D'Erlon's corps and that of Reille, supported by cavalry. Hougoumont was once more attacked, and the Allied line became engaged at several points.

But the greatest fury of the attack was directed against the centre at La Haye Sainte, which was most gallantly defended by the King's German Legion; and at length the divisions of Donzelot and Allix (Commanded by Quiot) succeeded in carrying this post, about 6 p.m., (according to Kennedy and others. There is, however, a good deal of discrepancy as to the hour when the farmhouse of La Haye Sainte fell, some as mentioned say it did so much earlier), partly owing to the supply of ammunition having failed.

This was a critical period of the battle. The French had established themselves within 60 yards of the main ridge, and kept up a sharp fire upon Alten's and Kempt's divisions, which had suffered heavy losses, Alten himself being wounded. The brigades of Ompteda and Kielmansegge were so weakened that there was practically a considerable gap in the Allied centre; and had Napoleon promptly supported his success with a powerful reserve the result might have been serious. He had not, it is said, perceived the advantage which he had gained; but even had he done so, he was hardly now in a position to act with great promptitude. D'Erlon's corps had suffered very severely, the cavalry terribly, while the Prussians were closing on his right flank. Bülow's corps was attacking Planchenoit, Ziethen coming up from Ohain; and to meet the Prussian advance 12 battalions of the Imperial Guard (chiefly the Young Guard) had been detached, and also the corps of Lobau.

In a very short time the opportunity for French success had passed away. During the last attacks Wellington had made several movements to strengthen his centre and right. (It is convenient now to turn to the last of the two plans of the battlefield). Du Plat's brigade, with Hugh Halkett's in support, had been pushed forward close to the Hougoumont enclosure, and Adams' brigade brought to the right of the Guards and thrown forward, (sometimes in squares, sometimes four deep; Kennedy), so as to flank a French advance against the right. Chassé's division had been ordered up from Braine-le-Leud, the brigade of D'Aubremé being posted behind Adams. The Brunswickers and Kruse's Nassau troops were placed on Kielmansegge's right; and Vandeleur and Vivian's brigades of cavalry brought from the left (Ziethen's Prussians having now come up on that flank) to between the Nivelles and Charleroi roads.

By 7.30 p.m. the immediate danger to Wellington's line had been met. Still, La Haye Sainte was in French hands; and the Guard and Lobau were holding their own, after very hard fighting, at Planchenoit: so, although Bülow, Pirch I., and Ziethen (52,000 Prussians with 104 guns) were now closing in, Napoleon determined to make one last effort for victory.

Then commenced the—

5TH PHASE: THE IMPERIAL GUARD ATTACK

Combined attack of infantry and cavalry, supported by a powerful artillery, upon the whole Anglo-Allied line (commencing about 7.30 p.m.)

This movement was covered by a cloud of skirmishers, and preceded by a furious cannonade. While from Hougoumont to Papelotte the French advanced to the attack, and the brigades of Best, Lambert, and Kempt were assailed from the direction of La Haye Sainte, Ney, with 10 battalions (two were left in reserve; the remainder were engaged with the Prussians), of the Imperial Guard (Middle and Old), accompanied on the march by field-guns, which kept up a heavy fire, moved from La Belle Alliance by the east of Hougoumont against the Anglo-Allied right.

These battalions, according to Kennedy, Chesney, Hooper, Siborne, and Houssaye, (Houssaye says that instead of forming one single column, Marshal Ney left the battalions divided), were formed in two columns; but Ropes is convinced that one column only advanced, though the rear battalions of this column inclined to their left (they moved in *échelon*), and thus presented the appearance of a second and separate column.

In any case, the attack was made by two distinct bodies, (which we will here term columns). The first approached Maitland's brigade, lying in four-deep formation, concealed along the ridge. Suddenly, twenty paces ahead, "a red wall loomed before them," (Houssaye), as the British Guards, at Wellington's order, rose in their front and poured in a volley which caused them the loss of 300 men.

★★★★★★

Wellington disclaims having said, "Up, Guards, and at them," as is usually stated. "What I may have said and possibly did say," he told Croker, "was 'Stand up, Guards,' and then gave the order to attack." (*How England saved Europe*, W. Fitchett, 1902).

★★★★★★

Shattered by grape and case from the field batteries, and by the

151

THE ATTACK OF THE FRENCH GUARD.

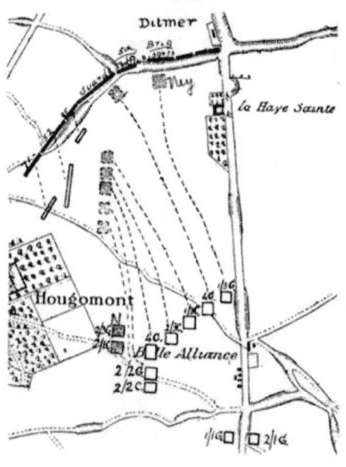

infantry musketry-fire, the column tried in vain to deploy; and then, as Maitland's Guards advanced with the bayonet, the veterans of Napoleon gave way in confusion.

The second column advanced rather after the first, supported by a body of cavalry, and mounted the ridge between the brigades of Maitland and Adam. (Both in four-deep formation, by Wellington's order). Its head was met by the fire of the former, while the 23rd Light Dragoons and other bodies of Allied cavalry fell upon and repulsed the French horse.

At this moment Colonel Colborne, (often before mentioned in these pages, and who subsequently became Lord Seaton), of the 52nd, in Adam's brigade, greatly distinguished himself. Wheeling up his regiment, he poured volleys into the flank of the column, which halted and endeavoured to deploy, but soon broke and fled before a bayonet charge.

Then Adam, with the whole of his brigade—52nd, 71st, and 95th Rifles (now Rifle Brigade)—followed the disordered battalions diagonally, in an easterly direction, as far as the Charleroi road. Kennedy writes that the march was directed so that the left of the 52nd came upon the Charleroi road so near to the orchard of La Haye Sainte that part of the 95th, who were on Colborne's left, got into the orchard.

Finally, the cavalry of Vandeleur and Vivian, moving down past the north-east corner of Hougoumont, dashed at various bodies of the French which were endeavouring to reform and renew the combat; and now commenced what may be termed the—

6TH PHASE: THE ADVANCE

Advance by Wellington of his whole line, and pursuit by the Prussians.

Having directed this advance, Wellington galloped off to Adam's brigade; this, as it neared the Charleroi road, met three battalions of the first column of the Imperial Guard, which had reformed; and Wellington, coming up at the moment, ordered the 52nd to attack them. They charged, and the French broke and dispersed.

The victory was now won. The Prussians were turning the French right; Ziethen had taken Smohain and Papelotte, driving Marcognet and Durutte before him; and his guns were on the ridge, close to where Pack's brigade had stood at the beginning of the battle. Bülow and Pirch I. were heavily engaged at Planchenoit, where Lobau, holding out gallantly for some time longer, gave to the rest of the French

Army an opportunity to retire, though in great disorder.

Napoleon left the field under cover of a determined stand of two battalions of his Guard left in reserve; but narrowly escaped capture, the road being choked with guns, waggons, and retreating troops. He reached Charleroi at about 6 a.m. on the 19th, and Paris on the 21st. Ney, too, escaped, having had, it is said, six horses killed under him during the battle.

As darkness was closing in, Wellington and Blücher met, not at La Belle Alliance, as is often stated, but four miles beyond it, after 10 p.m., at Genappe (*Supplementary Wellington Despatches,* 1863, vol. x.); and the pursuit through the night was entrusted to Gneisenau, with the Prussians.

It was so energetically conducted that probably no beaten army was ever more completely routed.

> Sometimes with horse and foot, sometimes with June 18, horse alone, always with drums and bugles, he (Gneisenau) kept close on the heels of the enemy, and the sound of the bugle and beat of the drum alone sufficed to drive the French from nine bivouacs. When his infantry were exhausted he mounted the drummers; and with these and a few squadrons, went clattering along the *pavé*, and drumming through the night. At dawn he halted—the French had disappeared.—Hooper.

Thus were Ligny and Jena fully avenged.

Only 40,000 of Napoleon's troops escaped across the Sambre. Two eagles, and the whole of the French artillery, with the ammunition train, fell into the hands of the Allies. The loss on both sides was very great—that of the French about 30,000, of Wellington's army 15,000, and of the Prussians 7,000. Very many officers of rank were killed or wounded, including almost all of Wellington's staff. Sir W. De Lancey died of his wounds, Lord Uxbridge had a leg shattered, and Lord Fitz-Roy Somerset lost an arm. Excepting the pursuing troops, the Allied armies bivouacked on the field; and Wellington returned for the night to his headquarters of the previous evening at Waterloo.

COMMENTS

As an illustration of tactics the Battle of Waterloo must always be specially instructive to soldiers. The superiority in fire-power of the line over the column; the combined employment of the three arms (cavalry, infantry, and artillery) upon the one side, contrasted with the comparatively isolated action of each upon the other; the value of well-situated advanced posts; the importance of rapidly following up a success when gained, of utilising ground to conceal and protect troops, and of retaining reserves in hand as long as circumstances will allow,—are all prominently brought out.

Waterloo was a most closely contested battle, a hand-to-hand struggle; and this fact, together with some of Wellington's own expressions with regard to it, such as, "Never did I see such a pounding match; both were what the boxers call 'gluttons.' Napoleon did not manoeuvre at all," (Letter to Lord Beresford, July 2nd, 1815—*Wellington Despatches*, 1852, vol. viii.), have contributed to create with many an impression that it was simply a gigantic stand-up fight, in which there was little scope for the skill of any general. No idea could be further from the truth. The battle was won by the way in which Wellington placed and fought his troops, even more than by the gallantry of the troops themselves. At this period other generals did not dispose their line of battle, or conduct a battle, entirely as Wellington did.

We have but to contrast Ligny with Waterloo to see this. In the former battle the troops (Prussians) were exposed to view and fire, in the latter they were concealed and protected; in the former the fire of columns was employed, in the latter that of the line; in the former the Prussian reserves were rather freely expended, in the latter Wellington's were cautiously held back.

Sir Harry Smith, who was present at the battle, writes, (*Autobiography of Sir Harry Smith*, by G. C. Moore-Smith), that the hard, close, defensive fighting which distinguished it had the effect, after the peace, of undoing much of what had proved valuable in the Peninsular contest, as it led subsequently to the undue employment of rigid formations in drill, such as squares, and of neglect of the work of light troops and the utilisation of cover—a point which it is well to note, although what Sir Harry Smith deplored when he wrote has since been corrected.

At the same time, it is evident that in the Waterloo campaign, as far as Wellington himself was concerned, there was a thorough appreciation of the importance of a due, not undue, use of cover. We see also that his subordinate generals and commanding officers were not afraid, as is sometimes supposed, to take responsibility upon themselves; and that, when he deputed authority, he did not unnecessarily interfere with its exercise.

Baron Marbot writes:

When the French have to defend a position they first garnish the front and flanks with skirmishers, and then crown the heights conspicuously with their main body and reserves—which has the serious inconvenience of letting the enemy know the vulnerable part of the line. The method employed in similar cases by the English seems to me to be preferable, as it was demonstrated in the Peninsular War. After having, as we do, garnished their front with skirmishers, they post their principal forces in such a way as to keep them out of sight, holding them all the time sufficiently near to the key of the position to be able to attack the enemy at once, if they come near to reaching it.—*Memoirs of Baron Marbot*, translated from the French by J. A. Butler (1892), vol. ii.

It was Wellington who principally, at all events on any large scale, employed this system; and its efficacy has been illustrated more than once in the campaigns described in these pages. Can it be supposed, had his army been drawn up on the exterior slopes of the ridge at Waterloo, exposed to view and to artillery, that Napoleon would have attacked it in the manner he did, or that, however gallant, it would have been victorious?

At the same time, this due employment of cover certainly did not lead, in the Peninsula or at Waterloo, with Wellington's troops, to its abuse, which must, of course, be guarded against. They were ready enough to come out for a counterattack upon the enemy.

With respect to the assumption of responsibility by officers under Wellington, we find Colonel Colborne, of the 52nd, wheeling up his regiment without orders from General Adam (though he subsequently approved) to attack the Imperial Guard; also Baron Constant de Rebecque directing to Quatre Bras, without authority, the Belgian troops, where the Prince of Orange retained them. We have instances also of this assumption of responsibility by senior officers in the Peninsula—*viz.* by General Kempt at the Nive, as well as with Picton and Craufurd on more than one occasion.

With junior officers he did not allow this latitude, for, at the period of the Peninsula and Waterloo, it was seldom necessary to do so, as, owing to the comparatively short range of firearms, those in command could frequently see much of an entire battlefield for themselves.

The difference between the extent of the battle front (*i.e.* the usual extent; at the passage of the Bidassoa, however, the fighting front extended nearly 12 miles, at the Battle of the Nive, about 9; at the Nivelle, about 14; and in the Battles of the Pyrenees much more than this), in the present day and at that period is illustrated in the following words of Lord Roberts, referring to Waterloo, ("The Army as it was, and as it is," *Nineteenth Century Review*, January, 1905), where the front of battle did not extend much beyond three miles. He writes:

It was possible for both commanders to be kept fully informed throughout the battle (of Waterloo) of all that was going on, and from first to last they had complete control over the troops. . . . In South Africa, on more than one occasion, with considerably less than half the number of troops engaged at Waterloo, the front extended for more than 20 miles.

Regarding the fact that when Wellington deputed authority, he did not interfere with its full exercise, we have this statement of Lord Uxbridge, commanding the cavalry at Waterloo:

I received no order from the Duke of Wellington to make the first charge, or any other, during the day. I felt that he had given me *carte blanche,* and I never bothered him with a single question respecting the movements it might be necessary to make.—*Waterloo Letters.*

At the same time the entire army recognised that it was Wellington who was watching, directing, and supervising all; and nothing is more noticeable in the various accounts of the battle than the consensus of opinion among his subordinates that the result of the day was mainly attributable to his skill and personal exertions.

His tactics throughout the whole of the great battle; the hawklike vision with which he detected each coming attack; the swift, unfailing resource with which he met it . . . there is nothing finer than all this in the history of war.—*How England saved Europe,* by W. Fitchett (1902).

We need not enlarge further upon Wellington's Waterloo tactics. His management of the three arms in combination has been generally admitted to have been masterly, and practically no adverse criticism has been directed against his arrangements. (One should except, perhaps, the criticism that the troops towards Hal should have been ordered in, to take part in the battle; but to this we shall refer later on).

It was somewhat in contrast to the separate use made of the infantry and cavalry by Napoleon, who, by not fully supporting one arm with the other, is considered by many writers upon Waterloo to have acted incomprehensibly, and by it to have wrecked his chances of success. D'Erlon's first infantry attack was not duly supported by cavalry, and the cavalry attacks not duly supported by infantry; the consequence being that the French squadrons were used up, and unable to give due aid to the last final effort of the Imperial Guard. It may be added that, when La Haye Sainte was carried, no adequate effort was made to secure with reinforcements the success obtained, and profit by it.

From all this, the conclusion has been often drawn that at Waterloo Napoleon's military genius was on the decline.

There may be some truth in this; but still, to receive it as a full explanation of his tactics at Waterloo is difficult. No one up to. the close of 1814 was a more complete master of the art of war than Napoleon; and the broad principles governing the use and combination of the three arms could scarcely, within those few months of 1815, during which he showed such energy in his concentration upon the Belgian frontier, have entirely passed from his mind under the influence of physical weakness.

It seems more probable that he was, from the first, completely surprised and disconcerted by the manner in which the Allied position was occupied and his attacks met by Wellington—as well as by the disquieting approach of the Prussians towards his right flank.

The position itself has been a good deal altered since the battle by the removal of earth along the main ridge in order to form the mound upon which the Belgic Lion now stands, and in other ways; but enough of its former character remains to show that, although well suited to Wellington's system of defence, there was little in the ground itself likely to impress Napoleon with an idea of its strength, or the difficulty of forcing it.

He may doubtless have heard from others of Wellington's method of concealing and handling his troops, but he had no personal experience of it; and at more than one stage of this campaign the conviction of his mind seems to have been, that before the French legions, led by himself, Wellington's army must necessarily give way, even if it had (which up to the last he doubted) the resolution to give battle before the Prussians had joined. In this respect it was probably unfortunate for France that he had never met Wellington in Spain.

If he exhibited failings and short-comings on the day of Waterloo, they were, it would seem, less connected with strategy or tactics than with his dominant, self-confident character, which, though it had contributed to his success on many other fields, ruined him on this. It did not permit him to profit by the experience of those generals who had fought long in the Peninsular War.

Oman writes, that his heavy column formations did not please his subordinate leaders as a mode of attack against the English; but that he replied to Soult with an insulting outburst:—

"You were beaten by Wellington, and so you think he is a great general: but I tell you that Wellington is a bad general, and the English are bad troops; they will merely be a breakfast for us."

"I earnestly hope so," replied Soult.

★★★★★★

The Cambridge Modern History (1906), "The Hundred Days," 1815, ch. xx. See also Houssaye to the same effect. The statement seems to be taken from the MS. notes of Lieut. -Colonel Baudus, on the staff of Marshal Soult.

★★★★★★

As he gazed at Wellington's position he could see very little of the troops which held it. As D'Erlon's dense columns mounted the slope in the first great attack of infantry, they were received by a superiority of fire which, though it might have been anticipated by D'Erlon himself, who had been at Fuentes d'Onor, Vittoria, the Pyrenees, Nivelle, and Nive, was not expected by Napoleon.

Had another leader of another army held that ridge, D'Erlon's columns would probably have been met by other columns, with a musketry fire no superior to their own; and judging by the way in which D'Erlon's troops attacked Picton, Kempt, and Pack, they might well have broken those columns.

But when, under the volleys of the Allied infantry, the sudden rush of Ponsonby's cavalry, and the fierce resistance at Hougoumont, both D'Erlon and Reille had failed, how then could Napoleon combine infantry with his cavalry to any great extent, except by employing his reserve? His whole first infantry line was more or less disorganised and required time to rally, while the corps of Lobau had been detached towards Planchenoit against Bülow.

But it was yet early in the afternoon, and it can be well understood that, with the Prussians closing upon him, he would be most reluctant to call upon the Imperial Guard, until it had been seen whether his massed squadrons, filling the entire space between the Charleroi and

Nivelles roads, could not ride over the thin lines which appeared to occupy the ridge.

The failure of his cavalry attacks upon the Allied squares must have much embarrassed him; and as it was during the confusion consequent on their defeat that La Haye Sainte fell, his attention was probably too much occupied to allow him to benefit at once by that success.

When both infantry and cavalry had been repulsed, it was with beaten troops that he had made his next attack with these two arms combined; and when the final advance of the Imperial Guard, closed the day, it was carried out when he had to face in two different directions against enclosing enemies.

It would rather seem that Napoleon was overthrown with a great defeat in June, 1815, less because he had lost his old genius and energy, than because he had met throughout the campaign, in Wellington and Blücher, with men whom he had from the first underrated, and was opposed on the field of Waterloo itself by a system of tactics which, even if it was not unknown to him, he was unprepared for. But for this Great Britain is mainly indebted to Wellington and his talent as a leader.

The close manner in which Wellington watched every phase of the battle, and his quickness to meet emergencies, were evinced repeatedly throughout the day. His order to the artillery to leave their guns and take shelter temporarily within the infantry squares was not a usual one; neither was that to the Guards and 52nd to form a four-deep instead of a two-deep line, before the combined attacks of the French cavalry and infantry. The full object of this last order has scarcely, perhaps, been sufficiently dwelt upon.

The two-deep line was, and still is, the normal formation of British infantry. Against infantry alone Wellington would have employed it, as he had done scores of times; against cavalry alone he would as a rule have formed square, having, if possible, his own cavalry ready to follow up the repulsed enemy: but at the time of this order his infantry lines had been greatly thinned, and his cavalry had suffered heavily. As he writes himself:

> It was obvious that the troops would require extension of line (*i.e.* something more than the front of a square) to engage with the infantry, and solidity to meet the cavalry.

So he directed one subdivision of each company to move behind the other, and the companies to close, forming a four-deep line.

Ropes, in alluding to Ney not having sufficiently supported the last attack of the Imperial Guard with cavalry, says:

If this attack of the Imperial Guard had been supported on the right by cavalry, this resistance on the part of Halkett's and Maitland's commands could not have been encountered.

And again:

A charge of cavalry would have forced the 52nd to form square.

The idea seems to be very generally entertained that the whole intention of this four-deep line was that square to meet cavalry could be more quickly formed from it; also that the flank march of the 52nd would have been frustrated had more cavalry been employed, because they must have stopped and formed squares, while the front of their fire would, moreover, have been much reduced.

But is this idea well founded? We imagine that the 52nd might not have formed square; and that Wellington's order was meant to provide against their being obliged to do so, although they might, if necessary, have thrown back a flank company temporarily, or faced about the two rear ranks. (The 44th Regiment, when attacked suddenly by cavalry at Quatre Bras, faced about the rear rank and held their ground).

★★★★★★

It may be added that, although the front of fire must have been diminished by the four-deep formation as compared with the two-deep line, its volume would not have been so wherever the ground permitted of the third and fourth ranks, as well as the two ranks in front of them, using their muskets.

★★★★★★

With regard to the part which the Anglo-Allied and Prussian Armies respectively bore in the great battle, it is natural that some misapprehension should exist in both England and Prussia. Men, while absorbed in their own duty in a close contest, see little of their comrades to the right and left. Many in the Allied Army did not know when the Prussians arrived on the field, nor of the hard fighting at Planchenoit, nor of the way in which Napoleon had to weaken his reserve to oppose Bülow.

On the other hand, the Prussians are said not to have been aware (from their position on the French right) of all the circumstances attending Wellington's final attack, or advance, of the whole line; or of the movements of Adam's brigade, or of Vivian's cavalry brigade.

But in all that has been published, nothing puts the share borne by the Prussians more clearly than Wellington's despatch, (to Earl Bathurst—Waterloo, June 19th, 1815, the italics are ours), written immediately after the battle:—

Having observed that the troops retired (this was after the last French attack) in great confusion, and that the march of General Bülow's corps by Frischermont upon Planchenoit and La Belle Alliance had begun to take effect, and as I could perceive the fire of his cannon, and as Marshal Prince Blücher had joined in person with a corps of his army to the left of our line by Ohain, I determined to attack the enemy; and immediately advanced the whole line of infantry, supported by the cavalry and artillery. The attack succeeded at every point; the enemy was forced from his position on the heights. . . .

I should not do justice to my own feelings, or to Marshal Blücher and the Prussian Army, if I did not attribute the *successful result of this arduous day to the cordial and timely assistance I received from them*. The operation of General Bülow upon the enemy's flank was a *most decisive one*; and even if I had not found myself in a situation to make the attack which produced the final result, it would have forced the enemy to retire if his attacks should have failed; and would have prevented him from taking advantage of them, if they should, unfortunately, have succeeded.

Sir Hussey Vivian's remarks, also, are very valuable, as he was on the extreme left flank of the Allied line, from whence he could see the Prussian approach through the greater part of the day (Letter to Captain Siborne, in *Waterloo Letters* by Major-General H. T. Siborne, 1891):—

That the Prussians were seen advancing to our support long before their arrival on the field there can be no doubt. That its being an understood thing between the duke and Blücher that they were to support us, and that such understanding was a necessary part of our remaining in our position and risking a battle, is equally certain. Any attempt, therefore, to throw doubt on the combination by which their assistance was afforded to us is quite absurd.

The first Prussians that came into action, I should say, were the advanced guard of a corps, not exceeding two regiments, and supported by another; they passed the hedge of Papelotte, and drew up across the valley in line almost at right angles to us. They were directly under where I stood, and I saw the operation as plainly as if at a field-day.

The French at once advanced against them (their left flank, rather), and drove them back. They then occupied the village of Smohain or Papelotte—I forget exactly the name. This must have been somewhere between 5 and 6 o'clock—I should say nearer 5. It was a considerable time after this that the Prussians appeared in force. We remained long enough for me to see the French reserve and right form line *en potence* in order to meet the attack on Planchenoit, and I was surprised to see the tremendous fire the French were able to direct against the Prussians. It was just as this took place that I moved to the right. If anyone can tell you exactly about the time we advanced, it will give you the time of the Prussians being generally engaged; but I should certainly say that they were before Planchenoit very soon after half-past seven, if not as early. (They were there earlier).

In truth, I care not what others say, we were greatly indebted to the Prussians, and it was their coming on the right and rear of Napoleon that gave us the victory of Waterloo. We might have held our ground, but we never could have advanced but for the Prussian movement.

When, at about 8 p.m., Wellington moved forward in the final advance of his army, it was an attack, not merely an advance. (His line was scattered and uneven; but his casualties having been 15,000 out of 68,000, he probably had at least 40,000 men able to advance, if not more). Adam's brigade, crossing by La Haye Sainte to the east of the Charleroi road, met three formed battalions and broke them; Vandeleur's and Vivian's cavalry attacked and dispersed other bodies of the French; and the reason why the pursuit was not kept up longer by Wellington, was not solely that the troops, who had been fighting for ten hours, were fatigued, but also because Marshal Blücher had expressed his intention of following the enemy himself throughout the night. (*Supplementary Wellington Despatches,* 1863).

Houssaye attributes the French retreat to "the check to the Middle Guard," the "irruption of the Prussians," and the "forward march of Wellington." Rose also writes that the French "have always attributed their final rout to the timely and spirited advance of Vivian's and Van-deleur's cavalry." (Houssaye; and *Napoleonic Studies*, by J. Holland Rose 1904). Vivian pursued till stopped by Wellington near Rossomme.

On the other hand, it was because he saw the Prussians closing in force on the French right that Wellington (as he himself says) felt in a position to make this attack.

The arrival of the Prussians on the French flank endangered Napoleon's retreat; and compelled him to detach Lobau and a large portion of the Guard to meet it, drawing these away from Wellington, as Wellington at Quatre Bras had kept Ney's troops away from Blücher at Ligny.

Thus the Prussians contributed greatly to the victory, which their pursuit turned into disaster.

Within the limited space of a short despatch Wellington could not duly notice many of the brilliant actions performed by the troops; but he says, "The army never, upon any occasion, conducted itself better," and a special medal (the Waterloo Medal) was issued to all ranks present in the actions of June 16th, 17th, and 18th, 1815.

In connection with the eagles taken in the battle, it may be of interest to mention that the reference to them made by Wellington in his Waterloo despatch is made to run thus in one edition of the *Wellington Despatches* (Despatch from Waterloo of June 19th, 1815—ed. 1852, vol. x.):

I send with this despatch 3 eagles, taken by the troops in this action.

This, perhaps, has led to the assertion in several works that three eagles were captured, and in some to statements as to how and when three were taken; although in other accounts but two eagles are alluded to.

At the Royal Hospital, Chelsea, two eagles only are deposited in the chapel; and there being an uncertainty as to what might have become of the third, the writer, who was then there, was permitted to refer to the original despatch. In this what is written plainly—in words, not figures—is "two eagles," and clearly the idea that three were sent arises merely from a copyist's or printer's error.

★★★★★★

Such errors will occur occasionally, in spite of the care of authors, copyists, and printers. It is not impossible that the idea that Wellington says in one letter that the Battle of Waterloo began at 10 a.m., and in another at 11 a.m., may have arisen from the figure in one letter having been written like, and copied as, 1.

★★★★★★

Some of the arguments and counter-arguments as to the Waterloo campaign have been based upon discrepancies between copies of instructions and orders as given in various works. A comparison between the instructions for the movements of the army on June 15th (orders of 5 p.m. and 10 p.m. on that day), as given in Siborne, App., (2nd ed., 1844, vol. i., possibly altered in later editions), with those given in the *Wellington Despatches*, (ed. 1852, vol. viii.), will show this. In the former no orders appear as sent out to the 2nd (Clinton's) Division at 5 p.m.; in the latter they are given. In the former no orders appear as sent out to the reserve in Brussels at 10 p.m.; in the latter they are given,—and so on; and occasionally, variations in different editions of one work are found.

CHAPTER 5

The Battle of Wavre,
June 17th–July 6th, 1815

We have already said, with regard to the campaign of Waterloo, that there is no other in which, as to many incidents, more conflicting opinions have been, and are still, expressed; and we might add that in this campaign the remark is especially applicable to the movements of Grouchy subsequent to June 16th, 1815. As carried out, these movements affected little the Battle of Waterloo—as those of D'Erlon had affected little the Battle of Ligny; but it is necessary to enter into them, because while some writers have entirely justified Grouchy's conduct, and exonerated him from all blame, others have stigmatised him as a traitor, or as incompetent; and attributed the defeat of Napoleon to the manner in which he interpreted, and acted upon, the emperor's orders.

Grouchy left the field of Ligny at about 2 p.m. on June 17th, 1815, under instructions to pursue the Prussians and ascertain their movements. Whatever directions may have been given to him verbally, he certainly left under what is termed the "Bertrand order" (Appendix B, VII.), which was a written one dictated by the emperor to Marshal Bertrand, in the temporary absence of Soult, the chief of the staff.

★★★★★★

It is stated that for many years Grouchy denied the receipt of the Bertrand order, asserting that he had received none but verbal ones before he set out (Ropes). It was, however, published in 1842, and has since 1864 been acknowledged in the memoirs of Marshal Grouchy by his son.

★★★★★★

This order has been the subject of so much discussion, that it should be considered very closely and carefully, and especially so because it was in reality the only order which Grouchy received between the time he left and the afternoon of June 18th (Ropes)—when it had become too late for him, whatever course he took, to reach the battlefield of Waterloo before nightfall. He received it before he left Ligny, and after Napoleon had heard that a Prussian corps (no doubt Thielemann's) had been seen at Gembloux.

It directed Grouchy to proceed to Gembloux; to explore ("*Vous vous ferez explorer,*" are the words used), in the direction of Namur and Moestricht; to pursue the enemy; and to communicate with Napoleon, who was to be at Quatre Bras, by the Namur-Quatre Bras road. It was (the order continued):

> Important to penetrate into what the enemy wished to do— whether to separate from the English, or to unite with them in order to cover Brussels and Liege, and try the fate of another battle. (It is not easy to understand how a position covering both these points could be taken up. Possibly the reading should be "Brussels or Liege.")

It is clear that this order, although it pointed out the importance of ascertaining where the Prussians were and their intentions, contains a definite instruction to explore the roads to Namur and Moestricht; also that it was written by Napoleon without any conception that Blücher, with the bulk of the Prussian Army, had fallen back from the field of Ligny upon Wavre, by Tilly and Gentinnes—miles to the west of Gembloux, and north of where he himself had dictated the Bertrand order.

Grouchy did not get off from Ligny, mainly owing to Napoleon's delay in giving him his instructions, until about twelve hours after the Prussians had commenced their retreat; and rain soon began to fall heavily. Fields and country roads which, even in that low-lying district, had been comparatively firm and hard, when the Prussians moved over them, soon became almost impassable for the French, and thus the start which the Prussians had obtained was in reality greater than is fully represented by twelve hours of time. This again illustrates how materially the nature of this section of the Belgian country influenced the operations of the campaign.

Grouchy, if he wished to catch up the retiring Prussians at all upon the road to Moestricht (which also branches off near Hannut to Liege), or Namur, had no time to lose; and owing to the state of the country, it took him till nightfall (9 p.m.)—*i.e.* seven hours—to get to Gembloux, a distance of about eight or nine miles. From thence he sent out patrols to Sauvenieres and Perwez, on the road to Liege and Moestricht; but not—and this should be noticed—towards the north-west, where the Prussians had passed through Mont St. Guibert, north of Gentinnes. In that direction he did not look for them at all.

Thus, on the night of June 17th, he did not ascertain their true line of retreat, and this is the first point for which he has been blamed.

But at Gembloux he heard a good deal from the inhabitants of the district as to the Prussians. Thielemann had, as a fact, passed through Gembloux; Bülow through Sauvenieres to the north of it, towards Dion le Mont; Pirch and also some small bodies of Prussians had, after Ligny, been seen on the Namur road. Incorrect reports were based upon this, and as a result Grouchy wrote to Napoleon at 10 p.m. on the 17th from Gembloux (Appendix B, VIII.), that, from information received, he thought the Prussians had divided into two columns, one of which had taken the road by Sart à Walhain to Wavre, and the other that to Perwez; also that a further column, with some artillery, had retreated to Namur. He writes:

> It may perhaps be inferred from this that one portion of the army is going to join Wellington, and that another, which is the army of Blücher, is retiring on Liege.

He adds that, after he had received the reports of his cavalry that night, he would decide how to act. If the bulk of the Prussians had fallen back on Wavre he would follow them, "so that they should not gain Brussels, and in order to separate them from Wellington"; if they had fallen back on Perwez, then he would proceed there.

More than one writer upon this campaign has dwelt upon the absurdity of the idea, to which Grouchy here gives expression, that he could, by following behind the Prussians on the road to Wavre, prevent their reaching Brussels, or interpose between them and Wellington; and it has been viewed as contrary to common sense that he could expect to intercept the Prussians on their march by pursuing them along a road upon which they had a start equivalent to over twelve hours of time.

But admitting the full force of this, it is just to Grouchy to consider the matter in other lights.

He was at Gembloux in accordance with Napoleon's order, and it may be here said that, though he only arrived there at nightfall on the 17th, and some have accused him of want of energy, there is no proof that, with his tired troops, and under the acknowledged difficulties of roads and weather, he could have marched more rapidly. Being at Gembloux, the sole question for him was, what course could he now best pursue in order to prevent the Prussians reaching Brussels or joining Wellington. There was but small chance of success in any case, but he could not stand still, and he had, at some point or other, to cross the River Dyle.

★★★★★★

Grouchy's command had been heavily engaged at Ligny on the day previous to this march, but Napoleon would not detach fresher troops in pursuit of the Prussians—such, for instance, as the corps of Lobau—wishing to keep these with him during his operations against Wellington and towards Brussels.

★★★★★★

It has been repeatedly said that his one prospect of attaining his object was to make immediately for Moustier, (see map), and the passages over the river close to that point, and march in the direction of Lasne and St. Lambert; and it has been also urged that he should have seen more clearly that this was his proper course because, by a letter written to General Pajol, at daybreak on June 18th, he shows that he had then become convinced that Blücher's army was not meaning to retire towards Liege, but would endeavour to join Wellington. (Ropes).

It can be seen, with *the knowledge we have now* of the intentions of Wellington and of Blücher, that this would have been his best course; but in examining Grouchy's movements the following all-important fact must constantly be kept in mind: Grouchy's impression no doubt was, as Napoleon's impression had been, that Wellington would probably *not* stand to fight where he did, but would take up a position further north. That this was the emperor's impression is to be clearly gathered from his letter to Ney on June 16th (Appendix B, II.), in which he evidently expects that there may be but slight opposition to Ney's advance upon Brussels; and states that he wishes to arrive there himself the following morning. His surprised satisfaction also on the night of June 17th, when he found that Wellington was in position in his front, is mentioned by all historians.

It must be remembered, too, that it was the original proposal of General von Kleist, commanding the Prussian Army before Blücher had joined it, (as mentioned earlier), that Wellington should, on Na-

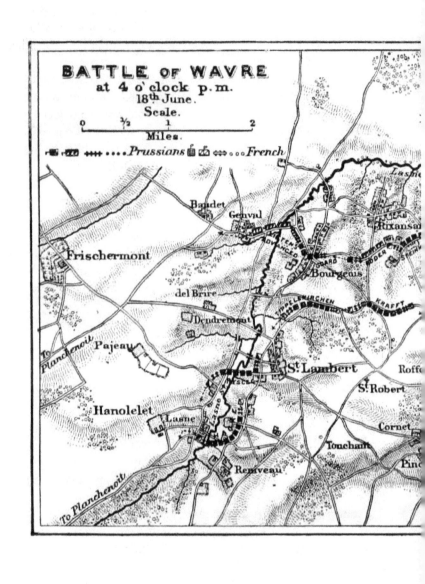

BATTLE OF WAVRE
at 4 o'clock p.m.
18th June.
Scale.

0   ½   1   2
Miles.

···· *Prussians*   ···· *French*

Baudet

Genval

Frischermont

Rixansa

del Brire

Bourgeois

Dendrement

Pajeau

St Lambert   Roffe

St Robert

Hanolelet

Lasne

Cornet

Touchant

Reuveau

Pin

To Planchenoit

To Planchenoit

Rosieres
Barriere
Stadt
La Bavette
Louis Delou
Chambre
Stream
Bas Wavre
R. Dyle
KAMPFEN
PIRCH II
Lanont
JAGOW
HONKEL
St. Juan WAVRE
Point de Juan
Bierge
BRAUSE
RECKOW
JURGASS
Mill of Bierge
Vandam
S. Antoine
St. Anne
C. des Delburg
EGELMANS
Marnil
Prefond Sart
Grand Sart
Dion le Mont
Sart
Limate
Trou Dehoux
Louvrange
Limelette
l'Auzel
Chocquroux
HULOT
R. Dyle
la Baraque
To

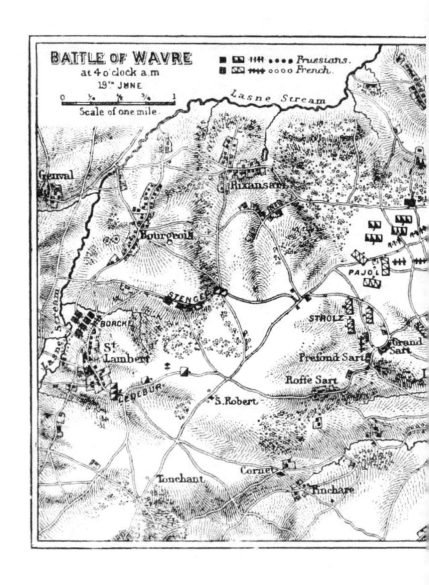

BATTLE OF WAVRE
at 4 o'clock a.m
19ᵀᴴ JUNE

Prussians.
French.

Lasne Stream

Genval

Rixansart

Bourgeois

STENGE

BORCKE

St.
Lambert

LEDEBUR

S. Robert

Tonchant

PAJOL

STROLZ

Grand
Sart

Presond Sart

Roffe Sart

Cornet

Finchare

poleon's advance, fall back *behind* Brussels; and that the Prussian army should effect a junction with his *east* of Brussels. Of course, when this proposal was made the circumstances were different, as the Prussian Army was lying to the east of the Meuse; but it is one worth alluding to, because it indicates that the advisability of a joint position being taken up to the north and east of Brussels was at one time entertained. It was a possible plan to follow still.

If it is said that the Prussians, in proceeding from points near Wavre to join Wellington east of Brussels, would take the direct Wavre-Brussels road, the answer is, not necessarily; for to move through Louvain, or some point south of it but north of Wavre, would be safer, while Louvain also was on the high road of Prussian communication from Brussels to Liege and Moestricht. (See *Operations of War,* by Sir E. Hamley, on this head. Ropes differs from Hamley's views).

Now, had the plan alluded to been adopted, Grouchy might, by at once passing the Dyle at Wavre, have effected what he aimed at, though the chance of his being able to do so was not great; but in any case—and this is the real point—there would have been no advantage whatever in his marching from Gembloux, through the country roads by Moustier, south of Wavre.

Apart from the difficulty of these country roads, and the chance of being delayed on them, or at the passages of the Dyle, by the Prussians, the distance from Gembloux to Moustier is, as the crow flies, not three miles less than from Gembloux to Wavre, and this last road was good and less intricate. There was, at least, a possibility also that the Prussians might have halted at Wavre, or would delay there to fight him.

Grouchy, at all events, determined when at Gembloux to march on the morning of the 18th, not towards Moustier, but upon Wavre. This is another point for which he has been blamed; but whether this decision of his was an absurd or wrong one, under the knowledge which he possessed, must hang a good deal upon whether it was absurd to imagine that Wellington would not stand so far south as Waterloo, but would retire to or even behind Brussels.

It will be seen further on, that Napoleon himself, writing to Grouchy from the field of Waterloo at 10 a.m. on the morning of June 18th, and although he then knew (which Grouchy did not know) that Wellington meant to stand and fight there, still approved of Grouchy marching upon Wavre. It has been said that Grouchy, following upon the track of the Prussians, should have known more than Napoleon knew, or could know, at Waterloo, of their intentions; but we have shown under what circumstances of difficulty Grouchy was pursuing the Prussians far behind them.

Setting out from Gembloux for Wavre at between 6 and 7 a.m., (possibly he might have got off earlier, and should have done so; but his troops were fatigued by their exertions of the previous days), and having arrived at Sart à Walhain, Grouchy wrote from thence to Napoleon at 11 a.m. the letter given in Appendix B, IX.

In this he reports that three Prussian corps were said to have passed through that place, some making for the plain of La Chyse, which lies about eight or nine miles north-east of Wavre, near the road to Louvain. He adds that he hopes to reach Wavre in the evening, and thus, he continues, "find myself between Wellington, whom I presume to be retreating before Your Majesty, and the Prussian Army."

From this it may be inferred that he then conceived that the Prussians were making for Louvain, or between that and Brussels (Bülow having moved to Dion le Mont might have given rise to this idea, the information that the Prussians were at La Chyse appears to have been imparted to Grouchy by a retired French officer; see Houssaye); and although we now know how incorrect this idea was, yet what has been already said shows that there was at least the possibility that they were doing so, and in that event there were good grounds why he should march on to Wavre. When at Sart à Walhain, or at Walhain, (as Ropes contends), a village to the west of it, he and his staff heard the cannon of Waterloo; and he was informed, at about the same time, that a strong Prussian force held Wavre as a rearguard.

He was now much perplexed as to the line of action to adopt. There was certainly more reason than before to believe that a decisive battle might be going on in the direction of the guns. Some of his staff were in favour of marching towards the sound of the cannonade, but others were opposed to it, on account of the difficult nature of the intervening country: there was also no certainty that the firing did not proceed from Wellington's rearguard, covering the retreat to Brussels and pressed by Napoleon.

Grouchy decided to press on to Wavre. This is another point for which he has been most severely blamed; and because he did not, at this juncture, proceed towards the sound of the guns, in the direction of the field of Waterloo, he has been, by some, held responsible for Napoleon's defeat, and practically accused of treason. In justification of this decision he has stated that he felt certain that he could not arrive where the firing was going on in time to be of any service to

Napoleon there—an opinion in which many others consider that he was right (see further on); and therefore that it was his duty to march to attack the Prussians where he believed he could reach them—*i.e.* at Wavre.

It is, doubtless, a sound general principle that, when one force is endeavouring to join another in order to aid it in battle against a common enemy, it should march to the sound of the guns which marks the position where the battle is being waged; it is usually the bold and proper course to take. But Grouchy's situation was exceptional: he was not marching to join Napoleon; on the contrary, he had been ordered away by him to reach and fight the Prussians: he was not, in taking a direction from the guns, shirking battle; on the contrary, he was marching to attack the Prussians, as he did at Wavre.

From Walhain to Wavre is ten miles; and as Grouchy drew near at about 4 p.m., (the hour given by Ropes; Houssaye says, "between 3.30 and 4 p.m.," as do the Grouchy memoirs; some accounts make its receipt earlier), Thielemann, who had retired to Wavre from La Baraque, defended the bridges over the river. This brought on what is occasionally termed the "Battle of Wavre," and by some the—

COMBATS OF WAVRE
June 18th and 19th, 1815

The French numbered in these combats about 32,000, the Prussians under 16,000, and the contest was fierce. On the afternoon and evening of June 18th the French were repulsed eleven times in their efforts to carry the bridges. On the 19th they succeeded in gaining the left bank of the Dyle; and, after hard fighting, Thielemann was forced back along the road to Louvain, halting on the night of the 19th at St. Achtenrode, Grouchy pursuing him.

At about 11 a.m. on June 19th Grouchy was informed by a despatch from Napoleon of the destruction of the French Army at Waterloo. He then acted with much decision, marching at once for Namur, which he occupied. The Prussian corps of Pirch I., which, after Waterloo, had marched to cut him off, assaulted the town, and lost, in an attempt to carry it, 1,500 men; but Grouchy made good his retreat, and reached France, at Givet, on June 21st.

Thus ended the operations of Grouchy; and it may be repeated here that it will assist anyone towards their just consideration to bear in mind that he was, up to the actual moment when he was about to attack Thielemann at Wavre, acting solely upon the order (Appendix

B,VII.) termed the "Bertrand order," under which he had set out from Ligny; and that Wellington's intention to give battle at Waterloo was not then certain.

But we should add, before making more comments upon Grouchy's movements, that as he was about to attack Thielemann at Wavre on June 18th, he received a letter, (Zenowicz, the bearer, says that he handed this to Grouchy at between 3.30 and 4 p.m.), from Soult (Appendix B, X.), written by Napoleon's order, which is of some interest in association with his movements, though it apparently did not influence them. It was written from the farm of Caillou, on the field of Waterloo, at 10 a.m. on June 18th, and in it Soult says that information had been received that a fairly strong column of Prussians had retired after the Battle of Ligny by Gentinnes upon Wavre, distinct from any columns which Grouchy had mentioned in his letter from Gembloux of 10 p.m. on June 17th (Appendix B, IX.), the receipt of which letter he acknowledges. This is the first intimation we have that the French had become aware that any of the Prussians had retired in this direction.

Soult further says:

> His Majesty desires that you direct your movements *upon Wavre* in order to draw near us, and connect our communications, driving before you the Prussian corps which have taken that direction, and may have halted at Wavre, *where you should arrive as soon as possible.*

This letter shows that Soult, and it may be assumed Napoleon also, in whose name he wrote, thought at 10 a.m. on the 18th, with Grouchy, that his proper course of action was to press on to Wavre; and this, although Napoleon then knew what Grouchy did not, that part of the Prussian Army had, after Ligny, retired by Gentinnes, and that he (Napoleon) was about to attack Wellington, who was in position in his front.

Grouchy, when he received this letter (or order, or instruction, whichever it may be termed), just as he was about to attack Thielemann, must have felt that, in acting as he had done, he had anticipated the emperor's wishes; and that, had he taken another course, he would have acted at variance with them.

Subsequently he received a further letter from Napoleon (Appendix B, XI.) written from the field of Waterloo at 1 p.m. on June 18th, directing him to manoeuvre towards him, and fall upon the corps of

Bülow, which had then been perceived upon the heights of St. Lambert; but this did not reach him until between 6 and 7 p.m., too late for him to act upon it with any effect. (Ropes).

COMMENTS

It can be seen that what led chiefly to the non-success of Grouchy's movements was that he was despatched from the field of Ligny too late, under difficulties of bad roads and bad weather, and under a false impression as to the line of retreat of the Prussians. Next to this, that he did not, on the night of the 17th, or early on the 18th, reconnoitre westward from Gembloux, as well as towards Namur, Moestricht, and Liege.

Whether, under the terms of the order under which he acted (the Bertrand order, Appendix B, VII.), he should unquestionably have done so, or might clearly have been expected to do so, is a point upon which, for now over sixty years, (the full Bertrand order was published in 1842), historians of repute, both soldiers and civilians, have continued to differ.

Putting everything else aside, what does this imply, except that the order dictated to Marshal Bertrand might reasonably at all events be interpreted in the way which Grouchy did interpret it. Had there been any idea that the Prussians might have retired from Ligny, by Tilly and Gentinnes, as they had, why should Grouchy have been ordered to Gembloux at all? Gembloux was altogether away from this line. We know, however, that there was at first no such idea.

It is clear that the dominant thought throughout the order is that the Prussians would be found in the direction of Namur or Moestricht, and that by exploring those roads he would ascertain their intentions. Of course, Grouchy's discretion to reconnoitre other roads was not shut out, and he might have reconnoitred that through Gentinnes and Mont St. Guibert, though his troops were tired and the weather bad. It is true also that a man of great intuitive grasp and exceptional energy might possibly have ascertained the movements of the Prussians with greater correctness than Grouchy; but more it seems unfair to say.

As to the decision of Grouchy, on hearing at Walhain (at 11 a.m. on June 18th) the cannon of Waterloo, not to march in that direction, we must touch upon what were then the chances of his being able to effect anything at Waterloo.

As to this, authorities again materially differ. Sir James Shaw-Kennedy holds that, owing to the intricacy and state of the roads, as well as the opposition he would almost certainly have met with from Thielemann, who was aware of his vicinity, he could have effected little or nothing. Wellington is stated to have expressed the same opinion.

★★★★★★

Diary of the Hon. J. H. Stanhope—quoted by Sir F. Maurice in paper upon Waterloo, *United Service Magazine*, September, 1890. Wellington's opinion seems to have been founded upon the amount of time which the Prussians took to reach the field of Waterloo from Wavre— a point much closer to it than Walhain is; but some writers regard this time as having been excessive.

★★★★★★

Ropes, on the other hand, holds the view that he might have been of service.

Having closely considered roads, time, and distance, he believes that, had Grouchy sent Pajol's cavalry and a division of infantry to threaten Thielemann at Wavre, and taken himself the high road to Wavre as far as La Baraque (so as to avoid the intricate ground by Mont St. Guibert) he could then, without much difficulty, have crossed the Dyle at Moustier by 4 p.m., at which hour Bülow's corps was part in the wood of Paris, near Frischermont, and part between Lasne and St. Lambert. Grouchy could then, he thinks, although he would have been far outnumbered by the Prussians, have so delayed their advance that they would not have carried Planchenoit before dark.

If this view is correct it would mainly show that, had Grouchy been aware of the situation of the Prussians, of the bridges they held over the Dyle, of the intention of Wellington to stand at Waterloo, and of the comparative character of the various country roads leading to these bridges, he could, had he marched without hesitation, have delayed the Prussian attack on Planchenoit. He was not, we know, in possession of the necessary knowledge to act thus promptly, and therefore it must be presumed that he would, had he moved upon Moustier, have advanced slowly, reconnoitring the country, as Bülow had done. Moustier is some miles from the wood of Paris, or Lasne; and it must in consequence be most uncertain whether his appearance upon the field, at the hour he really would have reached it, could have effected much. (Charras considers that it would only have involved him in the French rout of Waterloo). With respect to the charge that Grouchy could have prevented the defeat of Napoleon at Waterloo, a very recent French writer on this campaign says that to blame him for this defeat is "one of the greatest iniquities of history." (*La critique de la*

Campagne de 1815, *par* Lieut. -Col. A. Grouard, 1904).

It is to be remarked, with regard to the letter written by Napoleon to Grouchy (Appendix B, X.) on June 18th at 10 a.m. from the field of Waterloo, that although that letter did not reach Grouchy in time to allow of his taking any part in the struggle at Waterloo, (as mentioned earlier), still it has been discussed by more than one writer as if it had done so; and that he had disregarded Napoleon's desire, expressed in it, that while moving to Wavre he should do it by a road nearer to him than the one he took.

Sir James Shaw-Kennedy considers (*Notes on the Battle of Waterloo*), that the expressions used in this letter, to the effect that while moving upon Wavre Grouchy should keep towards, and in close communication with, the emperor:

> ....have been absurdly construed into an instruction to march towards Napoleon, while they simply and clearly meant that he should keep up his communication with him by patrols, as was evidently proper; and by no possible perversity of construction will it bear the other meaning.

This is the view of a soldier who both served in the campaign, and who wrote in 1865, after many works discussing the operations of Grouchy had been published.

Houssaye also writes:

> Napoleon, blinded as Grouchy was, imagined that the Prussians were going to halt at Wavre, or that they would make for Brussels, and not for Mont St. Jean. . . . Ingenious efforts have been made to read more into this letter (Appendix B, X.) than it ever meant—*viz.* an order to Grouchy to manoeuvre upon his left, so as to draw nearer to the bulk of the French Army. The emperor does say, 'in order that you may draw closer to us'; but it is obvious that, in marching from Gembloux to Wavre, Grouchy must draw nearer to the emperor. It is clear that the emperor, at 10 in the morning (of the 18th), neither summoned Grouchy to his battlefield nor expected him to appear there.

It has been contended that he did expect him on the field, and gave orders to Baron Marbot on the morning of the 18th to patrol towards Moustier, to look out for him; but it is not generally accepted that to watch for Grouchy was the object of the orders to Marbot (Houssaye); neither is it, as Houssaye asserts, to be gathered from Napoleon's letter of 10 a.m. on June 18th (Appendix B, IX.) that he then expected him *via* Moustier.

THE MARCH TO PARIS
(See map next chapter)

Although the Battle of Wavre and the retreat of Grouchy closed the military operations in Belgium, and the campaign of 1815 was decided upon the field of Waterloo, hostilities did not cease immediately after that battle.

It was necessary to prevent Napoleon from regaining his power; to place in other hands the supreme authority in France; and to exact from the French Nation, which had welcomed his return from Elba, compensation for the bloodshed and heavy expense which this had entailed upon Europe.

To this end, the armies of Wellington and Blücher at once entered France, and marched upon Paris; while those of the other European Powers who had taken part in the Congress of Vienna began also to pour across the French border at several points.

On June 19th, 1815, Blücher was at Gosselies, and Ziethen at Charleroi. On the 20th they were across the French frontier, the corps of Pirch I. having been detached (but unsuccessfully, as we have already mentioned) to endeavour to cut off Grouchy retreating from Wavre. Wellington was at Nivelles, and the army, marching by Mons and Binche, entered France at and west of Malplaquet.

The dispersed troops of Napoleon's beaten army had now begun to get together again at Avesnes and Philippeville, and on the 22nd some 20,000 had collected at Laon, where the corps of Grouchy was soon to join them.

On June 23rd Wellington was at Cateau Cambresis, and Blücher at Catillon-sur-Sambre; at which last place they met together to concert further operations.

It now became a question for decision whether to turn aside towards Laon, and attack the rallied French troops in that direction, over whom Soult had assumed chief command; or to pass them by, and, crossing the Oise below its confluence with the Aisne, interpose between them and Paris.

It was determined to follow the latter course, leaving in rear a considerable force under the Prince of Orange to blockade the frontier fortresses from the Scheldt eastwards, and trusting to the probability that, with the armies of the Coalition threatening France at so many points, the rallied troops of Napoleon would not act with any energy on the offensive.

On the night of June 24th Cambray was carried by escalade by the 4th Division (Colville), with a loss of 35 men; and on this day a message was received from the governor of Valenciennes that Napoleon had abdicated in favour of his son, and requesting that, as a provisional government had been formed, there might be a suspension of hostilities.

But the onward march of the Allies was not stayed on this account. Wellington on the right, and Blücher on the left, they moved towards Paris. Peronne was stormed by the 1st Division (the Guards), and Ham taken by the Prussians.

By June 26th Soult and Grouchy had moved to Soissons, Wellington was at Mattignies, and the Prussians at Noyon.

Grouchy had sent D'Erlon to occupy the bridge over the Oise at Compiegne; but Ziethen, by a forced march, forestalled him at that point. Then Grouchy, with Vandamme's corps, occupied Villers Cotterets, where his rear-guard on the 28th had an action with the Prussians, losing many prisoners. Eventually Grouchy, with the remains of D'Erlon and Reille's corps, falling back by Nanteuil and Le Bourget, reached Paris on June 29th. On this day the advanced guard of Wellington was at Senlis, and his headquarters west of Noyon: Blücher being more forward at Gonesse, (see Environs of Paris, on map), near St. Denis, whence he seized Aubervilliers, an outpost for the defence of Paris.

On the evening of June 29th Wellington again conferred personally with Blücher.

It is convenient at this point to allude briefly to the political events which had occurred in Paris between June 21st, when Napoleon re-entered the capital, and June 29th, when Wellington and Blücher arrived before its walls. Napoleon, who had at first hoped that the French Nation would continue him in power, had to experience the bitter truth that a crown which rests mainly on military success must be maintained by it. For the third time he had returned to Paris, leaving behind him a defeated army—*viz*. after the retreat from Moscow in 1812, after Leipsic in 1813, and now after Waterloo in 1815.

The representatives of the French Nation were in no mood at the moment to trust the fate of the country further to his hands; and knew also that the Powers of Europe would make no peace with France, while he remained at her head.

The Chamber of Deputies—the chief official body now existing in Paris—gave him one hour in which to send in his abdication; on failure to do which his deposition would be declared.

It is difficult to realise what the feeling of Napoleon must have been on receiving this ultimatum. For a moment he is said to have hesitated whether to dissolve the Chamber by military force, with the aid of his troops in Paris, or to obey its decision; but in the end he yielded and abdicated.

The Chamber would not directly recognise his son as his successor, though they did so to a qualified extent; and in reality the days of the First Empire were numbered.

In addition to the forces of Wellington and Blücher, at the very gates of Paris, the Austrians, Russians, Germans, Piedmontese, and Spaniards were invading France; and, by the middle of July, 1815, 800,000 men of the armies of the Coalition were on French territory, quartered upon its inhabitants.

In did not in truth rest with the Chamber to nominate a successor to Napoleon on the throne, for the Allies, although anxious in the interests of tranquillity to consult the wishes of the French Nation, were yet determined to insist on that succession which would offer to Europe the best guarantee for a lasting peace; and in the opinion of Wellington this peace would most probably be secured in the restoration of Louis XVIII., who had now left Ghent and was in the vicinity of Paris.

On June 29th the commissioners sent from the Chamber were informed that a suspension of arms would be sanctioned solely on the condition that the French regular troops marched out of Paris and retired behind the River Loire, (South of Paris, see earlier map), leaving the National Guard to hold the city until King Louis XVIII. should order otherwise.

Pending a reply to the conditions offered, the Allies continued their military operations, Blücher, for his part, being much disinclined to grant any terms, short of the unconditional surrender of Paris and the army.

Wellington and he, being now in front of Paris, on the north side, had to determine whether to (1) attempt to carry the northern defences of the city, or (2) cross the Seine to the south side. The northern defences, from Charenton, above Paris, to St. Denis below it, were formidably strong, and to man them 70,000 regular troops of various descriptions were available, in addition to the National Guard. The southern side of the city was, however, almost open.

It was, therefore, decided that the Prussians should cross the Seine; but this operation involved some risk, as not only might the French obstinately defend the bridges over the river, but the Prussian Army, when across it, would be divided by the broad and winding Seine from that of Wellington.

To lessen the chance of the Allied intentions being discovered, Thielemann and Ziethen marched at night towards St. Germains, and a bridge below it at Maisons, which the French had left undestroyed, and here the passage of the Seine was safely effected on June 30th; on July 1st Bülow followed, and Wellington, having relieved Bülow, took up a position towards Bondy. Some French cavalry on the south side of the Seine came into collision with the Prussian cavalry near Versailles, and the Prussian loss was here rather severe, two squadrons of Hussars being cut up; but beyond this, little opposition was made.

On July 2nd Blücher moved to Versailles, pushing on from thence towards St. Cloud, and Wellington threw a bridge over the Seine at Argenteuil, thus establishing better communication with Blücher. The Prussian Army now stretched from Plessis-Piquet to Meudon and Les Molineaux, with advanced posts at Catillon and Issy, and a reserve at Versailles.

On July 3rd Vandamme attacked the Prussians at Issy, and there was some loss on both sides, but this was the last encounter of the campaign. A suspension of arms was upon this day agreed upon at St. Cloud, between commissioners representing the French and the Allies. It is termed "The Convention of Paris," and was signed by Wellington, Blücher, and Marshal Davoust.

The chief provisions of this convention were that the French Army should, within eight days, withdraw to the south of the River Loire, and that Paris should be placed in the hands of the Allies. This secured to the latter the power of exacting such securities for future peace as they deemed essential.

Between July 4th and 6th the French Army marched out of Paris towards the Loire; on the 7th the Allies took possession of the city; and on the 8th Louis XVIII. re-entered the Tuilleries, and was restored to the French throne.

Napoleon, while the Allies were yet at some distance from Paris, had left the capital for Malmaison, a country house about seven miles distant from it, on the left bank of the Seine.

On July 2nd he set out for Rochefort, (west coast of France, between the Loire and the Garonne), where on July 14th, as he was about to be arrested by the Bourbon Government, he surrendered himself to Captain Maitland, commanding H.M.S. *Bellerophon*, off that port.

Subsequently, by decision of the Allied Powers, he was conveyed to St. Helena, where he landed on October 16th, 1815, and remained until his death on May 5th, 1821, his body, in 1840, being removed to Paris, where it was re-interred under the dome of the Invalides.

By the conditions of peace, afterwards ratified under the Treaty of Paris, signed in November, 1815, the French frontiers were limited to those of the year 1790, and a large indemnity was required from France. (Seven hundred and thirty-five million *francs*, or about thirty million pounds sterling, with the restoration of the works of art which Napoleon had removed from the cities of Europe).

While the rest of the troops returned to their respective countries, an Army of Occupation, numbering 150,000 men, (thirty thousand from each of the four great powers, and from the minor German states), of the Allied Powers, the command of which was conferred upon the Duke of Wellington, was to occupy the French frontier for five years, the expense being borne by the French Government. Ultimately, under the Convention of Aix-la-Chapelle, on October 9th, 1818, the Allied troops forming the Army of Occupation were withdrawn after three years, and on November 30th, 1818, they evacuated French territory. For the campaign of Waterloo Wellington was created Prince of Waterloo by the King of the Netherlands. (He had also conferred upon him at various times the Garter, and the high orders of almost all the European Powers).

After peace had been made under the Treaty of Paris, it was deemed essential by the government of King Louis XVIII. to bring to trial some of the most prominent of those in high official position who, upon Napoleon's escape from Elba, had deserted the trust confided to them by the king and joined him.

Ney was one of these. He had voluntarily entered the service of King Louis, and had been entrusted with the command of the troops sent to oppose Napoleon on his entry into France. He had declared that he would bring him back to Paris in chains (or in a cage); but in the end, finding that his troops were determined to join the emperor's standard, he did so likewise.

His treason, therefore, was clear; and having been arraigned before the Chamber of Peers, he was found guilty and sentenced to death.

On December 6th, 1815, he was shot in the gardens of the Luxembourg. Labedoyère was also executed, and Lavalette was sentenced to death, but escaped by contriving to change clothes in prison with his wife.

There is no more tragic history than that of Ney during the last nine months of 1815. The temptation to which he succumbed was great, and carried away others, though not all, as it did him. (Marshal Macdonald was one, among others, who resisted it; and who, though a strong Napoleonist, would not break his allegiance, once given, to the king). From the time he yielded fortune apparently deserted him; the failure of Napoleon's plans was, by many, laid upon his shoulders; and, in the end, he was condemned and put to death by his own countrymen, though he had so largely contributed, on a score of battlefields, to the triumph of the French arms.

Nevertheless, there was no question of his treason and of its marked character.

Wellington has been occasionally blamed for not having interfered officially to prevent his execution; but sympathy with Ney's heroic conduct as a soldier tends, perhaps, to blind some to Wellington's position, its duties, and its limits.

In that position he had no standpoint from which to concern himself with Ney's sentence. The King of France was now an independent sovereign; and Wellington, commanding the bayonets which had placed him on the throne, had to bear this in mind: the more so as his interference in French affairs had become, it is said, somewhat unwelcome to the king.

What he could fittingly do privately he is stated to have done; but in consequence of a refusal of the king's ministers to advise the king to show clemency to Ney, he felt that he could not act further, and that to do so would have been an undue official interference between the king and his ministry, as well as useless.

COMMENTS

We need comment little upon the operations connected with the march to Paris. They were steadily and firmly carried out, and involved, as we have seen, the reduction of more than one fortress and some loss of life.

On some occasions, also, the situation called for the exercise of much decision and military judgment as to the course to be pursued.

One of these was when, on June 23rd, 1815, Blücher and Wellington had to determine, at Catillon-sur-Sambre, whether to turn aside to attack and disperse the rallied French Army under Soult, or to march on, without doing so, to Paris. Another was when, on reaching Paris, they had to decide whether to attack the city from the north, or cross the Seine with part of their joint force to the south bank.

On both occasions the bold course was adopted and was successful. It had been realised by Wellington and Blücher that irresolution and divided counsels prevailed to a great extent both in the rallied army of Napoleon and in the capital; and they therefore judged that the measure of crossing the Seine, approaching Paris on its weak side, and cutting it off from supplies and succour from without, was the one best calculated to lead quickly to the surrender of the city, and the termination of the campaign.

CHAPTER 6

An Overview of the Waterloo Campaign, 1815

In these concluding comments upon the campaign it is desirable to revert occasionally to certain points already touched upon in previous chapters.

Considering the campaign of Waterloo as a whole, we see that there were two or three periods in it of special importance as regards their bearing upon its course and issue.

One of these was the early morning of June 16th, when Wellington's force at Quatre Bras was greatly inferior in strength to that of Ney, and a large portion of his army at a distance from that point.

Another was the early morning of June 17th, when the Prussians were withdrawing, unobserved and unpursued, from the field of Ligny in the direction of Wavre.

Another was when, late at night on June 17th, (or, possibly, between midnight of the 17th and 2 a.m. of the 18th), it was decided by Blücher to march with his whole available army upon Ohain and St. Lambert to support Wellington.

It can be confidently said, that had Wellington's concentration at either Nivelles or Quatre Bras been effected 12 hours sooner than it was; had the Prussians been kept in view and pursued through Tilly and Gentinnes after Ligny; or had Blücher been unwilling or unable to support Wellington as he did at Waterloo—the whole character and course of the campaign, whatever might have been its final issue, must have been affected. For this reason, we refer again more especially to these periods.

Oman, who has given much consideration to Wellington's campaigns, says, (*Cambridge Modern History*, 1906, "The Hundred Days"), with respect to the concentration of the Anglo-Allied army at Quatre Bras on June 16th, "If the troops from Ghent, Audenarde and Ath had started 12 hours earlier, Ney must have been destroyed"; and it is at all events probable that had they so started, Wellington, after defeating Ney, would have attacked Napoleon at Ligny.

We have entered into the causes of the delay in Wellington's concentration and how far these were unconnected with the disposition of his troops.

It has been pointed out that the primary cause, leading to others, was the defective transmission of reports from the advanced posts to Brussels on June 15th. To refer once more to this, the Rev. G. R. Gleig writes—

An orderly dragoon whom Ziethen had early despatched to announce the commencement of hostilities, lost his way; and, but for the delivery of despatches from Prince Blücher to General Müffling, it is impossible to guess when the true state of the case might have been communicated to the Duke of Wellington—*Waterloo*, by the Rev. G. R. Gleig,

Oman, (*Cambridge Modern History*, 1906, "The Hundred Days"), adds that after sending the message, Ziethen, "engrossed in the details of the fighting, forgot to keep the British headquarters informed of the developments of the French attack."

Every military student, in considering Wellington's plan for the defence of Belgium, with the disposition of the troops on June 14th, 1815, which formed part of it, should examine into,—

1st, How far that plan was the one which best safeguarded, upon the whole, all the interests of the Allies—not merely into what risks were involved in it.

2nd, How far the delays in the concentration of the Anglo-Allied army on June 16th resulted from the plan itself, and how far from defects and mischances in its execution, hardly to be anticipated.

3rd, Whether, if the time lost from defects or mischances in execution had been saved, the full design of the plan would have been attained—*viz.* the concentration of the armies of Wellington and Blücher, in close touch with each other, by the Nivelles-Namur road.

Upon these points it may be expected that opinions will differ;

and it is not one of the least advantages of the Waterloo campaign as a study for soldiers, that upon these and other matters occurring in it (such as the movements of Grouchy) there has been so full a criticism in so many works.

From this criticism and the facts upon which it has been based, students can form their own independent judgment, and this it is one great object of the study of military history to elicit and foster.

The above points have been discussed, and the view expressed for what it may be worth, that the imperfect execution of the plan of concentration, and not the disposition of the troops on June 14th, prevented the design of Wellington and Blücher from being fully, though it was to some extent partially, attained.

With regard to the Prussians having been permitted to retreat from Ligny unobserved, and so long unpursued, with all the after-consequences which this involved, most historians have concurred in the view that Napoleon, in not completing his victory by a more active pursuit, made his greatest error in this campaign. It has been said that "it was rather at Ligny than at Waterloo that the fate of the campaign was decided." (*Strategie Napoléonienne—La Critique de la Campagne de 1815*; by Lieut.-Colonel A. Grouard, Paris, 1904).

In endeavouring to find out some reason for this inactive pursuit, other than the somewhat disputed one of the failure of mental or physical power, we must recollect that the strategic plan of campaign which Wellington and Blücher jointly adopted and followed was not one which Napoleon, from his experience of the effect in Continental warfare of his own method of offensive attack, would probably have anticipated.

That method is referred to by Wellington himself in an interesting memorandum upon the campaign in Russia of 1812. (*Memorandum upon the War in Russia*, by the Duke of Wellington, given in Appendix to *Personal Reminiscences of the Duke of Wellington*, by the Rev. G. R. Gleig, published in 1904).

Without entering into details, it may be said that, as a rule, Napoleon's method was to fall in strength suddenly, and by forced marches, upon his enemy; endeavouring frequently to separate his opponent's force. This vehement onset usually succeeded; but after it there was a necessary pause to prepare for a further advance, and a certain reaction after the tension of a great effort. In the meantime, his adversaries fell back, generally upon their line of supplies and reinforcements. It was not in the Waterloo campaign only, or for the first time, that Napoleon resorted to this general method of attack.

General von Caemmerer, speaking of the Napoleonic strategy, writes:

> As soon as Napoleon once got between two army portions or corps, their fate was sealed as a rule. He deceived one of his adversaries by a weak but resolutely acting detachment, and fell upon the other with united forces in such a determined manner that the enemy was unable to resist. If this one was beaten he turned against the enemy whom he had hitherto only held in check. *In this way he began in 1796, and he still acted in accord with the same principles in 1815.—Development of Strategical Science during the 19th Century*, by Lieut. General von Caemmerer; translated by Karl von Donat (1905).

The Waterloo campaign forms but one illustration among others of Napoleon's method of war, as above described, although, as his ultimate object in this campaign was to march upon Brussels, he made Ney's force, detached towards Wellington, stronger than a mere detachment.

After his success at Ligny he had fair reasons, from former experience—to say nothing of Pajol's report and the capture of the Prussian battery on the Namur road, to suppose that Blücher would retire upon his communications. Further than this how could he reasonably have foreseen that the Prussian Army would entirely escape as it did, even from his very late pursuit on June 17th?

Is there another example in history of a beaten army of over 60,000 men being able to draw off in this way without the line they had taken being left unmistakably clear? (The Prussian strength at Ligny was about 87,000, and their casualties 12,000. Therefore, it is allowing a large margin to place the number retreating towards Wavre at 60,000). It is now known that under a combination of skill and energy, with special conditions of weather, they did so draw off: but without that knowledge it seems no exaggeration to say that it would have been deemed impossible. Colonel F. N. Maude, in referring to the little fear that Napoleon appears to have entertained that the Prussians, after Ligny, would be any real danger to his flank at Waterloo, says:

> Hitherto when operating against allies, the defeat of one had almost invariably led to the sympathetic retreat of the other; and having already failed to appreciate the extent to which the Prussians had profited by his teaching, it is not to be wondered

BRUSSELS
Louvain
Waterloo
Wavre
Mont St Jean
Gembloux
Nivelles
Gosselies
Mons
Binche
Namur
Malplaquet
Sambre
R.
Charleroi
Dinant
Maubeuge
Beaumont
Philippeville
Landrecy
Givet
Avesnes
Catillon
Meuse
Henappe
Oise R.
Rocroy
Fl.
Guise
Vervins
Mezières
Sedan
Laon
Aisne River
Rheims
Marne River
Chateau Thierry
Chalons sur Marne
Vitry

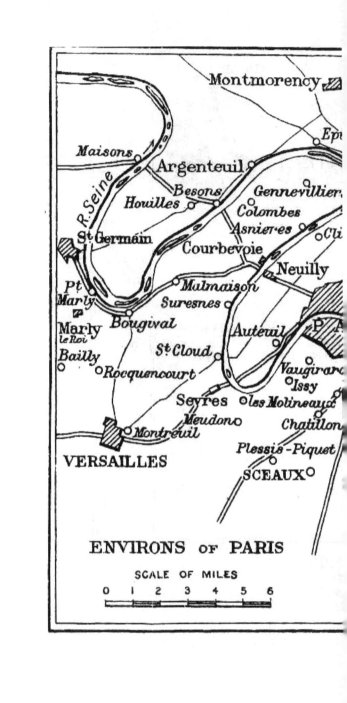

ENVIRONS OF PARIS

SCALE OF MILES

0   1   2   3   4   5   6

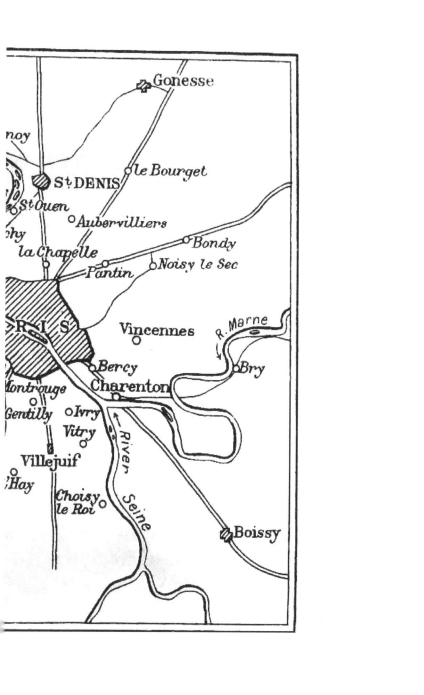

at if, at first, he paid little attention to the threat of their presence on his flank.—*Paper (M.S.) upon the Campaign of Waterloo,* by Colonel F. N. Maude, C.B.

Although Napoleon did not at first expect that Blücher had retreated to Wavre, he afterwards, as the following extract from his *Mémoires*, put together at St. Helena, shows, considered that the course which should have been followed by the Allies was one comprising this retreat.

What ought the English general to have done after the Battle of Ligny, and the combats of Quatre Bras? There cannot be two opinions on the subject. He ought on the night of the 17th and 18th (June) to have traversed the forest of Soignies by the Charleroi high road, while the Prussian Army was traversing it by the Wavre one: the two armies could then unite at daybreak before Brussels, leaving rear-guards to defend the forest; gain some days to give those of the Prussians who had been dispersed by the Battle of Ligny time to rejoin the army; obtain reinforcements from the 14 English regiments which were either in garrison in Belgium or had just landed at Ostend on their return from America; and leave the emperor of the French to manoeuvre as he liked. Would he, with an army of 100,000 men, have traversed the forest of Soignies to attack on the other side of it the two hostile armies united, more than 200,000 strong and in position? (See Ropes on *Correspondance de Napoléon,* vol. 31).

These remarks of Napoleon are of great interest. The plan he suggests as being better than that which Wellington and Blücher did follow, is one which General von Kleist would almost certainly have adopted; which many critics of this campaign have given approval to; and which on several grounds was the safest. It was natural that Napoleon, who had never been opposed to Wellington, should imagine on the morning of June 17th that the Allies would follow it; and that, if endeavouring to unite again, they would not seek to do so as far south as Waterloo.

But nevertheless, Wellington's Peninsular campaigns show us that with the exception of his occupation of the Lines of Torres Vedras in 1810—for the special purpose of retaining a permanent position in Portugal—his system of defence was never a passive one of the above description.

His construction of those Lines, and their success, may have given rise to a different impression in some minds; but Wellington on all occasions assumed the offensive immediately he could—struck, and struck hard.

He did not enter upon a campaign with the idea of awaiting attack in a strong position. At Waterloo, as elsewhere, his strategy was the result of profound calculation. It was undoubtedly risky, but if risk is to be always avoided, nothing great will be achieved.—*Some Notes on Wellington*, by Lieut.-Colonel G. F. R. Henderson (author of *Life of Stonewall Jackson*): paper read before the Military Society of Ireland, 1897.

In other words, that description of judgment which merely enables a leader to choose correctly the safest course, does not of itself make a great commander, but rather that insight which, among various risks, can decide upon the one which, when faced successfully, will lead most surely to the desired end.

The risks involved in the Allied strategy in this campaign were certainly not slight. One was that, at the outset, the line of concentration (the Nivelles-Namur road) was far advanced towards the enemy; it would have been much safer to have concentrated further back.

Another was that at Waterloo the Prussians might not have been able to arrive on the field in sufficient time; it would have been safer to have united further north.

But, on the other hand, this strategy had these advantages, which were great: it was not what may be termed a normal form of strategy—*i.e.* not one to be anticipated, and not the one which Napoleon expected; it gave him no time to arrange his plans and manoeuvre; it disconcerted him, and it brought him quickly to a decisive battle which crushed him. Surely a strategy which does this (and succeeds even under certain defects in its execution) is a good strategy.

From the first it was part of the plan of Wellington and Blücher to bring on a decisive battle with Napoleon as rapidly as possible, if they could do so with reasonable prospect of success.

Wellington, though Napoleon did not understand this, was quite as anxious as Blücher to come to battle; and there is little question that had the Allies been able to concentrate sooner on the 16th they would have attacked Napoleon, had he not attacked them.

Wellington, as his correspondence shows, ("Memorandum upon the Battle of Waterloo," by the Duke of Wellington), was aware that the plan of campaign which Napoleon has indicated as the one which the Allies should have adopted, would "have left the Emperor of the French to manoeuvre as he liked." He further saw that the latter's policy, were he permitted to collect his army south of the forest of Soignies, might possibly be not to seek, but even to avoid a decisive battle, while the Allies united, and waited for him north of it. But he considered that this would give the French an undesirable advantage.

There were many good reasons for the Allied desire to come to battle. One was that Napoleon, though circumstances had made him the aggressor in this campaign, had nevertheless, for the moment, not desired war. In the interests of his dynasty he had sought for peace, in order to consolidate his position in France, for he was facing an almost overwhelming coalition of the Powers who had declared war upon him.

There seems no reason to doubt that he told the simple and whole truth when, on the voyage out to St. Helena, he said to Rear-Admiral Cockburn (*Buonaparte's Voyage to St. Helena*, comprising the diary of Rear-Admiral Sir George Cockburn, 1815), that on entering upon this campaign his chief hope was, by a success (especially against the English), the might be able to create a situation such as would lead to the chance of a general truce, or produce a change of administration in England which would terminate the war. A cessation of hostilities (he said) was really his "first object," for France was hardly equal to the effort which she was then making.

Napoleon's genius shone conspicuously in the initiative, and in rapid movements, and his army was more capable of manoeuvring quickly than those of the Allies. Had he been permitted to gain time after Ligny to ascertain more exactly the Allied strength and positions, to formulate his own plans, and intrigue in Belgium, he might have increased his prestige, and, after gaining some successes against Wellington or Blücher, have possibly attained his "first object," "a cessation of hostilities," but not in a manner which would have been to the permanent interest of the Allies.

Wellington also sought a cessation of hostilities, but knew that no lasting peace could be attained except by a decisive victory, which in his judgment would be rendered less probable by delay.

To show that the Allied strategy at the outset, though it certainly involved risks, was not what may be termed rash, it is sufficient to note that under the defects which marked the execution of his concentration, Wellington at Quatre Bras maintained his ground against Ney and drove him back, while Blücher's troops, under great tactical disadvantages and without the corps of Bülow, nearly maintained his at Ligny. (Bülow's corps, through some misunderstanding in the orders sent him, took no part in the Battle of Ligny).

With respect to the fact that Napoleon did not attack Wellington *early* on June 17th at Quatre Bras, the natural explanation is that he assumed, though it would have been safer to have made sure, that Wellington would have known on the night of the 16th of the retreat of the Prussians from Ligny, and fallen back himself. Napoleon could not have anticipated that through the mischance of the officer despatched by Blücher to Wellington being wounded, Wellington was left in some uncertainty of the Prussian intentions until the morning of the 17th.

The final triumph of the Allied strategy took place at Waterloo, and was the result of Blücher's resolution to march with his whole available army to support Wellington.

Whatever its risks, it forms an instance of a most successful concentration from separate points upon the battlefield itself.

The divergent lines of communication of Wellington and Blücher now enabled them "to deliver their blows in the most fatally decisive manner against the enemy's flank and rear." (Hamley's *Operations of War*).

The complete success of this movement was chiefly due to the resolute determination of Blücher to march with his whole available force from Wavre to co-operate with Wellington; and his orders in pursuance of this determination have been given in Chapter 20.

Gneisenau, Blücher having been unhorsed and left for a time upon the field of Ligny incapable of giving his orders, had conducted the retreat by Tilly towards Wavre with much ability; and by many writers it has been, not unnaturally, asserted that to him was due the credit, not only of ordering this line of retreat, but also of having taken this important and bold step, with the formed intention not merely of marching on Wavre, but of marching from Wavre to support Wellington, thus abandoning the idea of retreating towards the Rhine.

Of recent years, however, the opinion has gained ground that this assumption was an unjust one to Blücher. General von Lettow-Vorbeck, a very recent writer upon the Waterloo campaign, says (*Napoleon's Untergang*, by Major-General von Lettow-Vorbeck, 1904), that at earliest dawn on June 17th an officer of the Prussian staff (Lieutenant von Wüssow), who had been establishing order in the retiring columns, wrote from a few miles south of Wavre to General Grolman,

Quartermaster-General of the army, asking him for instructions, as it was "perhaps of importance to pass through the defile of Wavre in good time." Upon his letter itself Grolman wrote at once the following answer:—

The 1st Corps to bivouac at Bierges; the 2nd Corps before Wavre, at St. Anne; the 3rd Corps at La Bavette; the 4th at Dion le Mont (all these points are around Wavre). The reserve ammunition column to Moestricht. (Afterwards brought to Wavre).

★★★★★★

Bierges is about 1½ miles south-west of Wavre; St. Anne is about 2 miles south-east of Wavre; La Bavette is about 1 mile north and a little west of Wavre; Dion le Mont is about 3 miles to the east and a little south of Wavre. Thus the army was directed to assemble around Wavre, and not to pass through it, retreating by the road to Moestricht which was still open.

★★★★★★

Lettow-Vorbeck continues:

From this, results the undeniable proof that this ever-memorable resolution, decisive of the entire campaign—*i.e.* of assembling the whole army at Wavre, and renouncing the retreat homewards—was taken not on the evening of June 16th by Gneisenau, but first of all on the night of the 16-17th, in consequence of an army command; and therefore with the concurrence of Blücher. (*von dem armee-kommando, also unter mitwirkung von Blücher*).

And he further adds, alluding to the letter, (previously mentioned), which Blücher had directed Count Nostitz, his *aide-de-camp*, to write to Wellington at 9.30 a.m. on the 18th, and which was afterwards shown to Gneisenau:

This letter enables us to recognise in an undoubted manner, that Marshal Blücher alone, without any previous agreement with Gneisenau, took this decision—of grave importance as respects the issue of the war—of marching (to join Wellington) with his whole army, (*i.e.* his whole available army).

General Zurlinden, in commenting upon General von Lettow-Vorbeck's views, says:

Lettow has been forced, by deep and conscientious study, to

diminish a little the influence of Gneisenau upon the march of events, which hitherto had been looked upon as preponderant; and to raise still higher the part, already so glorious, played by Marshal Blücher.—"Ligny and Waterloo," review by General Zurlinden of *Napoleon's Untergang,* by General von Lettow-Vorbeck. *Revue des Deux Mondes,* January, 1906.

Gneisenau unquestionably directed the retreat after Ligny on the evening of June 16th, first upon Tilly and then upon Wavre. (It has been said that Wavre was mentioned because Tilly was not marked upon the map; but at all events the march was ordered to be by the road to Wavre); but it does not follow that this was done with any definite intention of afterwards joining Wellington at Waterloo. In fact, under the knowledge probably possessed at that moment of Wellington's own plans, it could scarcely have been so.

A letter from Thielemann (commanding the 3rd Prussian Corps) to Bülow, written at 6 a.m. on June 17th, contains these words:

I have no order from Prince Blücher, but I assume he is retreating by Wavre on St. Tron.—Sir F. Maurice, *United Service Magazine,* July, 1890; article on Waterloo and responsibility for French failure.

This shows that General Thielemann, at all events, did not consider that a retreat on Wavre would mean that the idea of falling back further through St. Tron to Moestricht had been abandoned. Colonel Sir H. Hardinge, British Commissioner at Blücher's headquarters, says also that as he was lying wounded on his bed on June 17th, Blücher burst into his room, (this was probably, but not certainly, at Wavre on the night of the 17th; Ropes) exclaiming, "Gneisenau has given way. We are to march to join Wellington."

But though the evidence seems to prove that it was owing chiefly to Blücher's determination that the whole available Prussian Army joined Wellington upon the field of Waterloo, it is still due to Gneisenau to remember that it was he who directed the army to Tilly and Wavre. What more, under the circumstances, could any chief of the staff have done?

This step left open to the commander-in-chief (Blücher) the final decision of whether to retire further along the Louvain—Moestricht road towards the Rhine, or to run the risk of uniting with Wellington. What that risk was it was Gneisenau's duty to point out, as he did, and to emphasise, as he did; but it was Blücher's province to decide whether he should incur or avoid it.

Passing from the strategy of the campaign to the tactics of the battle of Waterloo, we have already remarked that Wellington's occupation of the ground, and handling of the troops, was eminently calculated to disconcert Napoleon; and in the latter's attack upon the Allied position at Waterloo there seems very little to denote any important departure from his previous tactical methods, or to prove any failure of former tactical ability. We may add that this view has struck some French writers, (see Houssaye; defeat is attributed, not to Napoleon's tactics, but to Wellington's occupation of ground, etc., and to defective execution of orders), and is expressed in a paper by Colonel F. N. Maude, C. B., upon this campaign, (Paper (MS.) by Colonel F. N. Maude, C.B. (late R.E.), upon the campaign of Waterloo). Speaking of Napoleon's general type of attack, in his many battles, he says that as a rule the attack opened by his first line engaging the enemy along the whole front, he writes:

> This stage has generally been considered as a reconnaissance in force to determine the enemy's weakest point; but in reality it was a far more serious matter than the word would indicate, being designed to compel him to expend his reserves prematurely. Into this trap his adversaries invariably fell. The first-line troops were fought to the last ounce, Napoleon sternly refusing all requests for reinforcements. By degrees the enemy's reserves were weakened, whilst Napoleon still held the mass of his own in hand.

Then came:

> A concentrated artillery fire, the horse artillery dashing to the front.... A great gap was torn out of the human target through which the cavalry charged, followed closely by the Imperial Guard, the latter marching in heavy masses, ready to form front in any required direction to meet any possible counter-attack. Such was the broad idea, and its success was in proportion to the local circumstances enabling him to conform to it. Of his many battles, Ligny approximates most closely to the type.

At Waterloo, after a parade of the army which must have been to a great extent in full view of the Allies, we have the "reconnaissance in force"—in reality a heavy attack—designed to compel the enemy to show his position and expend his reserves prematurely. This occurred in the 1st and 2nd phases of the battle (mentioned earlier)—*i.e.* in the advance of Reille and D'Erlon; but it did not lead Wellington to support his advanced posts unduly, or to disclose his occupation of the ground, or to weaken his reserves. As Colonel Maude writes:

> The tactical skill of Wellington began to tell.

It threw out the calculations of the French emperor, based as they were on the experience, not of Peninsular, but of other battlefields in Europe.

The attacks of D'Erlon and Reille were completely repulsed by the tactics explained earlier, and nearly half the former's guns were put out of action.

The French artillery, though its fire was heavy throughout the day, found no massed and exposed columns to tear a gap through; and subsequently, in the 3rd phase of the battle, the infantry, successful on so many other fields, having failed and suffered severely, Napoleon resorted, before drawing further upon his reserves, to those great attacks of cavalry described by Sir James Shaw-Kennedy as:

> The most powerful efforts ever made by cavalry against infantry
> in the history of war.

But the French squadrons could not break Wellington's squares, acting in combination with the other arms, or clear the ground, as they had been accustomed to do, for the Imperial Guard. They also failed.

Then, at the close, came the normal advance in heavy columns of the celebrated Guard, shorn of half their strength to meet the advance of the Prussians; and not now, as on many previous battlefields, to follow up a success, or turn a doubtful day into a victory as at Ligny.

Once more the Peninsular tactics of Wellington were repeated. The English Guards sprang up from under cover; their destructive volleys, and those of Adam's flanking brigade, were poured in; the bayonet charge was delivered; and finally the pursuing cavalry of Vivian and Vandeleur were let loose.

It was thus at Waterloo that the army of Napoleon was defeated by another which, in composition, and perhaps also in manoeuvring power, was scarcely its equal; and this view seems to be embodied in such expressions of Wellington (Letter to Lord Beresford, Gonesse, July 2nd, 1815) as:

> Napoleon did not manoeuvre at all. He just moved forward
> in the old style in columns, and was driven off in the old style.

But it is a mistake to suppose that the "old style" of Wellington meant simply hard blows; it was the embodiment of tactics not at that period generally adopted. (In the Oldfield MSS., Major Oldfield, Brigade-Major R.E., who fought in the battle, attributes the victory to Wellington's skill, as well as the extraordinary bravery of his troops).

With respect to the supposition occasionally met with, that in the Battle of Waterloo Napoleon showed a want of personal energy, indicating physical or mental failure, it should be noticed that, after the exertions of June 14th, 15th, 16th, and 17th, he retired late to bed at the farm of Caillou on the night of the 17th, having previously dictated the order of battle to Soult for the following day; rose at 1 o'clock a.m. on the 18th, and made with Bertrand the round of his outposts in pouring rain (chiefly to assure himself that Wellington was still in position in his front); and only returned to his quarters at dawn. (Houssaye).

From all accounts he had certainly been subject, since 1806, to sudden fits of weakness, lethargy, and prostration; but it is to be gathered, at all events, that he was not suffering from one of these on the 18th, and that the delay in opening the French attack was not due to lethargy, but simply to the fact that the heavy state of the ground after the continuous rain made delay, in his opinion, advantageous.

Gleig, (*Life of Wellington*), writes:

Portions of the French corps were at work all night on June 17th, bringing up ammunition and even cannon, which came in but slowly, and were still out of gear for action long after the dawn of the 18th broke.

To compare great things with smaller, the truth which Napoleon was forced to realise too late at Waterloo was, it seems, much of the same character as that which has been brought home to the British Army by its campaigns in South Africa,—*viz.* that where its tactics are unsuitable to those of the enemy it has met, as at Isandahlwana in 1879; its marksmanship, and thus its fire-power, inferior to that of its adversaries, as in the contests with the Boers in 1881; or its skill in utilising or improvising cover not so great as that of its opponents, as was occasionally illustrated in its latest campaign—the British Army may have to pay heavily for it.

It has been related that Wellington, when asked in Paris, shortly after Waterloo, how he should have attacked had he been in Napoleon's place, replied:

I should have turned the flank—the right flank. I should have kept the English Army occupied by a demonstration to attack, or perhaps by slight attacks, whilst I was in fact moving the main body by Hal on Brussels—Sir F. Maurice, *United Service Magazine*, September 1st, 1890, on the authority of the MS. diary of Colonel the Hon. J. H. Stanhope.

And to this opinion he appears to have adhered throughout his life.

He was convinced that the French ought to have advanced by other lines than by the valleys of the Sambre and Meuse; and we gather that, even up to the last moment previous to the attack on his position at Waterloo, he anticipated as probable that Napoleon might endeavour to turn it by a march upon Hal. He held that after the Battle of Quatre Bras the French should have marched along the *chaussée* from Mons to Hal and Brussels. ("Memorandum upon the Battle of Waterloo," drawn up in 1842. *Personal Reminiscences of the Duke of Wellington,* by Lord Ellesmere, 1903). His orders to Prince Frederic of Orange also on June 17th, when directing him to occupy with his corps the position between Hal and Enghien, were that he was "to defend it as long as possible."

There seems no doubt that, from the commencement to the close of the campaign, what Wellington was most anxious to prevent was a turning movement round his right; and he probably considered that the most serious danger to the Allies—more serious than a pitched battle—lay in Napoleon's manoeuvring power, which he always recognised as exceptionally great.

This leads us naturally to allude to what several historians of this campaign has appeared unaccountable—*viz.* that Wellington left at Hal and Tubize, throughout the Battle of Waterloo, some 18,000 men, including part of the 4th (Colville's) Division.

The reason why this force was posted there seems to have been a double one:—

1st, To guard against a turning movement round the Anglo-Allied right, from Mons towards Brussels.

2nd, To cover and secure Wellington's retreat in case he fell back, after the battle, towards Ostend and not towards Brussels.

Wellington is reported to have spoken thus, in relation to his arrangements for a retreat if necessary—in the hearing of Lord Hatherton and Croker, and in a conversation noted down at the time:—

I knew that every yard of the plain beyond the forest (of Soignies) on each side of the *chaussée* was open enough for infantry and cavalry, and even for artillery, and very defensible. Had I retreated through it, could they have followed me? The Prussians were on their flank, and would have been in their rear. The co-operation of the Prussians in the operations which I undertook was part of my plan, and I was not deceived. But I never contemplated a retreat on Brussels. Had I been forced I should have retreated by my right towards the coast, the shipping, and my resources. I had placed Hill (Colville's division was in the corps of Hill, it was at first ordered to Hal, but in the end halted at Tubize), where he could lend me important assistance in many contingencies that might have been. And again I ask—If I had retreated on my right, could Napoleon have ventured to follow me? The Prussians already on his flank would have been in his rear. But my plan was to keep my ground till the Prussians appeared, and then to attack the French position—and I executed my plan.—*Links with the Past*, Mrs. Charles Bagot (1901).

Too much weight is not to be placed on recorded conversations of the above description; still, in this one, we have an intelligible reason given for the posting by Wellington of these troops at Hal. It was not solely to prevent his right from being turned, but to support a retreat to Ostend—a measure of prudence in case it was desirable, or necessary (in the event of Napoleon obtaining the command of the Brussels road), to fall back in that direction.

Napoleon made no decided attempt, at all events, to turn the Anglo-Allied right, and was unsuccessful in the battle in piercing their centre or gaining the Brussels road.

★★★★★★

It is curious that Napoleon, in his *Mémoires*, compiled at St. Helena and published in 1820, says that on the evening of the 17th he did detach 5,000 cavalry to endeavour to gain the roads from Enghien and Braine-le-Comte to Brussels; and in the *Additional Particulars of the Battle of Waterloo*, by Booth (1817), a similar statement is made. See *Waterloo, a Narrative and a Criticism*, by E. L. S. Horsburgh (1900). The Allies, however, never encountered this cavalry, and if it really ever went out, which is doubted, it must have fallen back on finding the roads occupied.

★★★★★★

In consequence, perhaps, Wellington has been criticised the more for having left a strong force throughout the day at Hal. (Chesney, Kennedy, and others, Ropes gives no opinion on this subject). It can, however, be seen, by reference to the map, that after Wellington's retreat from Quatre Bras on June 17th, it was perfectly in Napoleon's power, had he so determined, to move a large force to his left for the Hal-Brussels road. Therefore, comparatively few have contested the wisdom of the disposition made by Wellington up to June 18th.

But by several who do not do this it has been contended that by 10 or 11 a.m. on the 18th, when the battle commenced, it had become so evident that no attack was contemplated against the right, that the troops from Hal and Tubize should have been called in; or that Colville should have been given orders to move towards Wellington as soon as he had satisfied himself that he would not be attacked from the direction of Mons.

Under the above contention the question is narrowed to this. At what time on June 18th had it become impossible for Napoleon to have turned Wellington's right with a force, mainly of cavalry, say, by the Braine-le-Chateau, Hal, and Brussels road, (from Napoleon's left at Waterloo to Hal was under 10 miles), *had the latter been left unoccupied?* And at what hour on the 18th could Wellington have been certain, or could Colville at Tubize or the troops at Hal have been certain, that no such movement was practicable? This is a difficult point for anyone to decide with confidence, criticising after the event; but we can see this, that Hal was nearly ten miles from Mont St. Jean—*i.e.* about a four hours' march—and therefore from the time when Wellington might despatch a messenger to Hal, ordering the troops there to join him, nearly six hours must elapse before their arrival. To bring them to the field before 7 p.m., the order must have been sent off by 1 p.m.—*i.e.* before D'Erlon's first attack had been delivered.

But before 7 p.m.—indeed, much before 7 p.m.—Wellington expected the Prussians on the field. On their arrival he probably felt confident that he could hold his ground without the troops at Hal; and before their arrival he was principally anxious that his right by Hal should not be turned, and that his retreat through that point should be secured by their presence there. Horsburgh writes:

> Notwithstanding the weight of authority, there was much force, it is contended, in the duke's apprehensions; and much caution and good sense displayed in the measures which he took

to allay them.—*Waterloo, a Narrative and a Criticism*, by E. L. S. Horsburgh (1900).

Before leaving the subject of Wellington's precautions with respect to his right, it must be mentioned that some have held that it should have been clear that Napoleon would not attempt to turn that flank, because his object was to separate Wellington from the Prussians, who were upon his *left*; and also that, had Napoleon moved round Wellington's right, he would have exposed his own line of communications through Charleroi. But had Napoleon, on the night of June 17th, moved round Wellington's right, he would certainly have placed a greater distance between himself and the Prussians; and, had there been no force near Hal, could probably have forced Wellington to draw away from his ally, in order to protect the Hal-Brussels road. (Those who condemn the retention of the troops at Hal).

It would seem, also, that it was within the power of Napoleon, had he secured the roads leading through Braine-le-Comte and Nivelles to the French frontier, to have changed his own line of communications to one further west.

It was a cardinal point of Wellington's plan of battle to remain immovable in his position, ("To keep my ground till the Prussians appeared"); until the Prussians could come up and attack Napoleon in conjunction with him. Could he have done this with Napoleon moving round his right flank in the direction of Brussels? Apparently he could not have done so; and to have been obliged to move to his right, to manoeuvre against Napoleon for the protection of the Hal-Brussels road, would have entirely disarranged his plan for the junction of the Prussians on his left. Under those circumstances some other plan for that junction must have been adopted and in dangerous haste.

All these considerations tend to explain why Wellington may have determined to leave the force he did at Hal; and moreover, as Sir P. Maurice has pointed out, a large portion of these troops were Dutch-Belgians, ("Waterloo," by Sir F. Maurice, *United Service Magazine*, September, 1890), and it might not have been viewed as desirable to mass all these on the line of battle at Waterloo. Many were doubtful as to their sympathies being with the Allies.

The weather, as well as the character of the country, especially about the River Dyle—to which we have already sufficiently alluded—had a decided influence upon this campaign.

The heavy rain which fell on the afternoon and during the night of June 17th, making the ground difficult to traverse, was an element in favour of the Allies, insomuch as it much hampered Napoleon in his movements during Wellington's retreat from Quatre Bras to Mont St. Jean; and Grouchy, in his pursuit of the Prussians after Ligny.

On June 18th, also, it had so affected the surface of the fields that it caused Napoleon to delay his attack.

On the other hand—and this was to the advantage of the French—it greatly retarded the Prussian march from Wavre to Ohain and St. Lambert on the 18th, to co-operate with Wellington.

It thus affected both sides materially, but which to the most adverse extent it is hardly possible to determine, and various views have been held respecting it.

Lieut.-Colonel Henderson, whose comparatively recent death has been so great a loss to the army, (Lieut.-Colonel G. F. R. Henderson, author of *Stonewall Jackson and the American Civil War,* after serving in South Africa on the staff of Field-Marshal Lord Roberts, as Director of Intelligence, died in Egypt at Assouan, March, 1903), writes as follows with respect to the Peninsular and Waterloo campaigns:—

I hope you will not consider me exceedingly unpractical, lagging hopelessly in rear of modern thought and modern progress, if I say that in my humble opinion the campaigns of Wellington, not in strategy alone, but in tactics also, are prolific in instruction. It is perfectly true that, both in strategy and in tactics, important modifications have been brought about by modern science; but steam and the telegraph have scarcely touched the grand principles of strategy—they have only introduced new means of applying them; nor have modern weapons wrought a complete change in tactics. . . . To define my meaning exactly, in the selection of a defensive position we look for exactly the same features as in the days of Brown Bess, with the one exception that we demand a wider field of fire.

Otherwise, as regards cover, the protection of our flanks, lines of retreat, and lines of communication, we are guided by the same principles as our forefathers. . . . Outposts are still established on the system which obtained in the Peninsula; and, above all, the enemy is deceived, outwitted, and outmanoeuvred by exactly the same means as were adopted by the great generals of the pre-breechloader era. I would lay special stress on the fact, which none can gainsay, that human nature, the paramount consideration of all questions of either tactics or strategy, remains unaltered.

And the art of generalship, the art of command, whether the forces be small or great, is the art of dealing with human nature. Human nature must be the basis of every leader's calculations. When once an officer has mastered the theory of formation, and understands the effects of fire, the means of producing those effects and also of reducing them, he cannot do better than study the Indian, and the Peninsular, and the Waterloo campaigns. Then he will learn how to outwit, to outmanoeuvre, to deceive, and in one word surprise his enemy; and as has been well said, surprise is the deadliest of all foes.

I cannot conceive anything more useful to a soldier than to be thoroughly imbued with the methods of Wellington.—*Some Notes on Wellington*, read before the Military Society of Ireland, March 31st, 1897.

How completely Wellington's tactics as regards cover and reserve-fire are applicable appears in the following remarks from General Joubert to Assistant-General Botha, made in December, 1899:

It was always my endeavour as long as the enemy blustered with his guns to conceal my men as much as possible, and to strengthen them in their positions till the enemy's guns were tired and they then advanced and attacked us; then, and not before, when they were between their own guns and our men, the *burghers* sprang forwards, and shot them away by batches.— *Official History of the War in South Africa,* 1899-1902, by Sir F. Maurice (1906), vol. i.

It is of some interest to conjecture how far the campaign of Waterloo might have been altered in character had railways, motors, the field telegraph, etc., been in existence in 1815 in France and Belgium. Sir Edward Hamley, (Hamley's *Operations of War*), has entered into this with respect to the question of railways, his conclusions being that, although they certainly would have enabled Napoleon to concentrate and advance even more rapidly than he did, yet, as they would also have enabled both Wellington and Blücher to do the same, they would on the whole have favoured the defence. It can be seen, also, that many of those dangerous misunderstandings which resulted through the non-arrival of officers and others bearing messages, might possibly have been avoided by the use of the field telegraph.

There is, however, no certainty that at times modern improvements in communication may not fail us; and orders in the future, as at present, will probably have continually to be conveyed by staff-officers, mounted orderlies, and cyclists.

But to soldiers of the present day the most valuable teaching of all, perhaps, in the Waterloo campaign is the importance of arrangements for the rapid and secure transmission of reports; of staff supervision over the march of large bodies of troops; of sending more than one messenger in the case of orders of great consequence; of the clear wording of orders; and of the clear writing of orders.

If anyone reflects upon the occurrences which either bore gravely upon this campaign, or might easily have done so, he must be struck with the fact that events upon which the fate of Europe might have turned, were not great movements alone, but small matters of military detail.

Prominent among these were the miscarriage of Ziethen's message to Wellington on the early morning of June 15th; the delay in transmitting the reports from Mons; the miscarriage of Blücher's message to Wellington after Ligny (the officer bearing it being wounded); the crowding and jamming of the troops on the march to Quatre Bras; disputes as to the receipt of orders, or as to the meaning of orders, on the part of Ney, D'Erlon, and Grouchy; and also illegible handwriting in orders. It is a good adage,—

For the want of a nail the shoe was lost,
For the want of a shoe the horse was lost,
For the want of a horse the rider was lost,
For the want of a rider the battle was lost.
—*What to observe, and how to observe it,* by Colonel Lonsdale Hale.

Houssaye says that Soult's weak point (as chief of the staff) was that he wrote his orders without precision and clearness, so that they were not always understood. It is also said occasionally that Napoleon constantly forgot what verbal orders he had actually given, remembering only what in his own mind he had meant to say, although he might not have said it; and that it was one of Berthier's strongest points, when chief of his staff, that he could intuitively judge the emperor's real wishes and convey them more clearly than others could; also that he (Berthier) sometimes sent several officers with the same message of importance to ensure its receipt.

We can see that in the Waterloo campaign much hung upon the

orders sent out, their clearness or the reverse, and the measures taken to ensure, as far as possible, that they were safely delivered.

Houssaye attributes the wanderings of D'Erlon partly to bad handwriting, which pencilled notes on the field are apt to accentuate. (D'Erlon read "*sur les hauteurs*" as "*à la hauteur*"; and Grouchy states that he, his chief of the staff, and his *aide-de-camp* all read the words in Letter X., Appendix B, "*Bataille engagée*"—Battle now in progress, as "*Bataille gagnée*"—Battle has been won).

In an article on Lettow-Vorbeck's work, *Napoleon's Untergang*, 1815, Mr. Andrew Lang says, (article in *Morning Post*, February 9th, 1900, "Ligny and Waterloo"), that the writing-master of Alexandre Dumas used to tell his pupil:

> The emperor never lost a battle except by his bad handwriting (the remark applies rather, perhaps, to his staff, who wrote his letters): his officers could never make out what he meant.

Wellington's writing, though it was occasionally difficult to read in later years, was not so at this period, and his orders and dispatches are remarkable for their clearness.

There is no practical training for the soldier like that of war; but nevertheless, the study of history, practice in writing orders on staff rides, and the lessons of field manoeuvres in peace, should tend to reduce the chance of certain mistakes being committed in war; and it is of more value to British military students to realise this, than to weigh whether Napoleon, Ney, or Grouchy were most responsible for certain movements which have been the subject of criticism, interesting though these questions may be.

The campaigns of Wellington, while prominently illustrating the paramount importance of sea-power, show us also its necessary limitations. The former is brought out continually in the Peninsular War; the latter in this, that although the French Navy was practically destroyed at Trafalgar in 1805, the freedom of the Peninsula was only achieved by Wellington in 1814—*i.e.* nine years later—at Vittoria and the destruction of Napoleon's power at Waterloo.

A great empire must have an adequate army as well as navy, or it cannot strike that final blow against the enemy's land forces, or at the seat of his military power, which, when war has once broken out, makes most certainly, most rapidly, most economically, and most humanely for peace.

An examination of the Peninsular and Waterloo campaigns must convince many that the military genius of Wellington has scarcely been sufficiently recognised by all his countrymen.

Two of our most distinguished commanders-in-chief since Wellington's day bear their testimony to this. Lord Wolseley writes, (Introduction by Lord Wolseley to *Wellington and Waterloo*, by Major Arthur Griffiths, 1898), "What Wellington did for the Empire is not, I think, sufficiently remembered in these days"; and Lord Roberts, (*The Rise of Wellington*, by Lord Roberts), "As a commander, Wellington has been greatly underrated."

In the language of Sir A. Alison and Sir E. Hamley:

Long and severe was Wellington's trial, but great and glorious was his reward. He found it in the smiling and prosperous realms which he had protected by his arms; he found it in the wasted and desolate kingdoms which he had wrested from the enemy; he found it in the universal gratitude of the world.—*Essays—Political, Historical, and Miscellaneous*, by Sir A. Alison (1850), vol. iii.

For posterity, Wellington will always live most vividly in the events of Waterloo, succouring the hard-pressed garrison of Hougoumont, encouraging with word and look his shattered squares, calling on the Guards to arise and charge, leading his diminished line in the final advance, and embracing Blücher in the twilight while the last remnants of the foe were swept from the darkening field. . . . The great hereditary sovereigns of Europe were leading hosts into France; but no eye regarded them or anything else, except the great Englishman before whom the world's incubus had vanished into night.—*Wellington's Career*, by Sir E. B. Hamley (1864).

Appendix A

Strength and composition of the armies of Wellington, Blücher, and Napoleon, June, 1815. Also their disposition on June 14th, Orders issued on June 15th, etc.

ANGLO-ALLIED ARMY*

FIELD-MARSHAL THE DUKE OF WELLINGTON

Headquarters: Brussels

FIRST CORPS

GENERAL H.R.H. THE PRINCE OF ORANGE

Headquarters: Braine-le-Comte

Divisions.	Brigades.	Battalions.	Strength of divisions.	Position of divisions in cantonments on evening of June 14th.	Orders to divisions on afternoon and night of June 14th.†
1st Division Maj.-Gen. Cooke (4 battalions of Guards)	1st British Brigade 2nd Bat. 1st Guards, 3rd Bat. 1st Guards, Maj.-Gen. Maitland.	2	4,061	Enghien (headquarters), and towards Ath, communicating with 2nd British Division (Sir H. Clinton).	5 p.m.—Collect at Enghien, ready to march at a moment's notice and move to Nivelles.† 10 p.m.—Enghien to Braine-le-Comte.
	2nd British Brigade 2nd Bat. Coldstream Guards, 2nd Bat. 3rd Guards, Maj.-Gen. Sir John Byng.	2			
	Batts. Artillery attached Capt. Sandham (Foot) } Lieut.-Col. Maj. Kuhlmann (Horse) } Adye.				
3rd Division Lieut.-Gen. Count Alten (British, German Legion, and Hanoverians)	5th British Brigade 2nd 30th, 33rd, 2nd 69th, 2nd 73rd, Maj.-Gen. Sir Colin Halkett.	4	6,970	Soignies (headquarters), Mons, Roeulx, Braine-le-Comte, Enghien.	5 p.m.—Collect at Braine-le-Comte, ready to move at shortest notice on Nivelles, if that point has been attacked.† 10 p.m.—Move to Nivelles.
	2nd Brigade K.G. Legion Colonel von Ompteda.	4			
	1st Hanoverian Brigade M.-G. Count Kielmannsegg.	3			

Batts.	Artillery attached		Strength	Position	Orders
	Major Lloyd (Foot) Capt. Cleeve (Foot) } Lieut.-Col. Williamson.				
2nd Dutch-Belgian Division Lieut.-Gen. Baron de Perponcher	1st Brigade Maj.-Gen. Count de Bylandt.	5	7,533	Nivelles (headquarters), Genappe, Quatre Bras, and Frasnes, communicating with Prussian right.	5 p.m.—Collect at Nivelles.
	2nd Brigade H.S.H. Prince Bernhard of Saxe-Weimar.	5			
	Capt. Byleveld's Battery of Artillery (Foot), Major van Opstal commanding Artillery.				
3rd Dutch-Belgian Division Lieut.-Gen. Baron Chassé	1st Brigade Maj.-Gen. Ditmers.	6	6,669	Roeulx (headquarters), and between that and Binche.	5 p.m.—To Nivelles.
	2nd Brigade Maj.-Gen. d'Aubremé.	6			
	Batteries of Artillery Capt. Krahmer (Horse) Capt. Lux (Foot) } Major van der Smissen.				
Total 1st Corps		.	25,233, with 48 guns.	40 Battalions, 7 Batteries.	

* These tables are taken from Siborne's *History of the Waterloo Campaign*.

† For further orders issued on the early morning of June 16th, see pages 523, 524, and 570.

‡ This movement to Nivelles was not to take place until it was certain that the enemy's attack was upon the Prussian right, or Wellington's left.

SECOND CORPS
LIEUTENANT-GENERAL LORD HILL
Headquarters : Ath

Divisions.	Brigades.	Battalions.	Strength of divisions.	Position of divisions in cantonments on evening of June 14th.	Orders to divisions on afternoon and night of June 15th.*
2nd Division Lieut.-Gen. Sir H. Clinton (British, German Legion, and Hanoverians)	3rd British Brigade 1st 52nd, 1st 71st, 2nd 95th, 3rd 95th,† Maj.-Gen. Adam.	4	6,833	Ath (headquarters), Lens, between Mons and Ath, and along Ath-Tournay road, communicating with 1st British Division at Enghien.	5 p.m.—Collect this night at Ath and adjacents, and be in readiness to march at a moment's notice.
	1st Brigade K.G. Legion Colonel du Plat.	4			
	3rd Hanoverian Brigade Colonel Hugh Halkett.	4			10 p.m.—To Enghien.
	Batts. Artillery attached Capt. Bolton (Foot) ⎫ Lieut.-Col. Maj. Sympher (Horse) ⎭ Gold.				
4th Division Lieut.-Gen. Sir C. Colville (British and Hanoverians)	4th British Brigade 3rd 14th, 1st 23rd, 51st, Col. Mitchell.	3	7,212	Audenarde (headquarters), Renaix. The 6th Hanoverian Brigade garrisoned Nieuport, on the coast.	5 p.m.—Collect this night at Grammont, excepting troops beyond the Scheldt, who are to move to Audenarde.
	6th British Brigade 2nd 35th, 1st 54th, 2nd 59th, 1st 91st, Maj.-Gen. Johnstone.	4			
	6th Hanoverian Brigade Maj.-Gen. Sir James Lyon.	5			10 p.m.—Move to Enghien.

1st Dutch-Belgian Division Lieut.-Gen. Stedman ‡				
Batts, Artillery attached Major Brome (Foot) Capt. von Rettberg (Foot) } Lieut.-Col. Hawker.				
1st Brigade Maj.-Gen. Hauw.	6	6,389	Between Grammont and Ghent.	5 p.m.—Collect at Sotteghem, ready to move at daylight. The Prince of Orange to be desired to leave 500 men to occupy Audenarde.
2nd Brigade Maj.-Gen. Eerens.	5			
1 Foot Battery of Artillery attached.				
Dutch-Belgian Indian Brigade Lieut.-Gen. Anthing.	4	3,583	Between Alost and the Grammont-Ghent road.	5 p.m.—Collect at Sotteghem, ready to move at daylight.
1 Foot Battery of Artillery attached.				
Various men attached, Orderlies, etc.	16			
Total 2nd Corps		24,033, with 40 guns.		39 Battalions, 6 Batteries.

* For further orders issued on the early morning of June 16th, see pages 523, 524, and 570.

† Three battalions of the 95th Rifle Corps, which became, in February, 1816, the Rifle Brigade, served in the Peninsula and at Waterloo.

‡ This Dutch-Belgian Division and the attached brigade came afterwards under the command of Prince Frederic of Orange.

Divisions.	Brigades.	Batta-lions.	Strength of divisions.	Position of divisions in canton-ments on evening of June 14th.	Orders to divisions on afternoon and night of June 15th.*
5th Division Lieut.-Gen. Sir T. Picton (British and Hanoverians)	8th British Brigade 1st 28th, 1st 32nd, 1st 79th, 1st 95th, Maj.-Gen. Sir James Kempt.	4		Chiefly in and around Brussels.	5 p.m.—To be ready to march from Brussels at a moment's notice. The 5th Hanoverian Brigade to collect at Hal ready to move on Brussels at daylight.
	9th British Brigade 3rd 1st, 1st 42nd, 2nd 44th, 1st 92nd, Maj.-Gen. Sir Denis Pack.	4	7,158		
	5th Hanoverian Brigade Colonel von Vincke.	4			
	Batts. Artillery attached Maj. Rogers (Foot) }Maj. Heisse. Capt. Brawn (Foot)				
6th Division Lieut.-Gen. the Hon. Sir Lowry Cole (British and Hanoverians)	10th British Brigade 1st 4th, 1st 27th, 1st 40th, 2nd 81st, Maj.-Gen. Sir John Lambert.	4		In and around Brussels; 1 brigade apparently at Ghent.	5 p.m.—Hanoverian Bde. and 81st Reg. of British Bde. to be ready to march from Brussels at a moment's notice. The brigade at Ghent to march to Brussels.
	4th Hanoverian Brigade Colonel Best.	4	5,149		
	Batts. Artillery attached Maj. Unett (Foot) }Lieut.-Col. Bruckmann. Capt. Sinclair (Foot)				

218

			Strength		
7th Division	{	7th British Brigade	3	Garrisoning Antwerp, Ostend, Nieuport, Ypres, Tournay, Mons, etc.	5 p.m.—Collect between Brussels and Vilvorde this night.
		British Garrison Troops.	3	3,233	
		Advanced-Guard Battalion	1		
Brunswick Corps H.S.H. the Duke of Brunswick	{	Major von Rauschenplatt. Light Brigade	4	In and about Brussels.	
		Lieut.-Col. von Buttlar. Line Brigade	3	5,376	
		Lieut.-Col. von Specht. Batts. Artillery attached Capt. von Heine—Major mann (Foot) } Major Moll } Mahn. (Foot)			
Hanoverian Reserve Corps Lieut.-Gen. von der Decken	{	1st Brigade Lieut.-Col. von Bennigsen.	3	Garrisoning various places similarly to the 7th Division (see above).	
		2nd Brigade Lieut.-Col. von Beaulieu.	3	9,000	
		3rd Brigade Lieut.-Col. Bodecken.	3		
		4th Brigade Lieut.-Col. von Wissel.	4		
Nassau Contingent } Gen. von Kruse .		1 regiment.	3	In and about Brussels. 2,880	6 p.m.—Collect at daylight on the Louvain road, in readiness to move at a moment's notice.
Total Reserve . .				32,796, with 64 guns.	

Excluding 7th Division, 1 Brigade 6th Division, and Hanoverian Reserve Corps (Garrison Troops), there were with the Field Army Reserve 28 Battalions, 6 Batteries. To the above force 5 Batteries of British Reserve Artillery, Horse and Foot, were added—viz. those commanded—

Horse—by Lieutenant-Colonel Sir Hew Ross and Major Beane } Major Drummond.
Foot—by Major Morrison, Captain Hutchisson, and Captain Ilbert }

These were in Brussels, and received orders at 6 p.m. on evening of June 15th to be in readiness to march at daylight.

* For further orders issued on the early morning of June 16th, see pages 523, 524, and 570.

CAVALRY
LIEUTENANT-GENERAL THE EARL OF UXBRIDGE
Headquarters : Ninove

Brigades.	Regiments.	Strength of brigades.	Position in cantonments on evening of June 14th.	Orders on evening and night of June 15th.*
British and King's German Legion				
1st Brigade 1st and 2nd Life Guards, Royal Horse Guards, Lord E. Somerset.	4	1,226		5 p.m.—The Earl of Uxbridge (leaving the 2nd Hussars looking out between the Scheldt and Lys) to collect the whole of the Cavalry *this night* at Ninove, except Gen. Dörnberg's brigade (the 3rd) and the Cumberland Hussars, who are to march this night upon Vilvorde.
2nd Brigade 1st (Royals), 2nd (Scots Greys), 6th (Enniskn. Dgns.), Maj.-Gen. Sir W. Ponsonby.	3	1,181		
3rd Brigade 1st K.G.L.,† 2nd K.G.L., 23rd Light Dragoons, Maj.-Gen. Sir W. Dörnberg.	3	1,263		
4th Brigade 11th, 12th, 16th Light Dragoons, Maj.-Gen. Sir J. Vandeleur.	3	1,171	The British, King's German Legion, and Hanoverian cavalry at Grammont and Ninove and villages along the Dender.	
5th Brigade 2nd Hussars, K.G.L., 7th and 15th Hussars, Maj.-Gen. Sir Colq. Grant.	3	1,336		
6th Brigade 1st K.G.L., 10th and 18th Hussars, Maj.-Gen. Sir H. Vivian.	2	1,279		10 p.m.—The Cavalry to continue its movement from Ninove to Enghien.
7th Brigade 3rd K.G.L., 13th Light Dragoons, Col. Sir F. von Arentschildt.	2	1,012		
Hanoverian 1st Brigade Colonel von Estorf.	3	1,682		

220

Brunswick Cavalry 5 Squadrons, 1 being Uhlans.	2	922	Vicinity of Brussels.
Dutch-Belgian 1st Brigade Maj.-Gen. Trip.	3	1,287	Near Roeulx.
2nd Brigade Maj.-Gen. de Chigny.	2	1,086	Villages between Roeulx and Mons.
3rd Brigade Maj.-Gen. von Merlen.	2	1,062	S. of Mons, in direction of Maubeuge and Beaumont; part between Binche and Mons.
Total Cavalry			14,482, with 44 guns.

Of the Cavalry, the Dutch-Belgian, with some other regiments, appear to have been watching the frontier between the Lys and the Sambre; the Brunswick Cavalry to have been near Brussels; and the remainder about Grammont, Ninove, etc., on the Dender.

To the above force of Cavalry 7 Batteries of Horse Artillery were attached,—viz. those of Major Bull (Howitzers), Lieutenant-Colonel Webber-Smith, Lieutenant-Colonel Gardiner, Captain Whinyates (Rockets), Captain Mercer, Captain Norman Ramsay; and Captain Gey, with Dutch-Belgians.

In all, between the Batteries of Artillery with Infantry Divisions, Cavalry, and Reserve, there were 31 Batteries with the force—the Belgian Batteries having, as a rule, 8 guns each, the British and Hanoverian 6. Total, 196 guns.

The total strength of the army (including garrison troops) is thus made up:—

Infantry	. . . . .	82,062
Cavalry	. . . . .	14,482
Artillery	. . . . .	8,166
Engineers, Waggon-train, Staff Corps, etc.	. . . .	1,240
Grand total	.	105,950, with 196 guns.

* For further orders issued on the early morning of June 16th, see pages 523, 524, and 570.
† K.G.L. = King's German Legion.

221

PRUSSIAN ARMY

Field-Marshal Prince Blücher von Wahlstadt

Headquarters : Namur

Corps d'Armée.	Brigades,* etc.	Regiments.	Battalions.	Strength.	Position of corps in cantonments on evening of June 14th.	Orders to corps late at night on June 14th, and on June 15th.
1st Corps d'Armée Lieut.-Gen. von Ziethen	Infantry 1st 2nd 3rd 4th	3 3 3 3	9½ 9 9½ 6	27,887	Charleroi (headquarters); watched the Sambre from south of Binche to Moustier-sur-Sambre.	11.30 p.m., June 14th.— Retard enemy's advance across the Sambre. If compelled to retire, do so slowly to Fleurus, to give time for the other three corps to concentrate.
	Res. Cav. 1st Corps 1 1	3 4		1,925	Res. Cav., Sombref.	
	Res. Art. 1st Corps 12 Batteries (9 Foot, 3 Horse).†			1,019	Res. Art., Gembloux.	
					Advanced posts of this corps were pushed as far as Lobbes, Thuin, Gerpinnes, and Sossoye.	
Total . . .				30,831, with 96 guns.		

34 Battalions, 32 Squadrons, 12 Batteries.

* A "regiment," it will be seen, contained several battalions, and corresponded practically in strength to a British brigade, while a "brigade" (containing from two to four regiments) corresponded in strength to a division.
† Batteries of Foot and Horse Artillery had usually 8 guns each.

Corps d'Armée.	Brigades, etc.	Regiments.	Battalions.	Strength.	Position of corps in cantonments on evening of June 14th.	Orders to corps late at night on June 14th, and on June 15th.
2nd Corps d'Armée. Gen. von Pirch I.	Infantry 5th 6th 7th 8th	2 2 2 2	9 9 9 9	25,836	Namur (headquarters), confluence of Sambre and Meuse; watched the Meuse from Namur to Huy.	11.30 p.m., June 14th.— To Sombref.
	Res. Cav. 2nd Corps 1 1 1	3 2 4		4,463	Res. Cav., Hannut.	
	Res. Art. 2nd Corps 10 Batteries (7 Foot, 3 Horse)			1,454	Res. Art., on high road to Louvain (north of Namur). Advanced posts of this corps were pushed as far as Dinant, on the Meuse.	
Total . . .				31,758, with 80 guns.		

33 Battalions, 33 Squadrons, 10 Batteries.

PRUSSIAN ARMY (continued)

Corps d'Armée.	Brigades, etc.	Regiments.	Battalions.	Strength.	Position of corps in cantonments on evening of June 14th.	Orders to corps late at night on June 14th, and on June 15th.
	Infantry				Ciney (headquarters); watched the country from Dinant, by Ciney, to Asserre.	11.30 p.m., June 14th.— To Namur.
	9th	2	9			9.45 a.m., June 15th.— Continue march through Namur to Sombref on morning of 16th.
	10th	2	6			
	11th	2	6			
	12th	2	9	20,611		
3rd Corps d'Armée Lieut.-Gen. von Thielemann	Res. Cav. 3rd Corps				Res. Cav., between Ciney and Dinant.	
	1	3				
	1	4		2,405		
	Res. Art. 3rd Corps				Res. Art., Ciney.	
	6 Batteries (3 Foot, 3 Horse)			964	Advanced posts of this corps were pushed out as far as Fabeline and Rochefort.	
	Total .	.	.	23,980, with 48 guns.		

30 Battalions, 24 Squadrons, 6 Batteries.

PRUSSIAN ARMY (continued)

Corps d'Armée.	Brigades, etc.	Regiments.	Battalions.	Strength.	Position of corps in cantonments on evening of June 14th.	Orders to corps late at night on June 14th, and on June 15th.
4th Corps d'Armée Gen. Count Bülow von Dennewitz	Infantry 13th	2	9		Liege (headquarters); watched the country from Waremme to Liers.	11.30 p.m., June 14th.—Concentrate on Hannut.— 9.45 a.m., June 15th.—Move from Hannut upon Gembloux.
	14th	2	9			
	15th	2	9			
	16th	2	9	25,381		
	Res. Cav. 4th Corps 1	3			Res. Cav., Dalhem and Looz.	
	1	3				
	1	1		3,081		
	Res. Art. 4th Corps 11 Batteries (8 Foot, 3 Horse)			1,866	Res. Art., Gloms and Dalhem.	
Total . . .				30,328, with 88 guns.		

36 Battalions, 43 Squadrons, 11 Batteries.

Total strength { Infantry 99,715
Cavalry 11,879
Artillery 5,303

Grand total . . . . 116,897, with 312 guns.

FRENCH ARMY

UNDER NAPOLEON

Headquarters : Beaumont

Corps d'Armée.	Divisions.	Regiments, etc.*	Battalions.	Strength.	Position of corps in the field on evening of June 14th.	Orders to corps on evening of June 14th, or on June 15th.
1st Corps d'Armée Lt.-Gen. Count d'Erlon. Had been previously at Lille and had marched from thence.	1st Gen. Allix.	4	8			To move early on 15th up right bank of the Sambre and cross at Marchienne, or between that and Thuin.
	2nd Gen. Donzelot.	4	8		Close to Solre-sur-Sambre.	
	3rd Gen. Marcognet.	4	8			
	4th Gen. Durutte.	4	8	17,600		
	Cavalry 1st Division Lieut.-Gen. Jaquinot.	4		1,400		
	Artillery Batts.† 5 Foot, 1 Horse.			1,564		
Total . . .				20,564, with 46 guns.		

32 Battalions, 11 Squadrons, 6 Batteries.

* The infantry regiments consisted usually of two battalions, each battalion being between 500 and 600 strong. They thus correspond to weak British brigades.
† The foot batteries of artillery had generally 8 guns, the horse 6.

FRENCH ARMY (*continued*)

Corps d'Armée.	Divisions.	Regiments, etc.	Battalions.	Strength.	Position of corps in the field on evening of June 14th.	Orders to corps on evening of June 14th, or on June 15th.
2nd Corps d'Armée Lt.-Gen. Count Reille. Had been previously at Valenciennes and had marched from thence.	5th Gen. Bachelu.	4	9		Close to Solre-sur-Sambre.	To move early on 15th up right bank of the Sambre and cross at Marchienne, or between that and Thuin.
	6th Prince Jerome Napoleon.	5	13			
	7th Gen. Girard.	4	8			
	9th Gen. Foy.	4	10			
				19,435		
	Cavalry 2nd Division Lieut.-Gen. Piré.	4		1,865		
	Artillery Batts. 5 Foot, 1 Horse.			1,861		

Total . . . 23,161, with 46 guns.

40 Battalions, 15 Squadrons, 6 Batteries.

Corps d'Armée.	Divisions.	Regiments, etc.	Battalions.	Strength.	Position of corps in the field on evening of June 14th.	Orders to corps on evening of June 14th, or on June 15th.
3rd Corps d'Armée Lt.-Gen. Count Vandamme. Had been previously in and around Mezieres and had marched from thence.	10th Gen. Hubert.	4	12		Beaumont.	To march at 3 a.m. on 15th and cross the Sambre at Charleroi.
	11th Gen. Berthezene.	4	8			
	8th Gen. Lefol.	4	11			
				13,200		
	Cavalry 3rd Division Lieut.-Gen. Domont.	3		1,400		
	Artillery Batts. 4 Foot, 1 Horse.			1,292		

Total . . . 15,892, with 38 guns.

31 Battalions, 9 Squadrons, 5 Batteries.

Corps d'Armée.	Divisions.	Regiments, etc.	Battalions.	Strength.	Position of corps in the field on evening of June 14th.	Orders to corps on evening of June 14th, or on June 15th.
4th Corps d'Armée Lt.-Gen. Count Gérard. Had been previously about Metz, Thionville, etc., and had marched from thence.	12th Lieut.-Gen. Pecheux.	3	6		Philippeville, but not all quite concentrated at that point.	Cross the Sambre at Charleroi; afterwards altered to Chatelet.
	13th Lieut.-Gen. Vickery.	4	8			
	14th Gen. Hulot.	4	8			
				12,100		
	Cavalry 6th Division Lieut.-Gen. Morin.	3		1,400		
	Artillery Batts. 4 Foot, 1 Horse.			1,292		
Total . . .				14,792, with 38 guns.		

22 Battalions, 12 Squadrons, 5 Batteries.

Corps d'Armée.	Divisions.	Regiments, etc.	Battalions.	Strength	Position of corps in the field on evening of June 14th.	Orders to corps on evening of June 14th, or on June 15th.
6th Corps d'Armée Lt.-Gen. Count Lobau. Had been previously in and around Laon, and had marched from thence.	19th Lieut.-Gen. Simmer.	4	8		Beaumont.	March at 4 a.m. on 15th and cross the Sambre at Charleroi.
	20th Lieut.-Gen. Jeannin.	4	8			
	21st Lieut.-Gen. Teste.	4	8	9,900		
	Cavalry None.					
	Artillery Batts. 4 Foot, 1 Horse.			1,292		
Total . . .				11,192, with 38 guns.		

24 Battalions, 5 Batteries.

FRENCH ARMY (*continued*)

RESERVE CAVALRY

MARSHAL GROUCHY

The Reserve Cavalry had been previously between the River Aisne and the frontier, and had assembled from thence.

Corps.	Divisions.	Regiments, etc.	Strength.	Position of Res. Cavalry on evening of June 14th.	Orders to, on evening of June 14th, or on June 15th.
1st Lieut.-Gen. Pajol.	4th Lieut.-Gen. Soult.	3			
	5th Lieut.-Gen. Subervie.	3	2,500		
	Artillery Batts. 2 Horse.		300		
2nd Lieut.-Gen. Excelmans.	9th Lieut.-Gen. Strolz.	4			
	10th Lieut.-Gen. Chastel.	4	2,500	Beaumont.	Cross the Sambre at Charleroi; afterwards altered to Chatelet.
	Artillery Batts. 2 Horse.		300		
3rd Lieut.-Gen. Kellermann. (Count de Valmy).	11th Lieut.-Gen. L'Heritier.	4			
	12th Lieut.-Gen. Roussel.	4	3,300		
	Artillery Batts. 2 Horse.		300		
4th Lieut.-Gen. Count Milhaud.	13th Lieut.-Gen. Wathier.	4			
	14th Lieut.-Gen. Delort.	4	3,300		
	Artillery Batts. 2 Horse.		300		
	Total . . .		12,800, with 48 guns.		

87 Squadrons, 8 Batteries.

FRENCH ARMY (*continued*)

IMPERIAL GUARD

MARSHAL MORTIER *

Had been previously in Paris and had marched from thence.

Divisions.	Regiments, etc.	Batta-lions.	Strength.	Position of the Guard on evening of June 14th.	Orders to, on evening of June 14th, and on June 15th.
The Old Guard Lieut.-Gen. Count Friant.	4 (2 Grenadiers, 2 Chasseurs)	8	4,000		
The Middle Guard Lieut.-Gen. Count Morand.	4 (2 Grenadiers, 2 Chasseurs)	8	4,000		To march at various hours between 4 and 6 a.m. on the 15th; the cavalry at 8. To cross the Sambre at Charleroi.
The Young Guard Lieut.-Gen. Duhesme.	4 (2 Voltigeurs, 2 Tirailleurs)	8	4,000	Beaumont.	
Cavalry 1st Gen. Guyot.	13 Squadrons (Grenadiers à Cheval and Dragoons)		2,000		
2nd Gen. Lefebvre Desnouettes.	19 Squadrons (Chasseurs and Lancers)		2,000		
Artillery Batts. Gen. Devaux. 9 Foot, 4 Horse.			2,400		

Total . . . | 18,400, with 96 guns.

24 Battalions, 32 Squadrons, 13 Batteries.

* Mortier was left sick at Beaumont, so that General Drouot subsequently commanded the Imperial Guard.

Appendix B

Nos. I–VI

Orders or instructions to Marshal Ney from Napoleon, or Soult (his chief of the staff), Duke of Dalmatia.

Nos.VII–XI

Orders or instructions to Marshal Grouchy, and reports from him.:

I

To NEY *from* SOULT

À M. LE MARÉCHAL

PRINCE DE LA MOSKOWA

Charleroi, le 16 juin 1815.

Monsieur le maréchal, l'empereur vient d'ordonner à M. le comte de Valmy, commandant le 3ᵉ corps de cavalerie, de le réunir et de le diriger sur Gosselies, où il sera à votre disposition.

L'intention de Sa Majesté est que la cavalerie de la garde, qui a été portée sur la route de Bruxelles, reste en arrière et rejoigne le restant de la garde impériale ; mais, pour qu'elle ne fasse pas de mouvement rétrograde, vous pourrez, après l'avoir fait remplacer sur la ligne, la laisser un peu en arrière, où il lui serva envoyé des ordres dans le mouvement de la journée. M. le lieutenant général Lefebvre Desnoëttes enverra, à cet effet, un officier pour prendre des ordres.

Veuillez m'instruire si le 1ᵉʳ corps a opéré son mouvement, et quelle est, ce matin, la position exacte des 1ᵉʳ et 2ᵉ corps d'armée, et des deux divisions de cavalerie qui y sont attachées, en me faisant connaitre ce qu'il y a d'ennemis devant vous, et ce qu'on a appris.

Le major général,
Duc de DALMATIE.

231

II

To Ney *from* Napoleon
AU MARÉCHAL NEY

Mon cousin, je vous envoie mon aide de camp, le général Flahaut, qui vous porte la présente lettre. Le major général a dû vous donner des ordres ; mais vous recevrez les miens plus tôt, parce que mes officiers vont plus vite que les siens. Vous recevrez l'ordre de mouvement du jour, mais je veux vous en écrire en détail parce que c'est de la plus haute importance. Je porte le maréchal Grouchy avec les 3ᵉ et 4ᵉ corps d'infanterie sur Sombref. Je porte ma garde à Fleurus et j'y serai de ma personne avant midi. J'y attaquerai l'ennemi si je le rencontre, et j'éclairerai la route jusqu'à Gembloux. Là, d'après ce qui se passera, je prendrai mon parti, peut-être à trois heures après midi, peut-être ce soir. Mon intention est que, immédiatement après que j'aurai pris mon parti, vous soyez prêt à marcher sur Bruxelles. Je vous appuierai avec la Garde, qui sera à Fleurus ou à Sombref, et je désirerais arriver à Bruxelles demain matin. Vous vous mettriez en marche ce soir même, si je prends mon parti d'assez bonne heure pour que vous puissiez en être informé de jour et faire ce soir 3 ou 4 lieues et être demain à 7 heures du matin à Bruxelles. Vous pouvez donc disposer vos troupes de la manière suivante. Première division à deux lieues en avant des Quatre-Chemins, s'il n'y a pas d'inconvénient. Six divisions d'infanterie autour des Quatre-Chemins et une division à Marbais, afin que je puisse l'attirer à moi à Sombref, si j'en avais besoin. Elle ne retarderait d'ailleurs pas votre marche. Le corps du comte de Valmy, qui a 3,000 cuirassiers d'élite, à l'intersection du chemin des Romains et de celui de Bruxelles, afin que je puisse l'attirer à moi, si j'en avais besoin ; aussitôt que mon parti sera pris, vous lui enverrez l'ordre de venir vous rejoindre. Je désirerais avoir avec moi la division de la Garde que commande le général Lefebvre Desnoëttes, et je vous envoie les deux divisions du corps du comte de Valmy pour la remplacer. Mais, dans mon projet actuel, je préfère placer le comte de Valmy de manière à le rappeler si j'en avais besoin, et ne point faire faire de fausses marches au général

Lefebvre Desnoëttes, puisqu'il est probable que je me déciderai ce soir à marcher sur Bruxelles avec la Garde. Cependant, couvrez la division Lefebvre par les deux divisions de cavalerie d'Erlon et de Reille, afin de ménager la Garde ; s'il y avait quelque échauffourée avec les Anglais, il est préférable que ce soit sur le ligne que sur la garde. J'ai adopté comme principe général pendant cette campagne, de diviser mon armée en deux ailes et une réserve. Votre aile sera composée des quatre divisions du 1er corps, des quatre divisions du 2e corps, de deux divisions de cavalerie légère, et de deux divisions du corps du Comte de Valmy. Cela ne doit pas être loin de 45 à 50 mille hommes.

La maréchal Grouchy aura à peu près la même force, et commandera d'aile droite. La Garde formera la réserve, et je me porterai sur l'une ou l'autre aile, selon les circonstances. Le major général donne les ordres les plus précis pour qu'il n'y ait aucune difficulté sur l'obéissance à vos ordres lorsque vous serez détache ; les commandants de corps devant prendre mes ordres directement quand je me trouve présent. Selon les circonstances, j'affaiblirai l'une ou l'autre aile en augmentant ma réserve. Vous sentez assez l'importance attachée à la prise de Bruxelles. Cela pourra d'ailleurs donner lieu à des incidents, car un mouvement aussi prompt et aussi brusque isolera l'armée anglaise de Mons, Ostende, etc. Je désire que vos dispositions soient bien faites pour qu'au premier ordre, vos huit divisions puissent marcher rapidement et sans obstacle sur Bruxelles.

Charleroi, le 16 juin 1815.

N.

III

To Ney *from* Soult
À M. LE MARÉCHAL
Prince de la Moskowa

Charleroi, le 16 juin 1815.

Monsieur le Maréchal, l'empereur ordonne que vous mettiez en marche les 2e et 1er corps d'armée, ainsi que le 3e corps de cavalerie, qui a été mis à votre disposition, pour les diriger sur l'intersection des chemins dits les Trois-Bras * (route de

---

* This is " Quatre-Bras " or " Les Quatre Chemins," termed in some maps " Les Trois Bras."

Bruxelles), où vous leur ferez prendre position, et vous porterez en même temps des reconnaissances, aussi avant que possible, sur la route de Bruxelles et sur Nivelles, d'où probablement l'ennemi s'est retiré.

S.M. désire que, s'il n'y a pas d'inconvénient, vous établissiez une division avec de la cavalerie à Genappe, et elle ordonne que vous portiez une autre division du côte de Marbais, pour couvrir l'espace entre Sombref, et les Trois-Bras. Vous placerez, près de ces divisions, la division de cavalerie de la garde impériale, commandée par le général Lefebvre Desnoëttes, ainsi que le 1er régiment de hussards, qui a été détaché hier vers Gosselies.

Le corps qui sera à Marbais aura aussi pour objet d'appuyer les mouvements de M. le maréchal Grouchy sur Sombref, et de vous soutenir à la position des Trois-Bras, si cela devenait nécessaire. Vous recommanderez au général, qui sera à Marbais, de bien s'éclairer sur toutes les directions, particulièrement sur celles de Gembloux et de Wavre.

Si cependant la division du général Lefebvre Desnoëttes était trop engagée sur la route de Bruxelles, vous la laisseriez et vous la remplaceriez au corps qui sera à Marbais par le 3e corps de cavalerie aux ordres de M. le comte de Valmy, et par le 1er régiment de hussards.

J'ai l'honneur de vous prévenir que l'empereur va se porter sur Sombref, où, d'après les ordres de Sa Majesté, M. le maréchal Grouchy doit se diriger avec les 3e et 4e corps d'infanterie et les 1er, 2e, et 4e corps de cavalerie. M. le maréchal Grouchy fera occuper Gembloux.

Je vous prie de me mettre de suite à même de rendre compte à l'empereur de vos dispositions pour exécuter l'ordre que je vous envoie, ainsi que de tout ce que vous aurez appris sur l'ennemi.

Sa Majesté me charge de vous recommander de prescire aux généraux commandant les corps d'armée de faire réunir leur monde et rentrer les hommes isolés, de maintenir l'ordre le plus parfait dans la troupe, et de rallier toutes les voitures d'artillerie et les ambulances qu'ils auraient pu laisser en arrière.

Le maréchal d'empire, major général,

Duc de DALMATIE.

To Ney *from* Soult

À M. LE MARÉCHAL

Prince de la Moskowa.

Charleroi, le 16 juin 1815.

Monsieur le Maréchal,

Un officier de lanciers vient de dire à l'empereur que l'ennemi présentait des masses du côté des Quatre-Bras. Réunissez les corps des comtes Reille et d'Erlon, et celui du comte de Valmy, qui se met à l'instant en route pour vous rejoindre ; avec ces forces, vous devrez battre et détruire tous les corps ennemis qui peuvent se présenter. Blücher était hier à Namur, et il n'est pas vraisemblable qu'il ait porté des troupes vers les Quatre-Bras ; ainsi, vous n'avez affaire qu'à ce qui vient de Bruxelles.

Le maréchal Grouchy va faire le mouvement sur Sombref, que je vous ai annoncé, et l'empereur va se rendre à Fleurus ; c'est là où vous adresserez vos nouveaux rapports à Sa Majesté.

Le maréchal d'empire, major général,

Duc de Dalmatie.

To Ney *from* Soult

À M. LE MARÉCHAL

Prince de la Moskowa

En avant de Fleurus,
le 16 juin à 2 heures.

Monsieur le Maréchal, l'empereur me charge de vous prévenir que l'ennemi a réuni un corps de troupes entre Sombref et Bry, et qu'à deux heures et demie M. le maréchal Grouchy, avec les troisième et quatrième corps, l'attaquera ; l'intention de Sa Majesté est que vous attaquiez aussi ce qui est devant vous, et qu'après l'avoir vigoureusement poussé, vous rabattiez sur nous pour concourir à envelopper le corps dont je viens de vous parler.

Si ce corps était enfoncé, auparavant, alors Sa Majesté ferait manœuvrer dans votre direction pour hâter également vos opérations.

Instruisez de suite l'empereur de vos dispositions et de ce qui se passe sur votre front.

Le maréchal d'empire, major général,

Duc de DALMATIE.

Au dos de cet ordre est écrit :

À M. le Maréchal Prince de la Moskowa,

A Gosselies, sur la route de Bruxelles.

Et au crayon : Wagnée

Bois de Lombuc.

Un duplicata de cet ordre porte

À M. le Maréchal Prince de la Moskowa,

À Gosselies, sur la route de Bruxelles.

WAGNÉE.

RANSART.

VI

To NEY *from* SOULT

Monsieur le Maréchal, je vous ai écrit, il y a une heure, que l'empereur ferait attaquer l'ennemi à deux heures et demie dans la position qu'il a prise entre le village de Saint-Amand et de Bry : en ce moment l'engagement est très prononcé ; Sa Majesté me charge de vous dire que vous devez manœuvrer sur-le-champ de manière à envelopper la droite de l'ennemi et tomber à bras raccourcis sur ses derrières ; cette armée est perdue si vous agissez vigoureusement ; le sort de la France est entre vos mains. Ainsi n'hésitez pas un instant pour faire le mouvement que l'empereur vous ordonne, et dirigez vous sur les hauteurs de Bry et de Saint-Amand, pour concourir à une victoire peut-être décisive. L'ennemi est pris en flagrant délit au moment où il cherche à se réunir aux Anglais.

Le major général,

Duc de DALMATIE.

En avant de Fleurus, le 16 juin 1815, à 3 heures un quart.

VII

*T*o Grouchy *from* Napoleon *

"Rendez-vous à Gembloux avec le corps de cavalerie de général Pajol, la cavalerie légère du quatrième corps, le corps de cavalerie du général Excelmans, la division du général Teste, dont vous aurez un soin particulier, étant détachée de son corps d'armée, et les troisième et quatrième corps d'infanterie. Vous vous ferez éclairer sur la direction de Namur et de Maestricht, et vous poursuivrez l'ennemi. Eclairez sa marche, et instruisez-moi de ses manœuvres, de manière que je puisse pénétrer ce qu'il veut faire. Je porte mon quartier-général aux Quatre-Chemins, où ce matin étaient encore les Anglais. Notre communication sera donc directe par la route pavée de Namur. Si l'ennemi a évacué Namur, écrivez au général commandant la deuxième division militaire à Charlemont, de faire occuper Namur par quelques bataillons de Garde Nationale, et quelques batteries de canons qu'il formera à Charlemont. Il donnera ce commandement à un maréchal-de-camp.

Il est important de pénétrer ce que l'ennemi veut faire : ou il se sépare des Anglais, ou ils veulent se réunir encore, pour couvrir Bruxelles et Liège, en tentant le sort d'une nouvelle bataille. Dans tous les cas, tenez constamment vos deux corps d'infanterie réunis dans une lieue de terrain, et occupez tous les soirs une bonne position militaire, ayant plusieurs débouchés de retraite. Placez détachemens de cavalerie intermédiaires pour communiquer avec le quartier-général.

Ligny, le 17 juin 1815.

(Dicté par l'empereur, en l'absence du major-général, au grand-maréchal Bertrand.)

VIII

*T*o Napoleon *from* Grouchy

"Sire :

"J'ai l'honneur de vous rendre compte que j'occupe Gembloux, et que ma cavalerie est à Sauvenières. L'ennemi, fort d'environ trente mille hommes, continue son mouvement

---

* Dictated to Marshal Bertrand (the "Bertrand Order").

de retraite ; on lui a saisi ici un parc de 400 bêtes à cornes, des magasins et des bagages.

"Il paraît d'après tous les rapports, qu'arrivés à Sauvenières, les Prussiens se sont divisés en deux colonnes : l'une a dû prendre la route de Wavres, en passant par Sart-à-Wallain ; l'autre colonne paraît s'être dirigée sur Perwès.

"On peut peut-être en inférer qu'une portion va joindre Wellington, et que le centre, qui est l'armée de Blücher, se retire sur Liége : une autre colonne avec de l'artillerie ayant fait son mouvement de retraite par Namur, le général Excelmans a ordre de pousser ce soir six escadrons sur Sart-à-Wallain, et trois escadrons sur Perwès. D'après leur rapport, si la masse des Prussiens se retire sur Wavres, je la suivrai dans cette direction, afin qu'ils ne puissent pas gagner Bruxelles, et de les séparer de Wellington.

"Si, au contraire, mes renseignements prouvent que la principale force prussienne a marché sur Perwès, je me dirigerai par cette ville à la poursuite de l'ennemi.

"Les généraux Thielman et Borstell faisaient partie de l'armée que Votre Majesté a battue hier ; ils étaient encore ce matin à 10 heures ici, et ont annoncé que vingt mille hommes des leurs avaient été mis hors de combat. Ils ont demandé en partant les distances de Wavres, Perwès et Hannut. Blücher a été blessé légèrement au bras, ce qui ne l'a pas empêché de continuer à commander après s'être fait panser. Il n'a point passé par Gembloux.

Je suis avec respect
de Votre Majesté,

SIRE,   Le fidèle sujet,
(Signé)   Le Maréchal Comte de GROUCHY."

IX

To NAPOLEON *from* GROUCHY

Sart-à-Walhain le 18 juin, onze heures du matin.

SIRE :

Je ne perds pas un moment à vous transmettre les renseignements que je recueille ici ; je les regarde comme positifs, et afin que Votre Majesté les reçoive le plus promptement possible, je les lui expédie par le major La Fresnaye, son ancien page ; il est bien monté et bon écuyer.

Les 1er, 2e et 3e corps de Blücher marchent dans la direction de Bruxelles. Deux de ces corps ont passé à Sart-à-Walhain, ou à peu de distance, sur la droite ; ils ont défilé en trois colonnes, marchant à peu près de même hauteur. Leur passage a duré six heures sans interruption. Ce qui a défilé en vue de Sart-à-Walhain peut-être évalué à trente mille hommes au moins, et avait un matériel de cinquante à soixante bouches à feu.

Un corps venant de Liége a effectué sa jonction avec ceux qui ont combattu à Fleurus. (Ci-joint une réquisition qui le prouve.) Quelques-uns des Prussiens que j'ai devant moi se dirigent vers la plaine de la Chyse, située près de la route de Louvain, et à deux lieues et demie de cette ville.

Il semblerait que ce serait à dessein de s'y masser ou de combattre les troupes qui les y poursuivraient, ou enfin de se réunir à Wellington, projet annoncé par leurs officiers, qui, avec leur jactance ordinaire, prétendent n'avoir quitté le champ de bataille, le 16, qu'afin d'opérer leur réunion avec l'armée anglaise sur Bruxelles.

Ce soir, je vais être massé à Wavres, et me trouver ainsi entre Wellington, que je présume en retraite devant Votre Majesté, et l'armée prussienne.

J'ai besoin d'instructions ultérieures sur ce que Votre Majesté ordonne que je fasse. Le pays entre Wavres et la plaine de la Chyse est difficile, coupé, et marécageux.

Par la route de Wivorde, j'arriverai facilement à Bruxelles avant tout ce qui sera arreté à la Chyse, si tant il y a que les Prussiens y fassent une halte.

Daignez, Sire, me transmettre vos ordres ; je puis les recevoir avant de commencer mon mouvement de demain.

La plupart des renseignements que renferme cette lettre me sont fournis par la propriétaire de la maison où je me suis arreté pour écrire à Votre Majesté ; cet officier a servi dans l'armée française, est decoré, et parait entièrement dévoué à nos interêts. Je les joins à ces lignes.

X

To Grouchy *from* Soult

En avant de la ferme de Caillou, le 18 juin 1815,
à dix heures du matin.

Monsieur le maréchal, l'Empereur a reçu votre dernier rapport, daté de Gembloux.

Vous ne parlez à Sa Majesté que de deux colonnes prussiennes qui ont passé à Sauvenière et à Sart-à-Walhain. Cependant des rapports disent qu'une troisième colonne, qui était assez forte, a passé par Géry et Gentines, se dirigeant sur Wavres.

L'Empereur me charge de vous prévenir qu'en ce moment Sa Majesté va faire attaquer l'armée anglaise, qui a pris position à Waterloo, près de la forêt de Soignes. Ainsi, Sa Majesté désire que vous dirigiez vos mouvement sur Wavres, afin de vous rapprocher de nous, vous mettre en rapport d'opérations et lier les communications, poussant devant vous les corps de l'armée prussienne qui ont pris cette direction et qui auraient pu s'arrêter à Wavres, où vous devez arriver le plus tôt possible.

Vous ferez suivre les colonnes ennemies, qui ont pris sur votre droite, par quelques corps légers, afin d'observer leurs mouvements et ramasser leurs traînards. Instruisez-moi immédiatement de vos dispositions et de votre marche, ainsi que des nouvelles que vous avez sur les ennemis, et ne négligez pas de lier vos communications avec nous. L'Empereur désire avoir très-souvent de vos nouvelles.

Le maréchal duc de Dalmatie.

XI

To Grouchy *from* Soult

Du champ de bataille de Waterloo, le 18 juin,
à une heure après midi.

Monsieur le Maréchal,

Vous avez écrit, ce matin à deux heures, a l'Empereur, que vous marcheriez sur Sart-lez-Walhain ; donc votre projet était de vous porter à Corbais ou à Wavre. Ce mouvement est conforme aux dispositions de Sa Majesté, qui vous ont été communiquées. Cependant, l'Empereur m'ordonne de vous dire que vous devez toujours manœuvrer dans notre direction. C'est à vous de voir le point où nous sommes pour vous régler en conséquence et pour lier nos communications, ainsi que pour être toujours en mesure de tomber sur les troupes ennemies qui chercheraient à inquiéter notre droite et de les écraser.

Dans ce moment, la bataille est engagée sur la ligne de Waterloo ; le centre ennemi est à Mont-Saint-Jean ; ainsi manœuvrez pour joindre notre droite.

P.S. Une lettre qui vient d'être interceptée porte que le général Bülow doit attaquer notre flanc. Nous croyons apercevoir ce corps sur les hauteurs de Saint-Lambert ; ainsi, ne perdez pas un instant pour vous rapprocher de nous et nous joindre, et pour écraser Bülow, que vous prendrez en flagrant délit.

Le maréchal duc de DALMATIE.

LEONAUR

ALSO FROM LEONAUR
AVAILABLE IN SOFTCOVER OR HARDCOVER WITH DUST JACKET

ZULU:1879 *by D.C.F. Moodie & the Leonaur Editors*—The Anglo-Zulu War of 1879 from contemporary sources: First Hand Accounts, Interviews, Dispatches, Official Documents & Newspaper Reports.

THE RED DRAGOON *by W.J. Adams*—With the 7th Dragoon Guards in the Cape of Good Hope against the Boers & the Kaffir tribes during the 'war of the axe' 1843-48'.

THE RECOLLECTIONS OF SKINNER OF SKINNER'S HORSE *by James Skinner*—James Skinner and his 'Yellow Boys' Irregular cavalry in the wars of India between the British, Mahratta, Rajput, Mogul, Sikh & Pindarree Forces.

A CAVALRY OFFICER DURING THE SEPOY REVOLT *by A. R. D. Mackenzie*—Experiences with the 3rd Bengal Light Cavalry, the Guides and Sikh Irregular Cavalry from the outbreak to Delhi and Lucknow.

A NORFOLK SOLDIER IN THE FIRST SIKH WAR *by J W Baldwin*—Experiences of a private of H.M. 9th Regiment of Foot in the battles for the Punjab, India 1845-6.

TOMMY ATKINS' WAR STORIES: 14 FIRST HAND ACCOUNTS—Fourteen first hand accounts from the ranks of the British Army during Queen Victoria's Empire.

THE WATERLOO LETTERS *by H. T. Siborne*—Accounts of the Battle by British Officers for its Foremost Historian.

NEY: GENERAL OF CAVALRY VOLUME 1—1769-1799 *by Antoine Bulos*—The Early Career of a Marshal of the First Empire.

NEY: MARSHAL OF FRANCE VOLUME 2—1799-1805 *by Antoine Bulos*—The Early Career of a Marshal of the First Empire.

AIDE-DE-CAMP TO NAPOLEON *by Philippe-Paul de Ségur*—For anyone interested in the Napoleonic Wars this book, written by one who was intimate with the strategies and machinations of the Emperor, will be essential reading.

TWILIGHT OF EMPIRE *by Sir Thomas Ussher & Sir George Cockburn*—Two accounts of Napoleon's Journeys in Exile to Elba and St. Helena: Narrative of Events by Sir Thomas Ussher & Napoleon's Last Voyage: Extract of a diary by Sir George Cockburn.

PRIVATE WHEELER *by William Wheeler*—The letters of a soldier of the 51st Light Infantry during the Peninsular War & at Waterloo.

CPSIA information can be obtained
at www.ICGtesting.com
Printed in the USA
BVHW030300011119
562495BV00005B/87/P